BLACK EDGE

BLACK EDGE

*Inside Information, Dirty Money,
and the Quest to Bring Down
the Most Wanted Man on Wall Street*

SHEELAH KOLHATKAR

9 10

WH Allen, an imprint of Ebury Publishing,
20 Vauxhall Bridge Road,
London SW1V 2SA

WH Allen is part of the Penguin Random House group of companies whose
addresses can be found at global.penguinrandomhouse.com

Penguin
Random House
UK

Copyright © Sheelah Kolhatkar 2017

Sheelah Kolhatkar has asserted his right to be identified as the author of this
Work in accordance with the Copyright, Designs and Patents Act 1988

First published in the United Kingdom by WH Allen in 2018
First published in the United States by Random House in 2017

www.penguin.co.uk

A CIP catalogue record for this book is available from the British Library

ISBN 9780753552230

Printed and bound in Great Britain by Clays Ltd, Elcograf S.p.A.

Penguin Random House is committed to a sustainable future for our business, our readers
and our planet. This book is made from Forest Stewardship Council® certified paper.

MIX
Paper from
responsible sources
FSC® C018179

For Seth

CONTENTS

PROLOGUE

THE FLIP

One evening in July 2008, FBI Special Agent B. J. Kang sat hunched over a desk with headphones on, listening to a phone call. It was dark outside, and he hadn't eaten dinner. His stomach growled.

"Raj, you better listen to me," a woman said in a soft, breathy voice. "Please don't fuck me on this."

"Yeah," a male voice said.

"They're gonna guide down," the woman said. *Guide down*, Kang knew, was a common Wall Street term that meant the company was planning to announce that its earnings were going to be lower than expected—definitely bad news; the "they" was an $800 million Internet company based in Cambridge, Massachusetts, called Akamai Technologies. "I just got a call from my guy. I played him like a finely tuned piano."

"I'm short it, you know that, right?" the man said.

"I want you to be on top," the woman purred. "We need to be a team." She wasn't talking about sex, at least not this time. This was about money. "Let's just play this thing. Just keep shorting, every day."

Who was this woman? Kang thought to himself. She sounded cartoonishly conspiratorial. Kang listened and took notes. He was in the FBI's "wire room," a windowless den housing fourteen vintage Dell computers and an assortment of mismatched office furniture on the twenty-fourth floor of 26 Federal Plaza in lower Manhattan, home of the Bureau's New York field office. Along one wall was a metal shelf loaded with granola bars, Goldfish crackers, and Kit Kats—sustenance for the agents who spent hours there each day, monitoring live phone calls.

Listening to the wires was generally considered a crappy job, but Kang didn't see it that way. He understood it as a matter of patience; if you put in the work, it eventually paid off. A few months earlier, on March 7, a federal judge had handed Kang a gift, approving a wiretap application on the cellphone of a Wall Street titan named Raj Rajaratnam. Kang had been practically living in the wire room ever since, gathering evidence for a massive insider trading case. He wasn't in securities crime just to bust the seedy, small-time frauds he'd been working on for the previous two years. He wanted to take down someone big—someone like Raj—a significant player in the financial world.

The fifty-year-old co-founder of the Galleon Group, a $7 billion hedge fund, Rajaratnam was one of the more high-profile traders on Wall Street. Partly this was due to his size. Raj was obese and flamboyant, a man of outsize appetites. He liked to eat, and he liked to spend money, flying seventy of his friends to Kenya for a birthday safari and paying $250,000 for a Super Bowl party on Star Island in Biscayne Bay. Raj cut a stark contrast to Kang, the disciplined child of Korean immigrants, who was built like a block of concrete with black buzz-cut hair. Where Rajaratnam lived to schmooze and trade and brag about his exceptional skill at every opportunity, Kang was a quiet, tireless worker who spoke only when absolutely necessary. Even his closest colleagues at the Bureau hardly knew anything about him.

Six days after that phone call, Kang watched as Akamai announced to the world that its next earnings release was going to be a disappointment. Its stock dropped from $31.25 to $23.34 overnight. Raj, who was short 875,000 shares, made over $5 million in a week. The woman who gave him the tip, a trader named Danielle Chiesi, made $2.5 million. Kang wanted to know where she had gotten such valuable intelligence about what Akamai was going to do, so he subpoenaed her phone records. He could see, looking over her call logs, that she had spoken to a senior executive at Akamai just before she passed the information on to Raj.

"You did it in such a classy way," Rajaratnam told Chiesi afterward, when he called to thank her for the tip. "The way you worked the relationship."

Chiesi sighed. "It's a conquest."

Rajaratnam had been caught on tape doing something that was clearly illegal: getting confidential, inside information about Akamai, trading on it, and making a profit. There was no code or innuendo. All the pieces were laid out perfectly, ready to go into a criminal complaint: The call came on the night of July 24; Raj shorted 138,550 shares the next day, betting that the stock was going to go down, and he kept shorting more until the news came out on July 30. Based on that evidence alone, one of the most successful traders on Wall Street was probably going to jail. Kang could feel himself growing excited. If Raj and Chiesi were trading on inside information so casually and openly, there had to be others doing it, too.

Rajaratnam's phone line was usually busiest in the morning, right around the time the market opened, and Kang made a point to get in early and listen. Raj would call his friends and acquaintances, casting around for dirt. Some of the people he exchanged information with were former classmates from Wharton who were now out in the world running technology companies or hedge funds. Many of them were on his payroll. Kang watched as Raj collected information about upcoming earnings announcements and takeover offers that hadn't yet been disclosed and used it to make millions of dollars trading stocks. Within a few months, Kang had wires going on Rajaratnam's friends, too.

He and the other FBI agents on wire detail were shocked by what they were hearing. Was this normal behavior on Wall Street? Was inside information *that* easy to get? They had become accustomed to finding corruption in the financial industry, but these interactions were so blatant, so obviously illegal, and seemed to extend in every direction. Each time they discovered one insider trading circle, it would overlap with another, and they'd have a whole new list of suspects to go after. The problem was bigger than Raj. It was a large, complicated network.

As the agents listened and studied phone records and interview notes, one hedge fund kept coming up: SAC Capital Advisors. Kang decided to look into it.

The sign for the Embassy Suites in South San Francisco loomed overhead as B. J. Kang steered the midsize rental car out of the parking lot and drove south, toward Cupertino, pulling up about forty minutes later in front of a three-bedroom house on a quiet street. He and his partner, who was sitting silently next to him, had spent a good part of the previous night rehearsing the different scenarios that might take place once they arrived at their destination and knocked on the door. What if the person they were looking for wasn't home? What if he told them to go screw themselves? What if he had a gun? It was unlikely, but they had to be ready for every possibility.

It was April 1, 2009, and the sun was setting. Kang and the other agent—Tom Zukauskas, whom Kang referred to as his "wingman"—exited the car and strode up the front walk. They knocked on the door. A dark-haired man appeared.

"Ali Far?" Kang said. The man nodded, confused. Kang reached into his jacket and produced a badge, which he held up in front of the man's face. "My name is B. J. Kang. I'm with the FBI. We're here to talk about insider trading."

He paused for a moment or two to let that sink in.

Kang explained that Far was in a difficult position because of some of the things he had done, but there might be a solution. Kang and Far could help each other. Far's wife, two daughters, mother, and mother-in-law cowered in the background, watching with alarm. "We know you used to work for Raj Rajaratnam at Galleon and that you've been trading on inside information," Kang said. "We have you on tape."

Tape?

Kang then played an audio recording in which Far could be heard giving inside information about a semiconductor company to Rajaratnam. As the recording played, Far was speechless.

Far had left Galleon in 2008 to start his own hedge fund with his friend Richard Choo-Beng Lee, who was known as "C.B." by virtually everyone. Lee was a technology analyst who had previously worked at SAC Capital. Kang hoped that Far and Lee would lead him closer to SAC, which was one of the biggest hedge funds in the world. Kang had been learning more and more about the fund and its mysterious founder, Steven Cohen, hearing from other traders on Wall Street that Cohen was "always on the right side" of every trade—something that seemed, at least on the surface, to be impossible. No one in the industry understood how Cohen made so much money so consistently; his competitors were envious—and suspicious. Taking skills they'd developed at Galleon and SAC, Far and Lee had marketed their own fund, called Spherix Capital, to potential investors partly by advertising the access they had to executives at technology companies and the valuable information they could get as a result of those relationships. Kang knew all of this. He liked to say that he understood the difference between "the dirty, important hedge funds," the "dirty hedge funds you didn't need to waste time on," and the "not-important hedge funds." He had argued to his FBI colleagues that they should push their investigation beyond Raj Rajaratnam and Galleon to bigger and more powerful targets like Cohen. Kang thought that Far and Lee, who were well connected and seemed to be getting inside information directly from company employees, were from the first group, worth going after on their own. But to Kang, they were also a path to something bigger. All Kang had to do was convince them to flip.

Kang believed that Far, in particular, fit the profile of a potential FBI cooperator very well. He seemed like a decent person who would want to do what was best for his family.

"Do you really want to put your kids through this?" Kang asked.

He told Far to think carefully about his offer, as it was the best one he was going to get—definitely more appealing than going to jail. If he didn't do the right thing and cooperate, the next time FBI agents showed up at his house, it would be to arrest him. "Don't tell anyone about this," Kang added, before saying goodbye. "We'll be watching, and we'll find out if you do." The agents walked back to their car.

That night, Far was in distress. He couldn't sleep. Despite Kang's warning, Far placed a call to his partner, C. B. Lee. The voicemail answered. "The FBI just showed up at my house," Far said, then abruptly hung up.

It was critical to the FBI that word of the investigation and the wiretaps not leak into the hedge fund community. Kang had to talk to C. B. Lee as soon as possible in order to try to contain the disclosure. Lee lived with his mother just twenty minutes from Far, and two days later Kang went to see him. As soon as Lee answered the door, Kang told him that he knew he had been insider trading at Spherix.

At first, Lee refused to answer any of the FBI's questions. But by the end of their conversation, Kang felt confident that he would cooperate.

"We are going to help each other," Kang told him. "You're doing the right thing."

The telephone rang inside Steven Cohen's offices at SAC Capital. It was C. B. Lee on the line. He and Cohen hadn't spoken in a while.

"Hey, Steve, we had to shut our fund down," Lee told Cohen, trying to sound calm. He explained that he and Ali Far weren't getting along because they couldn't agree on how to share their profits. "I'd love to work with you again," Lee said. He tried to bring up memories of all the money they had made together years ago when Lee worked for Cohen. Lee suggested an arrangement whereby he would come back as a consultant to Cohen and they would split the profits if Lee provided good information. He listed several technology companies and bragged about his ability to get the secret internal numbers at all of them.

"I know people," Lee said. "I have people in sales and finance at Nvidia who keep me up on quarterly earnings, and I have a contact at Taiwan Semiconductor who gives me wafer data."

Cohen was intrigued. Lee had been one of his highest-performing analysts, someone who could be relied on to bring in moneymaking trading ideas, until he left SAC in 2004. Lee's research was so good that Cohen and one of his portfolio managers used to fight over it. But Cohen wasn't naïve. He wanted to be careful.

"I don't want to get into it on the phone," he said.

He was interested enough, though, that he had his head of recruiting call Lee back and talk to him about the logistics of returning to work at SAC. The two men spoke several times.

A couple of weeks later, Cohen mentioned to one of his research traders that he was thinking of rehiring C. B. Lee. The trader shuddered, but he didn't say anything. He had just heard some gossip about Lee from a friend who worked at Galleon, Rajaratnam's fund. The rumor was that federal agents had recently visited Lee and Far's hedge fund. "I don't know what's going on there," the Galleon trader had said when he mentioned it during a group dinner in Manhattan three days earlier. "It's weird."

The next morning, the research trader leaned over to Cohen and summoned up all his courage. He had no idea how his volatile boss might react to what he was about to say. "This might be totally off base," he said, "but there's a rumor that the Feds were in C.B.'s office. You might want to take a closer look at it."

"You mean the SEC?" Cohen said.

"No," the trader answered. "The FBI."

Cohen grabbed the phone and dialed the number of a friend of his, a former SAC portfolio manager who was close to Lee. "I heard C.B. might be cooperating with the Feds," Cohen told him. "We heard he's wearing a wire." It sounded like there might be a federal investigation of the hedge fund industry going on. Who knew where it might lead?

"Be careful."

It would be an investigation unlike any other in the history of Wall Street, a decadelong, multiagency government crackdown on insider trading focused almost entirely on hedge funds. It began with Raj Rajaratnam and the Galleon Group and quickly expanded to ensnare corporate executives, lawyers, scientists, traders, and analysts across dozens of companies. Its ultimate target was Steven Cohen, the billionaire founder of SAC Capital Advisors, possibly the most powerful hedge fund firm the industry had ever seen.

In 1992, the year Cohen started SAC, the average person had only the faintest idea of what a hedge fund was. Most funds like his began as tiny, informal operations founded by eccentric traders whose financial ambition couldn't be satisfied by even the mightiest investment banks on Wall Street. They had little patience for corporate culture and no interest in negotiating over their bonuses each year. Many of them wore jeans and flip-flops to work. Their aversion to the big banks and brokerage firms was a source of pride.

Hedge funds were conceived as a small, almost boutique service, as vehicles for wealthy people to diversify their investments and produce steady, moderate returns that were insulated from swings in the stock market. The idea behind them was simple: A fund manager would identify the best companies and buy their shares while selling short the stock of ones that weren't likely to do well. Shorting is a bet against a stock on the expectation that it will go down, and the practice opened up new opportunities to sophisticated investors. The process involves borrowing a stock (for a fee), selling it in the market, and then, if all goes well, buying the shares back at a lower price and using them to repay the loan. In a good market, when most stocks are going up, the gains on the longs eclipse the losses from the shorts; in a bad market, the shorts make money to help offset the losses on the longs. Being long some stocks and short others meant that you were "hedged." This strategy could be applied to other financial instruments in addition to stocks, such as bonds and options and futures, in any market in the world.

The losses on a short position are potentially limitless if a security keeps rising, so it's considered a high-risk activity. That, combined with the fact that many hedge funds employed leverage, or borrowed money, to trade with as they pursued different strategies in different markets around the globe, led regulators to decree that only the most sophisticated investors should be investing in them. Hedge funds would be allowed to try to make money almost any way they wanted, and charge whatever fees they liked, as long as they limited their investors to the wealthy, who, in theory at least, could afford to lose whatever money they put in.

For years hedge funds existed largely separate from Wall Street's operatic boom-bust cycles, but by the mid-2000s they'd moved to the center of the industry. Some started producing enormous profits each year. Over time, the name *hedge fund* lost any connection to the careful strategy that had given such funds their name and came to stand, instead, for unregulated investment firms that essentially did whatever they wanted. Though they became known for employing leverage and taking risk, the defining attribute of most hedge funds was the enormous amounts of money the people running them were taking in: The fees they charged were generous, typically a "management fee" of 2 percent of assets and a "performance fee" of 20 percent of the profits each year. Before earning anything for his or her investors, the manager of a $2 billion fund would be positioned to make $40 million in fees just to keep the place running. By 2007, hedge fund founders like Paul Tudor Jones and Ken Griffin were managing multibillion-dollar pools of money, building twenty-thousand-square-foot palaces to live in, and traveling on $50 million private jets.

To work at a hedge fund was a liberating experience for a certain kind of trader, a chance to test one's skills against the market and, in the process, become spectacularly rich. Hedge fund jobs became the most coveted in finance. The immense fortunes they promised made a more traditional Wall Street career—climbing the hierarchy at an established investment bank such as Bear Stearns or Morgan Stanley—look far less interesting. In 2006, the same year that Lloyd Blankfein, the CEO of Goldman Sachs, was paid $54 million—causing outrage in some circles—the lowest-paid person on the list of the twenty-five highest-paid hedge fund managers made $240 million. The top three made more than a billion dollars each. Cohen was number five that year, at $900 million. By 2015, hedge funds controlled almost $3 trillion in assets around the world and were a driving force behind the extreme wealth disequilibrium of the early twenty-first century.

The hedge fund moguls didn't lay railroads, build factories, or invent lifesaving medicines or technologies. They made their billions through speculation, by placing bets in the market that turned out to be right more often than wrong. And for this, they have gained not only extreme personal wealth but also formidable influence throughout society, in politics, education, the arts, professional sports—anywhere they choose to direct their attention and resources. They manage a significant amount of the money in pension and endowment funds and have so much influence in the market that CEOs of public companies have no choice but to pay attention to them, focusing on short-term stock performance to keep their hedge fund shareholders happy. Most of these hedge fund traders don't think of themselves as "owners" of companies or even as long-term investors. They are interested in buying in, making a profit, and selling out.

If there was one person who personified the rise of hedge funds, and the way they transformed Wall Street, it was Steven Cohen. He was an enigmatic figure, even to those in his own industry, but his average returns of 30 percent a year for twenty years were legendary. What was especially intriguing about him was that his performance wasn't based on any well-understood strategy, unlike other prominent investors such as George Soros or Paul Tudor Jones; he wasn't famous for betting on global economic trends or predicting the decline of the housing market. Cohen simply seemed to have an intuitive sense for how markets moved, and he entered the industry at precisely the moment when society reoriented itself to reward that skill above almost all others. He traded in and out of stocks in rapid-fire fashion, dozens of them in a single day. Young traders longed to work for him and rich investors begged to put their money in his hands. By 2012, SAC had become one of the world's most profitable investment funds, managing $15 billion. On Wall Street, "Stevie," as Cohen was known, was like a god.

Word quickly spread about this new way to become wildly rich, and thousands of new hedge funds opened up, all staffed with aggressive traders looking for investments to exploit. As the competition became more intense and the potential money to be made ballooned, hedge fund traders started going to extreme lengths to gain an advantage in the market, hiring scientists, mathematicians, economists, and shrinks. They laid cable close to stock exchanges so that their trades could be executed nanoseconds faster and employed engineers and coders to make their computers as powerful as those at the Pentagon. They paid soccer moms to walk the aisles at Walmart and report back on what was selling. They studied satellite images of parking lots and took CEOs out to extravagant dinners, digging for information. They did all this because they knew how difficult it is to beat the market, day after day, week after week, year after year. Hedge funds are always trying to find what traders call "edge"—information that gives them an advantage over other investors.

At a certain point, this quest for edge inevitably bumps up against, and then crosses, a line: advance knowledge of a company's earnings, word that a chipmaker will get a takeover offer next week, an early look at drug trial results. This kind of information—proprietary, nonpublic, and certain to move markets—is known on Wall Street as "black edge," and it's the most valuable information of all.

Trading on it is also usually illegal.

When one trader was asked if he knew of any fund that *didn't* traffic in inside information, he said: "No, they would never survive." In this way, black edge is like doping in elite-level cycling or steroids in professional baseball. Once the top cyclists and home-run hitters started doing it, you either went along with them or you lost.

And just as in cycling and baseball, the reckoning on Wall Street eventually came. In 2006, the Securities and Exchange Commission, the Federal Bureau of Investigation, and the Manhattan U.S. Attorney's Office declared they were going to go after black edge, and before long their search led them to Cohen. Whatever it was that everyone was doing, they realized, he was clearly the best at it.

This book is a detective story set in the back rooms of office parks and the trading floors of Wall Street. It's about FBI agents who followed hunches and set up wiretaps, flipping witnesses and working their way up the hierarchy until they reached the guys in charge. It's about idealistic government prosecutors facing slick defense lawyers making twenty-five times as much money a year. It's about young traders smashing their hard

PART
ONE

CHAPTER 1

MONEY, MONEY, MONEY

There tend to be two types of people who seek out jobs on Wall Street. The first are those with wealthy parents who were sent to the right prep schools and Ivy League colleges and who, from their first day on the trading floor, seem destined to be there. They move through life with a sense of ease about themselves, knowing that they will soon have their own apartments on Park Avenue and summer houses in the Hamptons, a mindset that comes from posh schooling and childhood tennis lessons and an understanding of when it is appropriate for a man to wear seersucker and when it isn't.

The second type call to mind terms like *street smart* and *scrappy*. They might have watched their fathers struggle to support the family, toiling in sales or insurance or running a small business, working hard for relatively little, which would have had a profound effect on them. They might have been picked on as children or rejected by girls in high school. They make it because they have a burning resentment and something to prove, or because they have the ambition to be filthy rich, or both. They have little to fall back on but their determination and their willingness to do whatever it takes, including outhustling the complacent rich kids. Some-times the drive these people have is so intense, it's almost like rage.

Steven Cohen came from the second group.

As he reported for work one morning in January 1978, Cohen looked like any other twenty-one-year-old starting his first job. He could hear the roar of the trading floor, where dozens of young men were chattering away on the phone, trying to coax money from the people on the other end of the line. The room was alive with energy. It was as if a great oak tree were shaking in the middle of an autumn forest and leaves of money were raining down. To Cohen it felt like home, and he ran right in.

Gruntal & Co. was a small brokerage firm located around the corner from the New York Stock Exchange in the gloomy canyons of lower Man-hattan. Established in 1880, Gruntal had survived the assassination of President McKinley, the crash of 1929, oil price spikes, and recessions, largely by buying up other tiny, primarily Jewish firms while also staying small enough that no one paid it much attention. From offices across the country, Gruntal brokers tried to sell stock investments to dentists and plumbers and retirees. When Cohen arrived, the firm was just starting to move more aggressively into an area called proprietary trading, trying to make profits by investing the firm's own money.

For an eager Jewish kid from Long Island like Cohen, Wall Street didn't extend an open invitation. Even though he was freshly out of Wharton, Cohen still had to push his way in. Gruntal wasn't well-respected, but he didn't care about prestige. He cared about money, and he intended to make lots of it.

It happened that a childhood friend of Cohen's, Ronald Aizer, had re-cently taken a job running the options department at Gruntal, and he was looking for help.

Aizer was ten years older than Cohen, had an aptitude for math, and had autonomy to invest the firm's capital however he wanted. On Cohen's first day, Aizer pointed at a chair and told his new hire to sit there while he figured out what, exactly, he was going to do with him. Cohen sank down in front of a Quotron screen and became absorbed in the rhythm of the numbers ticking by.

The stock market distills a basic economic principle, one that Aizer had figured out how to exploit: The more risk you take with an investment, the greater the potential reward. If there's a chance that a single piece of news could send a stock plunging, investors expect greater possible profit for exposing themselves to those potential losses. A sure, predictable thing, like a municipal bond, meanwhile, typically returns very little. There's no reward without risk—it is one of the central tenets of investing. Aizer, however, found an intriguing loophole in this mechanism, where the two elements had fallen out of sync. It involved stock options.

The market for options at the time was far less crowded than regular stock trading—and in many ways, more attractive. Options are contracts that allow a person to either buy or sell shares of stock at a fixed price, before a specific date in the future. A "put" represents the right to *sell* shares of stock, which means that the owner of a put will benefit if the stock price drops, allowing him or her to sell the underlying shares at the agreed-upon higher price. "Calls" are the opposite, granting the holder the right to *buy* a particular stock at a specific price on or before the expiration date, so the owner of the call will benefit if the stock rises, as the option contract allows him or her to buy it for less than it would cost on the open market, yielding an instantaneous profit. Investors sometimes use options as a way to hedge a stock position they already have.

At Gruntal, Aizer had implemented a strategy called "option arbitrage." There was a precise mathematical relationship dictating how the price of the option should change relative to the price of the underlying stock. Theoretically, in a perfect market, the price of a put option, the price of a call option, and the price at which the stock was trading would be in alignment. Because options were new and communication between markets was sometimes slow, this equation occasionally fell out of line, creating a mismatch between the different prices. By buying and selling the options on one exchange and the stock on another, for example, a clever trader could pocket the difference.

In theory, the technique involved almost no risk. There was no borrowed money and relatively little capital required, and most positions

were closed out by the end of the day, which meant that you didn't develop ulcers worrying about something that might send the market down
overnight. The strategy would be rendered obsolete as technology im-
proved, but in the early 1980s it was like plucking fistfuls of cash off of
vines—and the traders at Gruntal enjoyed bountiful harvests. All day
long, Aizer and his traders compared the prices of stocks to their valua-
tions in the options market, rushing to make a trade whenever they detected an inconsistency.

"You could have IBM trading at $100 on the New York Stock Exchange
floor," explained Helen Clarke, who worked as Aizer's clerk in the early
1980s, "and the options that equal IBM at $100 trading at $99 in Chicago,
so you'd run to Chicago and buy it and sell it at the NYSE." If done enough
times, it added up.

Without the benefit of computer spreadsheets, the traders had to keep
track of everything in their heads. Aizer set up a system that required
minimal thinking. You didn't have to be good, he liked to say, you just
had to follow the formulas. It was tedious. A trained monkey could do it.

On Cohen's first day, he watched Aizer work with a trading assistant,
scouring the market for $0.25 or $0.50 they could make on their idiot-
proof options schemes. During a lull in activity, he stared at the market
screens. Then Cohen announced that he was looking at a stock, ABC. "I
think it's going to open higher tomorrow," he said. Even brand-new on
the job, Cohen was confident in his abilities as a trader.

Aizer snickered. "All right," he said, curious to see whether the new kid
with bushy brown hair and glasses had any clue what he was doing. "Go
ahead, take a shot."

Cohen made $4,000 that afternoon, and another $4,000 overnight; in
1978, this was a meaningful profit. Watching the price oscillate like a sine
wave, placing the bet, taking the risk, absorbing the payoff—his body
surged with adrenaline, and Cohen was hooked. Trading was all he
wanted to do.

Aizer was stunned. How could someone so inexperienced, someone
who couldn't even be bothered to iron his shirt, be this good at predicting
whether stocks would go up or down?

"I knew he was going to be famous within a week," Aizer said. "I never saw talent like that. It was just staring at you."

On Sunday afternoons, inside a four-bedroom split-level house in Great Neck, a little boy stood watch by his bedroom window, waiting for the sound of tires on asphalt. As soon as the Cadillac pulled up outside, he came flying down the stairs. He wanted to beat his siblings to the door when his grandparents arrived.

Walter and Madeline Mayer, Steven Cohen's maternal grandparents, lived partly off an investment portfolio of inherited money, and they came to see their grandchildren once or twice a month. They led an alluring life in Manhattan, one that involved fancy restaurants and Broadway shows. They represented escape and abundance and excitement, and when Steve was growing up, their visits were his favorite moments of the week. They were always talking about money, and Cohen listened carefully to the lessons that emerged, the idea that once you had money, banks would pay interest on it, and that money could be invested and it would grow, requiring little or no work on the part of the investor, who was left to be envied and admired by others. The freedom that his grandparents enjoyed was a sharp contrast to the pinched and pedestrian existence of Cohen's parents. When his father walked in the door after work each night, Cohen grabbed his *New York Post* so he could study the stock tables like his grandfather.

Born in the summer of 1956, Cohen was the third of Jack and Patricia Cohen's eight children. Great Neck was twenty miles from New York City, an affluent suburban enclave of progressive-minded Jewish professionals who expected their children to do well in school and go on to careers as doctors and dentists. F. Scott Fitzgerald settled there in 1922, and the area became partial inspiration for *The Great Gatsby*, which was set in the fictional "West Egg," based on Kings Point, Great Neck's northernmost tip on the Long Island Sound. Many of the fathers of Great Neck lived separate Long Island and Manhattan existences, which involved a lot of drinking and long train commutes and extended hours away from home. There were synagogues and good schools and grand estates.

In Great Neck, the Cohens were on the low end of the financial spectrum, which Steve was aware of from an early age. At a time when the Garment District still produced garments, Cohen's father, Jack, took the train every morning to one of his showrooms in Manhattan, where he ran a business called Minerva Fashions, which made twenty-dollar dresses for chains such as Macy's and J. C. Penney.

Cohen's mother, Patricia—Patsy—was a self-employed piano teacher. She advertised in the local *Pennysaver* for clients, mostly neighborhood children, and taught strictly popular music—"Hello, Dolly!" rather than Beethoven or Brahms. She was a harsh, uncompromising woman who dominated the family, known for a sense of humor that could cut like a blade and for periodically berating her husband: "Jackie, you gotta fuck them before they fuck you!"

Money was a constant source of stress in the Cohen household. Cohen's mother and father spoke openly about the inheritance they hoped was imminent from Patsy's parents, which they planned to use to introduce more comfort into their lives. Although he was small, Cohen was a gifted athlete, pitching for the baseball team, playing point guard in basketball. But his parents didn't have the means to help him make the most of his athletic potential—there wasn't much money for private lessons or time to drive him around to games. The junior high soccer coach ran a lakeside summer camp in Maine where several of the neighborhood children went. Cohen attended in 1968 and loved it. Camp was an enchanted world, a great equalizer where all the kids wore the same T-shirts and slept in little pine cabins, everyone on equal footing. There were no parents around fighting about the bills and telling the kids they couldn't do things. After that one summer, however, Steve's parents never sent him back; his classmates believed it was because they couldn't afford the fees.

Still, Steve was doted upon. His grandmother marked him as the brightest of the eight siblings and referred to him as the "sharpest pencil in the box," which made him glow with pride. He got good grades without spending a lot of time studying. Cohen's older brother Gary remembers their mother fixing steak for Steve while the rest of the kids got hot dogs. "I used to complain," he recalled, "and my mother said, 'Your brother Steve is going to support us someday.'"

In high school, Cohen discovered the one extracurricular activity that ignited true passion in him: poker. "A group of us, we started playing cards at each other's houses, all day, then all night," Cohen remembered. "The stakes started at, like, a quarter, fifty cents. Eventually we got up to five, ten, or twenty bucks a replacement card, and by tenth grade you could win or lose a thousand dollars in a night."

All this card-playing helped Cohen learn an important lesson about capitalism. There were relatively difficult ways to make money, like working as a stock boy at Bohack supermarket for $1.85 an hour, which he did one summer and found to be excruciating. And there were much easier ways to earn a buck, like beating his friends at the poker table, which he found to be quite enjoyable. Cohen would stumble home early in the morning with bundles of cash, making sure to return his dad's car keys in time for his father to make his morning commute to work. Watching his father trudge off to work each day, Cohen had one thought: *This life is not for me.*

Cohen was admitted to Wharton, and his parents were overjoyed. They had inherited some money from Jack's parents, freeing them from the burden of student loans, although Steve would still have to work to earn money for books and going out. As soon as he arrived on campus, he noticed that the parking lot was filled with BMWs and Mercedes that belonged to his fellow students. Once again, Cohen was in an environment where most everyone around him came from wealthier families than he did and he was shut out of the most elite social circles. His fraternity house became the center of his life.

The culture at Wharton was driven by the worship of money. Cohen's fraternity, Zeta Beta Tau, or ZBT, was the wealthier of the two Jewish fraternities on campus. Its nickname was "Zillions Billions Trillions."

Cohen spent most of his nights in ZBT's living room, which was transformed into a gambling den, with a dozen guys around a table. At the center of the table sat Cohen, leading the game, intensely focused amid clouds of smoke and clinking beer bottles. He was part of a core of five or six young men who dominated the table, while a rotating cast of losers filled the extra seats.

One night in 1976, a student from one of his classes sat across from him, sweat accumulating at the base of his back. Cohen cracked jokes and flashed his gap-toothed smile. He had become known as a snake charmer who specialized in separating his classmates from their inheritances. He wasn't cool and didn't have women paying attention to him, but he had earned the respect of the trust fund kids he was in school with. The stakes in the game were already into the hundreds of dollars, which Cohen's opponent, an occasional player, found to be a little rich for a game full of college students. Cohen's classmate swallowed hard and braced himself for another loss. Cohen won several thousand dollars from him over the course of the semester, and each time he lost, the classmate swore he wouldn't let it happen again.

While many of the fraternity brothers stayed up late dropping acid or drinking beer, Cohen rose early each morning to read *The Wall Street Journal*. He carefully tracked the stock market, but he considered school itself to be a waste of time. One day, during a statistics exam, while the others in the class were struggling to finish, Cohen stood up and marched out the door before he was done to check his closing stock prices. He thought he had no chance of competing with the prep school kids who spoke the same language and had all read the same books. He would have to outsmart them.

In between classes, Cohen roamed around the floor of the Philadelphia-Baltimore-Washington stock exchange in a T-shirt, walking up to the traders and annoying them by saying things like: "Hey, your spreads are off." He started skipping classes to visit the Merrill Lynch offices in Philadelphia, where he could watch the NYSE ticker. "I'd just stand there and stare," he said. "I could hear the tick tick tick of the tape, and you would watch a stock go by at, say, 50 . . . 50 . . . 50 . . . And then it might go up or down a tick. You could see the trade happening. You could just watch it happen in slow motion. And later, not right away, I found I was pretty good at guessing which way those numbers would go."

All around him, Cohen saw people who weren't as talented as he was succeeding. That tick tick tick of the tape became the key to the future he felt he deserved.

Elaine's was a smoky, oak-paneled restaurant that attracted artists and theater people on the Upper East Side, and Cohen was at the bar, sipping a drink. He was alone, on his birthday. He didn't have many friends. Rain was pouring down on the street outside.

It was June of 1979, and Cohen was exhausted from a day on the floor at Gruntal, where all day long people had been screaming "Stevie!" at him. The nickname made his skin crawl. Aizer had adopted "Stevie" as a way to distinguish Steve Cohen from Steve Ginsberg, the older brother of Kenny Ginsberg, Cohen's best friend from high school, who had recently started working with them. Aizer's little operation was becoming an important profit center at Gruntal, and they were given a lot of freedom by Howard Silverman, Gruntal's CEO, who adored Cohen. Silverman drove sports cars, spoke with arrogance and ambition, and liked people who shared his values. He could see that Cohen was hungry, and he wanted guys like him around.

Over the previous year, Cohen had started making more and more money trading at Gruntal, but he was still socially unhappy, permanently disappointed over the lack of recognition he felt he received. He didn't have many friends. Elaine's was crowded and Cohen looked around, contemplating the fact that he was now twenty-three years old and single, when someone caught his attention.

A woman had just walked in, dripping wet, in a white camisole and a silk skirt that clung to her legs. Cohen stared at her.

The woman looked around anxiously and smoothed her wet hair. She was supposed to meet a girlfriend for dinner. It was the sort of Manhattan rainstorm that made it impossible to find a cab, so her friend was late. She hovered by the bar and watched the door, keeping her eyes cast low to avoid the gazes of the men who were staring from different parts of the restaurant, a New York City survival tactic that came naturally to her. At one point, she noticed Cohen looking in her direction and angled herself so that she was facing the other way. Cohen watched her for a few minutes before he felt bold enough to approach her.

"Hello," he said, sidling up awkwardly. He tried to smile.

"Hello," she said, and looked at him quizzically. *Who* is *this guy?* she thought to herself.

Her name was Patricia Finke. She would never normally have bothered with someone like Cohen, who was so conservative, so corporate-looking. She had grown up in an artsy family in Manhattan and had been raised with a snobbish attitude toward the suburbs. Under different circumstances she would have completely ignored him. But he appeared harmless enough in his wrinkled shirt and unstylish shoes, and he seemed captivated by her. He gave off an aura of vulnerability that was appealing.

At first, Cohen tried to impress Patricia with stories about how he'd gambled all his bar mitzvah money in the stock market as a kid and how his bosses at Gruntal were upset about how much risk he took with his trades and how everyone at work thought he was too cocky. "They think I'm a cowboy," he said. For a while, Patricia kept looking over his shoulder, watching for her friend. But eventually, against her better instincts, she was drawn in. She and Cohen ended up talking for hours.

Before he left that night, Cohen convinced Patricia to give him her phone number. He spent the next few weeks pursuing her, calling three times a day, asking to know when they'd see each other again.

They dated for the next several months. Some of Patricia's friends couldn't understand what she was doing with Cohen, who seemed so unsophisticated, a money-obsessed schlub from Long Island. But Patricia had grown up without money, and she hadn't finished high school. She knew what it was like to worry about paying for all her expenses. She was supporting herself working for a publishing company and had a rent-controlled apartment in the West Village. She wasn't unhappy, but there was no denying that Cohen's drive for riches was attractive. She didn't have a clue about the stock market, but he talked about it endlessly, boasting about how much money he planned to make. He said that he would take care of her.

Cohen, for his part, had little else going on in his life. He lived in a one-bedroom apartment where most of the lightbulbs were burned out. He spent a lot of his free time by himself. He wanted a wife. He cared about Patricia, and he started suggesting they get married. Patricia finally agreed.

They told their parents that they had eloped. But in fact there was a tiny wedding, with just two guests, Patricia's maid of honor and Cohen's best man, at a small Unitarian church in Murray Hill, a quiet neighborhood in the middle of Manhattan. Not long after, in 1981, their first child, Jessica Lynn, was born. Finally, Cohen had his own family.

"Pick up the fucking phone!" Ron Aizer yelled.

It was a typical morning on Gruntal's trading desk, with Aizer's traders tapping on their keyboards. Usually, when a phone rang, everyone would wait to see who would be the first one to get too annoyed to ignore it and pick it up.

One of the assistant traders, who was trying to fill in trade tickets that were spread all over his desk, looked around, but there was no free phone within reach. "I don't have a phone!" he yelled.

The phone kept ringing.

Cohen, who was trying to make a trade, yanked his own phone right out of the wall and slammed it on the assistant trader's desk. "You want a phone? Here's a fucking phone!" Within seconds, they were both on their feet, inches apart.

"You motherfucker, what do you think you're doing?"

"You fucking piece of shit!"

A few minutes later, everybody was friends again.

It went like that every day. It was Aizer's job to manage the tension and keep his traders productive and busy. He divided the stocks of the Dow Jones index among them, usually reserving the biggest ones with the most volatility, such as IBM and Eastman Kodak and Honeywell, for himself. If no one appeared to be trading a particular security regularly, any one of the traders could gradually take it over until it became theirs. Most of the time, everyone respected these allocations. Everyone except Cohen.

One day, a trader came to Aizer to complain about Mesa Petroleum, one of his stocks. Mesa was a volatile company, with dramatic swings that created ample opportunities to make money, which meant that everyone else wanted to trade it, too. "Every time I try to trade, Steve's ahead of me," the trader complained. "Mesa's my best stock, and he's killing me!"

Aizer confronted Cohen. "Steve, you're making so much money, and these guys are not doing as well," he said. "Do you *really* need to trade Mesa?"

"Would the Yankees ask Mickey Mantle to bat eighth?" Cohen shot back. Aizer shrugged. It was hard to argue. Cohen was such a good producer that he became the exception to every rule.

Aizer had negotiated to keep 50 percent of the trading profits his team made, which added up to millions of dollars a month. They moved into a larger office adjacent to Gruntal's trading floor to accommodate all the new traders being hired. Many of them came from Drexel Burnham Lambert, where Michael Milken worked, which had developed a reputation for training aggressive traders. Even in the bigger space, though, there was a disproportionate number of men with volcanic tempers squished together so tightly that they were practically on top of one another.

Cohen and the rest of Aizer's employees couldn't have chosen a more opportune moment to begin a career in finance. Ronald Reagan's pro-business policies had strapped a jet pack on Wall Street and the traders and raiders who filled its ranks. Regulations were loosened, freeing companies to borrow money and buy their competitors, and the stock market began one of the most prolonged upward swings in its history. The pace of mergers and acquisitions increased, fueled in part by Milken's empire at Drexel Burnham Lambert, which had created a new way of financing corporate takeovers through high-yield debt, also known as junk bonds—which were ranked "below investment grade" by ratings agencies because they were riskier than other bonds. With these new instruments, companies that couldn't borrow money could suddenly issue junk bonds, which gave them the financial resources to launch hostile takeovers of their competitors. Every day, rumors of these leveraged buyouts sent companies' share prices soaring, earning millions for the traders buying and selling their stocks.

It didn't take long for Cohen to become emboldened by his success. He started day-trading stocks and built positions around events such as takeovers and initial public offerings, applying his instinct for the market to the industry shifts taking place. "He was the best trader I'd ever seen—just exceptionally better than anyone else," Aizer's clerk Helen Clarke said. "He had an ability to hold on to a position, without flexing. Sometimes you can be in a position, and someone slips on a banana peel in Pakistan, and suddenly everything changes. He never got out of a position because he was nervous."

It wasn't so much that Cohen was smarter than other traders, but he had conviction in his instincts and he acted quickly. "He had a natural talent," recalled Silverman, Gruntal's CEO, describing Cohen's skill as a "tape reader," someone who had an intuitive feel for supply and demand in the market gained from watching the physical ticker tape, which showed trades that had just been completed. "He really was brilliant."

Cohen became a star at Gruntal, someone who couldn't get himself fired no matter how many risk limits he violated or how many tantrums he threw while violating them. Cohen knew that he was right about where a particular stock price was going more often than not. He abandoned Aizer's riskless options strategy and stopped hedging his positions, making them both riskier and, usually, much more profitable.

Soon, Cohen was making $5 to $10 million a year. Oddly, though, while the money fueled his confidence on the trading floor, it did little for his private life. He would come home from work in an irritable state, and he and Patricia would argue. He was a disengaged father. He and his wife felt awkward in the fancy social settings their wealth now granted them access to. He complained to Patricia incessantly that everyone was trying to take advantage of him, recounting every trade he'd done that day, how he was shorted by some floor specialist, or how a broker had cheated him a quarter point on a stock.

His sense that everyone was out to get him wasn't entirely imagined; it was partly a result of the structure of the industry. On Wall Street, a trader at a small firm such as Cohen was competing with banks and brokerage firms filled with starched-shirt sharks. All day long, traders at firms much larger than Gruntal would call Cohen up, trying to sell him blocks of stock at prices they had set. It made Cohen crazy that they expected him to just agree to do whatever trades they offered him. "I can tell you what made him think, a typical situation," said a former colleague. "Goldman Sachs would call you and say, 'We're going to put up 100,000 shares at $90,' and you were supposed to take the other side of that," meaning buy some of the shares they were selling. In almost every instance, though, a buyer in Cohen's position knew that by taking the opposite side of a trade from Goldman he would be getting the worse end of the deal. It was like betting in a Las Vegas casino—the house always has the odds in its favor. Cohen did *not* want to be the guy making other people rich. He wanted to know why Goldman always seemed to have better information than everyone else. Instead of being used by the Goldmans and the Morgans, he wanted to compete with them. So when Goldman Sachs called, he made it clear that he wasn't going to do whatever they wanted. He wanted their best trades, their best prices, the information they kept to themselves.

By the mid-1980s, Cohen was generating so much in commissions with his trading that Goldman and the other big firms had no choice but to try to work with him. Finally, he was starting to get some respect.

As his stature on Wall Street grew, Cohen realized that he could make even more money by getting away from Aizer and going out on his own. He saw himself as destined for bigger things than Aizer. In 1985 Cohen negotiated a deal with Gruntal that put him in charge of his own trading group, which gave him authority to hire and fire his own traders and negotiate their compensation directly, excluding Aizer completely. Cohen's status as Gruntal's most lucrative trader allowed him to bargain for an unprecedented 60 percent share of his profits, plus a 2 to 4 percent "kicker" at the end of the year, depending on how well he did. This brought him one step closer to his dream of running his own fund—and keeping all of the money he made for himself.

Howard Silverman gave him $8 to $10 million of the firm's capital to invest and moved him into a larger office on the building's twenty-third floor, where Cohen set up a basketball hoop, a symbol of his independence. His best friend, Jay Goldman, from Wharton, whose nickname was "J-Bird," came to work with him, taking the seat next to Cohen on the trading desk. Cohen's younger brother Donald, an accountant, was hired to check Cohen's trading records and help him manage the administrative side of his operation. Cohen's golf pro did clerical work. An assistant filled out his trade tickets. His refusal to write his own tickets, which the brokerages needed to reconcile their trades each day, had almost gotten him fired several times before. Why bother with stuff like that when he could be making money trading?

Now that he was in charge, his moods and pet peeves became more pronounced. He kept the room at near-arctic temperatures, which he felt helped him think more clearly, and he didn't adjust it for anyone. His sister Wendy, whom he had hired as a trader, sat shivering in a corner with a portable heater under her desk. One day Cohen stormed in and ripped up all the carpeting in the office because it was distracting him. His group was a collection of strange personalities, mostly drawn from his Wharton or Great Neck past.

On the other side of a glass wall, Aizer's options group kept going for a few more years, then shut down. His no-risk trades were disappearing as the market became more sophisticated. Aizer didn't like the way the trading business was changing, so he moved to Florida. Cohen and the mentor who gave him his first job on Wall Street never really spoke again.

Beginning in the mid-1980s, the American stock market came to be dominated by mergers and acquisitions. Every day, the stock prices of large corporations like Carnation, Union Carbide, and Diamond Shamrock were sent on wild swings as rumors of takeovers surged across Wall Street. Like most everyone else trading stocks at the time, Cohen got caught up in the rumors. He had a hard time pulling himself away from his desk. According to one of his former traders, he almost missed the birth of his son Robert because he was on the phone at the hospital, giving out trade orders for Schlumberger while Patricia shrieked with labor pains in the background.

"Our job was to play," said the former trader. "You buy, man. It was deal mania, and every rumor was true."

Cohen loved to engage in market chatter as he watched his screens, exchanging stock ideas with his friends. He also had a habit of sharing stock ideas with his brother Donald, who administered Cohen's books from his office in Miami.

One morning in December 1985, Cohen phoned Donald and recommended that he buy shares of RCA, the parent of the NBC television network. "I heard there might be a restructuring going on," Cohen said. "These TV stocks are pretty hot." He then added, "If NBC is spun off, it could run up 20 points."

After studying RCA's stock chart over the weekend and looking through a few back issues of *Forbes,* Donald bought twenty March call options in his personal trading account at Fidelity. It gave him the right to buy RCA shares three months later at $50, an aggressive bet that its stock price was going to increase. Cohen had already made a similar investment in his own account. Patricia later said that he'd been telling people that a Wharton classmate had told him about an impending takeover offer for the company.

The movement of RCA's stock looked like the skyline of the Andes, a zigzag of dramatic spikes as investors kept buying more shares in response to rumors of the takeover. Six days after the conversation with Donald, General Electric announced a takeover of the broadcaster for $66.50 a share, which sent its stock price shooting up even more. Cohen made $20 million in profits on the trade.

Three months later, an envelope from the SEC arrived at the office of

Gruntal's legal counsel. It contained a subpoena. The agency had launched an investigation into possible insider trading in RCA before the takeover. It seemed obvious to the regulators looking at the stock activity that some traders in the market had known about the deal in advance. The SEC wanted Cohen to come in and testify.

In fact, the agency was looking at a handful of other stocks, too—Warner Communications, General Foods, and Union Carbide, all of which had recently been targets of takeover offers. Trading on material nonpublic information that was leaked by an insider who was supposed to keep it confidential was a violation of securities laws. The SEC noticed that a group of people connected to Cohen had accumulated shares of all three stocks, as well as RCA, right before public announcements had driven the prices higher. The agency suspected an insider trading ring of some sort.

Donald got a subpoena, too. Trying to stay calm, he called Steve demanding to know what was going on.

"Don't worry," Cohen reassured him. "Everyone that bought RCA at the time is being questioned."

Privately, though, Cohen was panicking. Days before, he and his traders had all watched in horror as Drexel's top mergers and acquisitions banker, Dennis Levine, was arrested and charged with orchestrating a massive insider trading scheme by paying off lawyers and bankers to leak him information about takeovers and other deals. The Levine arrest was just the beginning of the unraveling of Michael Milken's junk bond empire, an unprecedented series of prosecutions that would dominate news headlines for months. The SEC accused Levine of accumulating $12.6 million in illegal profits and froze all his assets, preventing him from paying his legal bills.

Around 6 P.M. on June 5, 1986, the same day that Levine pleaded guilty to tax evasion, securities fraud, and perjury and agreed to help the Justice Department by providing evidence against others committing crimes on Wall Street, Cohen arrived at 26 Federal Plaza, at Broadway and Worth Street, wearing his best suit. He was about to be deposed in the RCA investigation. Gruntal had arranged for Cohen to be represented by Otto

Obermaier, a former head trial lawyer for the SEC with a taste for expensive wine and Mozart. Obermaier was one of the most talented and well-connected defense attorneys in the field, and he was about to validate his reputation.

An SEC staff attorney and a financial analyst who evaluated trading data for the agency's enforcement division were waiting for Cohen in a conference room. After some awkward greetings, the staff attorney began the formal proceedings. "This is an investigation by the Securities and Exchange Commission entitled, 'In the matter of trading in the securities of RCA Corporation,'" the staff attorney said. "We are here to take testimony in this matter to determine whether there have been violations of certain provisions of the federal securities laws."

The staff attorney asked Cohen to raise his right hand. Cohen did, and he was sworn in. The staff attorney then turned to Cohen, introduced himself and his colleague, and asked: "Have you seen the subpoena?"

"*He* has," Cohen said, gesturing in Obermaier's direction.

The staff attorney looked at Obermaier, then turned to Cohen again. "Have *you* seen the subpoena?"

"I don't think so," Obermaier said, answering for Cohen. "It hasn't been shown to him."

The agency had sent a separate subpoena to Cohen requesting trading records and other documents as part of its investigation. The staff attorney mentioned this and then looked at Cohen again. "No documents have been produced. Do you plan to produce any documents today?"

"No," Obermaier said, again on Cohen's behalf. They had no intention of being helpful, although he didn't say that to the SEC lawyers. Instead, Obermaier told them that they would "decline the invitation to produce documents" based on his client's constitutional rights.

"Which constitutional right is that?" the staff attorney asked.

"The provision that no person shall be compelled to be a witness against himself," Obermaier answered.

"That's his 'Fifth Amendment right,'" the staff attorney said.

Frustrated, the SEC attorney tried to insist that Cohen answer the question about the documents himself. During depositions there was usually a struggle over this point. It was always a goal of the SEC to get a witness to admit that he was "taking the Fifth" on the record when he was refusing to answer their questions; it could be used later as an inference of guilt. If you were innocent, the thinking went, why wouldn't you use the opportunity to tell the SEC all about it? White collar defense attorneys were well aware of this, of course, so it was their job to resist and try to avoid letting the client say that he was "taking the Fifth," even when he *was* taking the Fifth, for precisely the same reason. It was standard legal maneuvering.

"He has to assert personally his right not to produce documents under the Fifth Amendment," the SEC staff attorney said, trying again.

"I don't think he does," Obermaier replied. He had no intention of letting Cohen say a word. "I'm responding as his lawyer."

"What is your date and place of birth?" the staff attorney asked.

Cohen and Obermaier had rehearsed this. "Upon the advice of counsel," Cohen said, "I respectfully decline to answer the question on the ground that I'm being compelled to be a witness against myself."

"Did you purchase securities on behalf of Gruntal & Co. in December of 1985 while in possession of nonpublic information concerning RCA?"

"Same response," Cohen said.

They went back and forth. The staff attorney asked more questions: Did Cohen purchase RCA shares in his own account in December 1985? Did anyone tell him that RCA would be involved in a merger with General Electric prior to the public announcement? Did Cohen, in December 1985, recommend that anyone else buy RCA shares? Each time Cohen repeated the same answer, taking the Fifth without saying that he was taking the Fifth.

Then the staff attorney asked, "Are you familiar with an entity known as J. Goldman & Company?" The attorney was referring to Cohen's close friend Jay Goldman, a.k.a. "J-Bird," who had formed his own trading firm after leaving Gruntal the previous year.

Cohen barely registered any recognition. "Same response," he said.

The testimony was over in twenty minutes. Riding the elevator back down to the lobby, Obermaier felt confident that he had done the best he could to save his client from prosecution.

Cohen, however, was badly shaken by the experience. Refusing to answer questions before a law enforcement agency usually made people sound guilty, even if they weren't. The RCA investigation was still ongoing. He felt he was now at risk of losing his livelihood. He was more irritable than usual during the day and spent most evenings at home, ranting about the SEC to Patricia. One weekend he could barely get out of bed. He was being unfairly persecuted, he complained, it wasn't right. Patricia, for her part, was anxious. But she believed her husband's assurances that he hadn't done anything wrong.

Then, one day, a letter arrived at their apartment from the phone company. It informed the Cohens that their phone records had been subpoenaed by the U.S. Attorney's Office. It was a sign that there was a possible criminal investigation under way in addition to the SEC's civil one. Patricia started screaming when she read it. The possibility of a criminal case went against everything Cohen had been telling her, that the worst that could happen was that he'd have to pay a fine. A criminal prosecution could result in jail time. Cohen assured her that he had learned the information indirectly, not right from the Wharton classmate who worked on the deal but from an intermediary, which meant that trading on it wasn't illegal. Still, the uncertainty affected the whole family. Patricia and the children would cower when they heard Cohen's key in the lock at the end of each day.

The government's RCA investigation was a source of constant embarrassment. "I'm just a stock trader, and I happen to have been trading in these stocks," Cohen complained to his friend on the golf course. "It's creating a lot of problems for my family, my children, and my personal life."

On Monday, October 19, 1987, Cohen came into work before 8 A.M., earlier than usual. He had a bad feeling. In spite of the distractions of the SEC investigation, Cohen's group had continued making money as the market, driven by hundreds of merger deals, climbed higher and higher. In the previous couple of weeks, though, fissures had started to appear, caused partly by the fact that lawmakers in Washington were debating the possibility of eliminating a tax loophole for interest payments on loans for financing hostile takeovers. If the mergers suddenly stopped, so would the ascent of the stock prices. Investors were nervous.

There were also geopolitical tensions to worry about, including a long-running war between Iran and Iraq. On the previous Thursday, October 15, Iran had blasted an American oil tanker near Kuwait with a missile, prompting debate about how the United States would respond. The Dow fell over 100 points. By Monday morning, markets around the world were crashing. It seemed to be the result of a combination of fear about the Middle East, falling oil prices, the end of the M&A boom, signs of a recession, and some computerized stock selling. Cohen was aware of all of this when he got to his desk and saw how badly the overseas and Asian markets were doing. The Hong Kong index was down, and all the numbers on the European charts were red. He had many short positions in the portfolio, which would offset some of his losses. He tried to calculate how much money they might lose as he stared at his screen.

When the market opened in New York, he started selling his holdings as fast as he could. The trouble was, with everyone else trying to do the same thing and a total absence of buyers in the market, stock prices lurched downward. Traders were rushing around the floor of the NYSE, knocking into one another. During the last hour of trading the selling accelerated, as investors panicked at the thought of holding shares overnight. Over the course of a single day that would become known as Black Monday, the Dow Jones Industrial Average fell 508 points, or 23 percent, the largest one-day decline in its history. Ten years of unrestrained borrowing was coming to a sudden, painful halt.

Gruntal, along with many other firms, was practically put out of business. Cohen's group lost almost half of its capital. Every one of its seven traders was nearly wiped out by losses.

When the financial stakes were high, though, Cohen demonstrated an almost inhuman ability to stay calm and make rational trading decisions.

As the chaos continued around him, he saw an opportunity. After trading had closed for the day, according to a former employee, Cohen turned to his traders who were rubbing their faces and staring at their monitors in shock. "From now on, no one is trading but me," he told them. "I'm the only trader, and you guys are my clerks." No one quite knew what he was talking about, but they didn't argue.

It was a fraught time. Fortunes were lost and people's lives were ruined. Two of their brokers at outside firms, including Kidder, Peabody, which was embroiled in the Drexel insider trading scandal, jumped out their office windows. The junk bond bubble was beginning to burst, as companies that had borrowed billions of dollars found they couldn't pay it back. The savings and loan crisis was also getting worse, causing the collapse of more than a thousand banks around the country. Wall Street was in crisis.

Cohen, however, remained in control. For the next month after the crash, as the NYSE floor specialists struggled to open trading in their securities every morning, Cohen's "clerks" would call them before the market opened and get quotes for where they thought particular stocks would start trading. Due to the ongoing shock of the crash, the biggest trading opportunities often came at the start of the day, when nobody knew what was going to happen and fear ran high. Could this be the day it all went to zero? Cohen would get his "look" conveyed to him from the floor specialists, as in, "Gillette's going to open up 2." Then as soon as the stock opened he'd short as many shares as he could—selling shares he didn't actually own and buying them back when the stock went down again. He did this over and over again for weeks, shorting nearly every stock in the Dow—DuPont, GE, IBM—making money almost every time as the prices went lower. It wasn't a patriotic move, when the market was struggling to recover, but his colleagues marveled at his ability to turn off his emotions.

Gruntal, and Cohen's trading group, ultimately survived. Cohen's marriage did not.

He and Patricia had been fighting bitterly for months and had gone in and out of couples therapy. Things got so tense that on June 22, 1988, Cohen moved out of his family's fifty-five-hundred-square-foot apartment on East End Avenue. It was the beginning of a year and a half of acrimonious divorce negotiations. While they were trying to come to a settlement, Cohen's lawyer recommended that he move back into the apartment to give him a stronger negotiating position, which he did. With twenty-eight rooms, the place was enormous, and Cohen argued that he should be able to live there until the divorce was official, since it seemed to be taking so long. The move was the beginning of a new phase of conflict between them.

The attorneys spent hundreds of billable hours arguing over a list of Cohen's assets and trying to figure out exactly how much money he had been making each year. He had never shared this information with his wife. They made offers and counteroffers. Cohen finally produced a spreadsheet showing that everything he had in the world was worth $16.9 million. Around half of that, $8.75 million, had been invested in a real estate deal with his friend Brett Lurie. Cohen said that the deal had been unprofitable, though, and that the entire $8.75 million was gone—so he valued it at zero. The remaining $8 million or so had to be divided evenly. Cohen offered to give Patricia their apartment, which he said was worth $2.8 million, and an additional $1 million in cash. He also agreed to pay around $4,000 a month for expenses for Jessica and Robert, in addition to paying for their camp and private school tuition. Patricia planned to sell the apartment and move into something smaller, and she waived her right to spousal maintenance.

Although Cohen made more than $4 million that year, he resented having to give any money to his former wife. He complained about her spending habits, her $80,000 in Bergdorf's bills. The day after he signed the final spousal agreement he showed up at work in a petulant mood and turned to his traders.

"I just got ripped off by my wife," he said, according to a person who was there. "I'm going to make it all back by cutting your payouts."

His employees couldn't believe what they were hearing. Cohen was taking 60 percent of the group's profits. Out of that pool he was paying each of them 30 percent on the profits on their own trades, leaving him a full half of the cut on trades he hadn't even made himself. Many of the traders had worked their way up from clerks' salaries. Cohen wanted to reduce what they were getting by 5 percentage points.

"You can't do that," one of the traders said.

"Fuck you," Cohen said. "I'm the boss."

Within a relatively short time, the gloom of Black Monday went away. The stock market started another long climb. The SEC's RCA insider trading investigation petered out, apparently without charges or sanctions against anyone. The same happened with the criminal case. Through it all, a lesson that many other suspects of financial crime would come to understand in the future had emerged: Taking the Fifth could take all the momentum out of a securities investigation.

CHAPTER 2

WHAT STEVIE WANTS, STEVIE GETS

"This is what we're gonna do," Cohen announced to his traders in 1992. "I want us to get out of Gruntal's broker dealer fiefdom. They're sucking our profits, they're holding us back." As long as Cohen's trading group was part of a registered broker, which Gruntal was, they were subject to heavy regulation that restricted their activities—they couldn't invest in initial public offerings, for example, which were becoming an important new source of profit. Cohen grinned. "We're doing this. We're going out on our own."

By this time, Gruntal had earned a reputation as a less than reputable firm and was the subject of multiple regulatory investigations. In an era characterized by unscrupulousness and outright lawbreaking on Wall Street, Gruntal's CEO, Howard Silverman, had given Cohen total freedom, and Cohen had thrived. Over fourteen years he had gone from being a junior trader to a Wall Street star. He was almost thirty-six years old, freshly divorced, and ready to make a change. It was time for him to go out on his own.

Cohen started SAC with around $23 million in capital and nine employees. He put in about $10 million of his own money, and his traders and friends and investors put in the rest. Many of his traders were in their late twenties and early thirties, with young kids at home. Some of their wives had been opposed to the decision to leave a stable job and take a chance on Cohen's new startup. They didn't have a big bank to help them in an emergency; it was their own life savings at risk.

During their first weeks in business, Cohen could tell that his new employees were nervous. Now that they were trading their own money, they became timid, hesitating over every buy and sell order, calculating and recalculating how much money they might lose if the market moved against them. Cohen tried to resist the temptation to scold and belittle them and instead tried to build up their confidence. "Come on," he told his traders. "There's nothing different about this!"

He wanted to have people around him who were comfortable taking risk. He loved hiring guys who were driven and competitive, especially those who'd played college sports. His dream was to have a room full of mini–Steve Cohens, men as fearless as he was. "Tell me some of the riskiest things you've ever done in your life," Cohen would ask his prospective traders. "I want guys who have the confidence to be out there, to be risk-takers."

The way to make money in the stock market, Cohen believed, was by taking intelligent risks. If you had a good investment idea but you were too scared to put a lot of capital behind it, you couldn't make abundant profits. Cohen figured that 5 percent of his trades accounted for most of the money he made. If he'd only placed those winning trades on a modest scale, those profits would have been considerably smaller. But what came naturally to him was a struggle for most people. It was practically a genetic anomaly, this ability to behave like a reptile while he was trading, as opposed to a human being prone to fear and self-doubt. When he interviewed potential new hires he tried to test for this quality as best he could.

Cohen's investing method was different from the ones employed by most other hedge funds. He absorbed vast amounts of information from every corner of the market each day, watched the bids and offers as they appeared in the market, then bought up tens or even hundreds of thousands of shares and sold them as soon as the price moved up. He did the same thing shorting, when stocks went down. He was a glorified day trader. It was a style that was almost impossible to replicate successfully, but if there was a model for Cohen's trade-making process it was probably the investing strategy employed by Michael Steinhardt, who'd started his hedge fund, Steinhardt, Fine, Berkowitz, in 1967. Steinhardt came into stock trading just as pensions were becoming popular, with ordinary people investing billions of dollars of new money in the stock market each year. The number of American workers with guaranteed benefit retirement funds tripled between 1950 and 1970, and all that money needed to be invested. Trading went from being an administrative job carried out by clerks in color-coded jackets to the fastest path to Wall Street superstardom. As one of few individual investors trading high volume at the time, Steinhardt demanded that big brokers with large blocks of stock to trade call him first and offer him better prices than ordinary investors could obtain in the open market. Steinhardt's intimate, and controversial, relationship with banks and brokerage firms provided much of his advantage over other investors, and his fortune.

For years, hedge funds had existed apart from mainstream Wall Street, populated mainly by eccentric men who avoided publicity. A few investing celebrities had emerged from hedge funds in the 1980s, including George Soros and Paul Tudor Jones, but what exactly they did was still unclear to most people. Eventually, it became known that these brainy oddballs were quietly amassing multibillion-dollar fortunes, and the media started to pay attention. They bought mansions the size of the Taj Mahal, traveled by helicopter to beach houses on Long Island, and collected artwork that belonged in the Metropolitan Museum. They became objects of extreme envy.

Cohen was a little different. He wasn't particularly fantastic at math, he didn't study global economies, he had no unique investing philosophy. He was just a great trader, one who was so good that a traditional Wall Street career couldn't contain him. Having his own hedge fund gave him an entrée to a new universe of wealth and power.

As SAC grew larger, with more money to trade and invest, established Wall Street firms began to notice. How could they not? Within three years, SAC had quadrupled in size, to almost $100 million. Cohen and his traders bought and sold so many shares each day that brokers started to worry they were missing out on a huge amount of revenue if they didn't trade with SAC. The problem the brokers had to overcome was that many of the big firms that employed them were suspicious of hedge funds in general, and Cohen in particular. There were rumors that SAC was making 100 percent annual returns. Traders at the big firms told each other that Cohen had to be cheating. J. P. Morgan refused to do business with him.

Cohen, meanwhile, wanted SAC to keep growing, which required finding new investors as well as salesmen who could help SAC get into IPOs or who could offer investment ideas they couldn't come up with on their own. He went out for steak dinners, golf and racquetball games. But Cohen didn't enjoy socializing for business purposes, and he wasn't good at building the kinds of relationships that would have helped the firm expand. He didn't really want to be part of the club. He needed to bring in a professional to do it for him.

He knew of one person who was perfect for the job. His name was Kenny Lissak, a blue-eyed, broad-shouldered stock salesman Cohen had hired during his last years at Gruntal. Lissak enjoyed golfing and going out drinking with brokers. He had developed contacts at Merrill Lynch, Goldman, Lehman, all the firms where Cohen was struggling to get people to treat him like an important client. In many ways, Lissak was the opposite of Cohen. They got along immediately.

Lissak had a more traditional perspective on trading than Cohen. Having worked at Shearson Lehman Brothers, one of the largest brokerage firms in the United States, Lissak understood how institutional research could influence stock prices. If Merrill Lynch put out an analyst report criticizing IBM, investors were likely to sell the stock and it would go down. Even if the substance of the report was wrong, the mere fact of the stock being upgraded or downgraded by a respected analyst had a powerful effect on its price. Not keeping track of these basic mechanisms was costing Cohen money.

Lissak met with brokers at Goldman Sachs and First Boston and pitched Cohen as a serious investor who should have access to their best research analysts. In exchange, Lissak told the brokers, there were huge trading commissions to be made. When he wasn't rushing to meetings, Lissak traded stocks himself, co-managing a portfolio with Cohen. They were best friends who worked hard all week and then spent the weekends relaxing side by side, golfing at the Glen Head Country Club on Long Island and taking ski vacations in Aspen.

Each morning the two of them arrived at the office and read the papers and checked the stock prices, deciding where they'd be making their money that day. If there was news about a company or a big buy or sell order coming into the market, Cohen prepared to take advantage of whatever momentum was created, buying shares as the stock ticked upward and selling as soon as it was ready to drop. Cohen was so good at it that traders at other firms began tracking what he was doing.

Cohen and Lissak spent hours analyzing their trades and trying to figure out how they could have done better. Lissak characterized their core philosophy in simple terms: It was all about improving their odds of earning a profit by eliminating the ways they lost money and increasing the ways they made money. The key to making money, they believed, was by intelligently controlling their losses. Academically, this was known as risk management.

Their trades usually went in their favor, but not always. One day after the market had closed, early in their relationship, Cohen and Lissak met at a frozen yogurt shop on the Upper East Side to talk through an especially difficult afternoon.

"What the fuck happened?" Cohen said morosely.

They had just experienced a huge loss in shares of Northern Telecom. The stock had gone from $38 to $31, but, reluctant to admit defeat, Cohen and Lissak bought more as it kept going lower. They'd been certain that the worst was over and that the stock would rebound. It was the sort of ego-driven stupidity that affects investors all the time, the fear of selling and realizing a loss, and believing, irrationally, that the moment you capitulate and sell, the stock will suddenly shoot back up. That one trade cost them close to $2 million. The loss wasn't going to cause them to have to shut down, but for Cohen, it was painful. He took each trade he made, every single day, very seriously. No miscalculations were forgivable.

"What are we going to do, drive a cab?" Cohen said.

After the Northern Telecom trade, Cohen implemented strict discipline when it came to losing money: If a trade is going against you, you set a limit, and then you sell, no matter what. Never let emotions get in the way.

The Hamptons, a longtime summer vacation spot for Manhattan's elite, comprise a handful of shingled villages stretching east from Westhampton to Montauk along the Atlantic Ocean, just eighty-eight miles from where Cohen grew up. By the time he founded SAC, Cohen could finally afford to be there. He and Lissak had started relocating their trading operation to East Hampton for the season. They rented a five-bedroom house with a pool and a housekeeper and took over an office above the Grand Café, a coffee shop in the center of East Hampton where rich ladies came in with their poodles. It would serve as their headquarters for July and August.

Cohen was sharing custody of Jessica and Robert every other weekend, trying to reconcile being a dad with his affluent bachelor lifestyle. His ex-wife, Patricia, didn't feel he paid enough attention to his kids when she wasn't around. Cohen lived alone and occasionally left the children by themselves while he worked out. One time, five-year-old Robert fell into the pool at Cohen's house in East Hampton, and Cohen had to jump in, fully clothed, and pull him out.

Cohen didn't like being alone, and yet he didn't enjoy the process of trying to meet women. He signed up for a dating service and sent out invitations in response to twenty of the profiles. Only one woman responded. Her name was Alexandra Garcia. She had long dark hair. They had their first date at a noisy Italian restaurant near Cohen's apartment in Manhattan, where they talked for several hours.

They started seeing each other regularly, but Alex made it clear that she wasn't interested in a casual relationship. She wanted to get married. On the surface, she was an unlikely match for a successful Wall Street trader. Alex was a struggling single mother raised in a large Puerto Rican family in Spanish Harlem. She had not gone to college. She had a son. She and Cohen had very little in common.

Cohen wasn't sure about getting married again after going through a painful divorce.

"I don't know what to do," Cohen said to Lissak one day at a pizza place near their summer house.

Alex was pressuring him to get engaged, he explained, but she didn't like the idea of signing a prenuptial agreement. Cohen was ambivalent for other reasons, too. He was still attracted to Patricia, for one thing. Cohen's friends compared his ex-wife to Margaret "Hot Lips" Houlihan, the sexpot army nurse on the TV show *M*A*S*H*. He also couldn't imagine getting married again without taking measures to protect his growing personal fortune. As Cohen agonized about what to do, Patricia and Alex developed an intense hatred for one another. They had to interact every time the kids were dropped off or were picked up from visitation with their father. The tension between them occasionally erupted into arguments on the street.

Lissak, though, could see that his friend was lonely and that Alex seemed to make him happy. "Just get her a ring," he advised Cohen. "What does it cost, three-eighths on $100,000? If it doesn't work out, you're out thirty grand."

Steve and Alex broke up at least four times in the intervening months, and each time, Alex fumed and made threats. It was now or never, she kept saying. Cohen finally took Lissak's advice and proposed to her. They were married on June 6, 1992, at the Plaza Hotel, an extravagant black-tie affair with three hundred guests. Lissak was the best man.

Alex immediately started to exert influence over her husband. Cohen was shy, someone who tried to avoid being the center of attention. Yet somehow, eight months after they were married, Alex convinced him to do something unthinkable: She signed them up to appear on a well-known Latin daytime TV program, *The Cristina Show,* that was doing a special on couples who were involved in toxic emotional entanglements with the husbands' ex-spouses. "Poor Alex has been married to Steven Cohen for only eight months," said Cristina, a blond, Latina version of Oprah. "She feels her battle with his ex-wife will *never* end. She says that she and his ex-wife despise each other so much, she only agreed to come here if we guaranteed that the supposedly insane ex-wife was not invited." Cristina leaned forward and paused theatrically. "Tell us, Alex, *is she that crazy*?"

Cohen, who showed up thinking they were going to talk about the challenges of parenting stepchildren, was mortified by the experience. Still, he did the best he could to acquit himself. When Cristina brought up the fact that Cohen had continued seeing his first wife after he and Alex had started dating, the audience gasped with disapproval. Cohen turned pale. "A lot of these things occurred in the first year of our relationship, where I still wasn't committed to Alex, and maybe I used the ex as a wedge," he sputtered. "I had gone through a pretty nasty divorce, and I wasn't ready. . . . We went back and forth for a while. And there were some financial difficulties. . . ."

Cohen's friends were stunned by the episode, both the embarrassing revelations and the fact that their cautious, shy friend had agreed to appear on a TV talk show in the first place. Cohen was the opposite of an exhibitionist. His colleagues at SAC saw the episode as a sign that Alex had complete control over him.

Cohen threw a Christmas party at his new apartment on East Seventy-ninth Street to celebrate the great year the firm had in 1993. Everyone was in a fine mood, feeling excited about the enormous amount of money they had just made. Bartenders poured drinks. Cohen touched Lissak on the shoulder. "Can I talk to you for a second?" he said. They went into an empty room.

Over the previous three years, Lissak had become Cohen's most dependable partner, the main person who communicated with investors and Wall Street banks, the head trader–recruiter–operations person and the one anyone who worked for them went to with a problem. "You're invaluable to running SAC," Cohen said, according to Lissak. "I'm making you a 20 percent general partner."

Lissak was thrilled. He loved working with Cohen, running the fund by his side and trading all day. Becoming a partner would offer security, but it would mean a lot more money, too—in the tens of millions of dollars, easily. They rejoined the party and started to tell SAC's employees about Lissak's promotion. The reaction was overwhelmingly positive. Lissak was widely liked and respected. Having someone like him implanted in the company made it seem more stable and legitimate.

"Steve was the mad scientist and Kenny was the people person," said Warren Dempsey, a trader who joined SAC in the early 1990s to help it build a presence investing in IPOs in Europe. "They were running the place. Kenny had real authority there. At least in my time there, I don't think Steve did much without talking to Kenny."

Two years later SAC moved to a new office at 520 Madison Avenue, a block away from the Museum of Modern Art. Cohen sat at the center of a T-shaped desk, with his traders seated in front of banks of monitors that stretched out to either side of him. San Pietro, a glitzy Italian restaurant with frescoes on the walls, was located downstairs. The SAC traders became some of its best patrons.

While SAC was prospering, nearly doubling every twelve months, Cohen continued to struggle with his own well-being. Even though he had achieved his life's dream of running his own firm, he was still unhappy, and he had become dependent on a psychiatrist named Ari Kiev to help him manage his moods.

In addition to treating depression, Kiev's other area of expertise was success and how to achieve it. He had worked as a psychiatrist and coach with Olympic basketball players and rowers trying to improve their performance and overcome their fear of failure. His background building athletic champions appealed to Cohen's unrelenting need to dominate in every transaction he entered into, and he started asking Kiev to spend entire days at SAC's offices, tending to his staff. Kiev was tall, with a bushy mustache and a portly midsection, and he would often appear silently at a trader's side and ask him how he was feeling. Sometimes the trader would be so startled to see Kiev there he'd practically jump out of his seat. Cohen asked Kiev to give motivational speeches to his employees, to help them get over their anxieties about losing money.

Basically, Kiev was there to teach them to be ruthless.

Once a week, after the market closed, Cohen's traders would gather in a conference room and Kiev would lead them through group therapy sessions focused on how to make them more comfortable with risk. Kiev had them talk about their trades and try to understand why some had gone well and others hadn't. "Are you really motivated to make as much money as you can? This guy's going to help you become a real killer at it," was how one skeptical staff member remembered Kiev being pitched to them. Kiev's work with Olympians had led him to believe that the thing that blocked most people was fear. You might have two investors with the same amount of money: One was prepared to buy 250,000 shares of a stock they liked, while the other wasn't. Why? Kiev believed that the reluctance was a form of anxiety—and that it could be overcome with proper treatment.

Kiev would ask the traders to close their eyes and visualize themselves making trades and generating profits. "Surrendering to the moment" and "speaking the truth" were some of his favorite phrases. "Why weren't you bigger in the trades that worked? What did you do right?" he'd ask. "Being preoccupied with not losing interferes with winning," he would say. "Trading not to lose is not a good strategy. You need to trade to *win*."

Many of the traders hated the group therapy sessions. Some considered Kiev a fraud.

"Ari was very aggressive," said one. "He liked money."

Patricia, Cohen's first wife, was suspicious of Kiev's motives and believed that he was using his sessions with Cohen to find stock tips. From Kiev's perspective, he found the perfect client in Cohen, a patient with unlimited resources who could pay enormous fees and whose reputation as one of the best traders on Wall Street could help Kiev realize his own goal of becoming a bestselling author. Being able to say that you were the trading coach to one of the most powerful traders on Wall Street was an amazing way to sell books and attract clients.

Kiev also served another purpose for Cohen, or so some of SAC's traders thought, as a sort of internal spy. He would target particular employees, wanting to know what was bothering them. Having practiced as a therapist for decades, he was skilled at drawing intimate confessions out of people, making them comfortable and earning their trust. But few at SAC felt comfortable opening up to him because it was understood that everything they said was reported back to the boss.

The economics of hedge funds are extremely favorable to the people running them, largely due to the exorbitant fee structure that they employ. Cohen made the decision early on to exploit this as much as he could. If investors wanted the best—*him*—they were going to have to pay for it. SAC was doing so well that he was able to charge higher fees than almost any other fund, keeping 50 percent of the profits at the end of the year. Most hedge funds charged 20 percent. But Cohen's investors did not complain. In fact, they fought to get in.

At the same time, Cohen grumbled constantly about the idea that other people were unfairly benefiting from his success. Almost every penny he gave to someone else, whether a commission to a broker or a bonus to a partner or a dollar in taxes, annoyed him. Finally, he decided that New York City's taxes were too high and Manhattan office space was too expensive. The firm needed to expand, and it would be much more cost-effective to leave the city. He told his employees that they were relocating SAC to Connecticut. He had already chosen the space, in the GE office park in Stamford. The economics of it made a lot more sense.

In addition to his taxes, some of the business arrangements he'd negotiated years earlier started to seem overly generous. Cohen would fire people who suddenly started to make what he regarded as disproportionately large sums of money, or he'd refuse to pay them what they thought they were owed. Eventually, he turned his resentment onto his partner.

One evening in October 1997, Cohen called Kenny Lissak with some shocking news: His wife, Alex, had accused Lissak of trying to instigate an affair with her. Alex told Cohen that he had to choose between his business partner and his marriage, according to Lissak, who said he was stunned by the allegation. Lissak denied it and said that he was happily married. He had just recovered from a series of medical crises and was physically weak. A year earlier, he had checked in to the hospital for routine back surgery after a series of injuries incurred playing basketball. While he was there, he contracted an *E. coli* infection in his spine that almost killed him and kept him bedridden in the hospital for a month. He had lost a hundred pounds.

During Lissak's absence, Alex had taken a more prominent role around the office. She issued memos to Cohen's employees and picked her husband up after the market closed. "It was clear that she was the queen and Steve was the king, that was the way it was," said a former trader. "I wouldn't want to have crossed her, let's put it that way." Another trader described her as a troublemaker. Some employees went out of their way not to make eye contact with her.

There had been an increasing amount of tension between her and Lissak, almost as if they were two girlfriends competing for Cohen's attention. But this was different.

After accusing his best friend and business partner of trying to have an affair with his wife, according to Lissak, Cohen told him to leave immediately. He barely seemed angry, he was just cold. Lissak says that he insisted that the story wasn't true and tried to persuade Cohen that he was making a mistake by firing him, but Cohen was unmoved. In a fog, Lissak packed up a box and walked out of the office, *his* office. He was in a state of anguish. Cohen never explained Lissak's departure to his employees, who were unsettled by it. But people soon heard about what had happened.

Afterward, Lissak found himself shut out of other Wall Street firms. It was understood by companies that wanted to keep Cohen as a client that they couldn't do business with both of them.

"That was the first sign of Steve's truly ruthless side," said a former trader. "When he dumped Kenny."

One Monday morning in 1998, a group of Goldman Sachs employees gathered for their division's weekly meeting an hour before the market opened. The man preparing to address the crowd was a Goldman securities salesman, the person responsible for keeping some of the firm's most important trading customers happy. He had urgent information to share about his most lucrative account.

"SAC Capital," he announced, "is now the single largest generator of commissions to the equity division."

The equity division was responsible for all of the stock trading on behalf of Goldman's clients, and during the technology boom of the late 1990s, this trading generated a significant amount of profit for Goldman. It was halfway through Bill Clinton's second term as president, and the country was in the midst of a stock market boom that had practically turned every New York City cabdriver with a copy of *Barron's* into a day trader. There seemed to be big IPOs for new dotcom companies every day, creating new millionaires who were lionized on magazine covers. Senior citizens were gambling their Social Security checks on the stock market. CNBC anchors eagerly reported that stock prices of technology companies like Qualcomm and Rambus were breaking new records on an hourly basis. It was as if the entire world was getting rich.

Up until that point, the hierarchy on Wall Street that determined who took whose phone calls and who got paid what had been clear. Huge mutual funds such as Wellington, Fidelity, and State Street, which managed trillions of dollars in retirement accounts, were the industry's most important customers. They were not in the business of lightning-quick trading. Their business was longer-term investing, incremental gains. They would build up large positions in stocks and hold them for months or years at a time, aligning their economic interests with those of the company. Firms like Goldman and Morgan Stanley and Salomon Smith Barney assigned salespeople to work with these fund managers by providing stock research compiled by the banks' analysts and by taking them out to Yankees games and sushi dinners. It was a comfortable arrangement, easily characterized, as one former investment analyst put it, as "fifty-year-old white guys getting research from other fifty-year-old white guys."

The Goldman securities salesman who was handling the SAC account was about to turn all of that upside down. SAC was a hedge fund, he explained to the confused Goldman employees, some of whom had never heard of the company. They don't just buy blocks of IBM to hold for months at a time while playing golf and collecting dividends, they *trade*. And they don't just trade. They trade hundreds of stocks a day, hundreds of thousands of shares at a time. They were not interested in a company's long-term health or whether the new products it had under development would enable it to hire more people in five years. SAC was interested in one thing: short-term movements in the stock price that it could exploit for profit.

For every one of those shares that Goldman might buy or sell on SAC's behalf, it collected six cents of commission. It didn't take a PhD to understand the implications. Although Fidelity was much bigger, SAC generated far more revenue, based purely on volume.

In exchange for giving Goldman Sachs millions of dollars of its business, SAC wanted something in return, the salesman said, something that was commensurate with its importance to the company. It wanted preferential treatment, particularly when it came to moves Goldman's analysts made that might affect a company's stock price. "If you change a penny or two on your estimates, you call SAC first," the salesman said. If an analyst was going to recommend that investors buy or sell shares in a company he or she covered, or revise the amount of money he or she estimated the company would make next quarter, SAC would like to know before anyone else. And when a Goldman analyst offered to jump on the phone for a "huddle" with important investors to help them interpret company events, why not do it first with SAC? Was that so much to ask?

A stock salesman at a rival brokerage firm who was responsible for the Cohen account described the dynamic this way: "If he was going to trade with you, he wanted *the* best price. He was willing to pay a lot of commissions. And he was willing to do so, so he could get the first call, any piece of information that could help him make money from you or your firm."

At Goldman Sachs, at least one analyst who heard the salesman's speech that morning was shocked by the brazenness of the arrangement. Nobody was proposing anything that was against the law, exactly. But it made the analyst uncomfortable. It gave SAC a huge advantage in the market. With early information about a new "buy" or "sell" rating that was coming on a stock, SAC could anticipate what other investors were going to do in response to the news and buy or sell a split second before anyone else, accumulating tiny crumbs of profit that could add up to significant sums. *Sleazy* might have been too strong a word for it; it was more like *distasteful*. Yet at the same time, the analysts and salespeople understood that their priority was to serve the firm's clients. Investment banks are hierarchies structured much like the military, where everyone must salute the person with the most stripes—or the department that brings in the most money.

The Goldman salesman's directive reflected an important shift on Wall Street, although its most entrenched players took a long time to recognize it. The new way to command power in the financial industry was to start a hedge fund. Doing so at the right time could turn someone who might have accumulated millions over the course of a twenty-year career at Goldman Sachs or Morgan Stanley into a billionaire almost overnight. In a matter of a few years, hedge funds went from a peculiar subculture on Wall Street to the center of the industry. They were far more demanding and difficult (and almost certainly more clever) than the Fidelitys and State Streets of the world, and the Goldmans and the Morgans had to go to a lot of trouble to keep them happy. But in the end, they were paid for it. If a hedge fund that generated hundreds of millions of dollars in revenue wanted the best access to the best research or the first call, you gave it to them. Or they'd take their business elsewhere.

On a clear, bright day in the spring of 1998, Cohen and Alex spent a few hours driving around Greenwich, Connecticut, with a real estate agent, looking for a new home that befitted their rising status. The couple was already living in Greenwich, in a refurbished six-thousand-square-foot ranch house that Cohen had purchased for $1.7 million in 1993, and they'd happily hosted many Thanksgiving dinners there. But Alex was pushing for more space. One person close to them at the time claimed that her intense interest in real estate was partly driven by a detail in the couple's premarital agreement stipulating that in the event of a divorce, Alex would receive the primary residence as part of her settlement. At least, that's what Cohen intimated when he joked about it at the office. "This is the carveout," he allegedly told a colleague. "This is her payout when she wants to get rid of me."

The couple also had a growing family to shelter. There was Alex's son from before she met Cohen, as well as her aging parents; Cohen's children from his first marriage visited on weekends; and Cohen and Alex now had three daughters of their own, including a set of young twins. When Alex first saw 30 Crown Lane, a large colonial on fourteen acres that had previously belonged to Sy Syms, founder of the Syms discount clothing chain, she gasped.

Greenwich was the obvious place for them to live. Since the 1920s, it has been home to men with more money than they knew what to do with, consistently ranking as one of the wealthiest zip codes in the country. It sits at a comfortable, leafy remove from Manhattan and once housed heirs to the Rockefeller and J. Pierpont Morgan fortunes, whose mansions were tucked discreetly behind hedges and stone walls, at the ends of long pebbled driveways. Eventually, the old money began to be supplanted by the new, as hedge fund moguls moved in, each one seeking to build his own Buckingham Palace. Paul Tudor Jones was one of the first, and one of the most ostentatious, when in 1994 he and his Australian-model wife bought a pretty mansion overlooking Long Island Sound for $11 million, tore it down, and replaced it with a much larger house that included a subterranean garage that could accommodate twenty-five cars. From the water, people frequently mistook it for the Belle Haven yacht club.

Although 30 Crown Lane had been sitting on the market for close to two years, it had recently drawn the interest of another financier, a partner at the old-line Wall Street investment bank Bear Stearns named Robert "Bobby" Steinberg. There was nothing particularly unique about the house, according to Jean Ruggiero, the real estate agent who was working with Steinberg, but there were very few properties on the market of that scale, with so much land attached. Steinberg was the head of Bear's risk arbitrage department. He and his wife, Suzanne, had a large family and had decided to make an offer on the house. That night, after contacting the selling broker with the Steinbergs' offer, Ruggiero called Steinberg back.

"You're not going to believe this," she said, "but someone else also made a bid on the house." This was a highly unusual situation. There were few houses on the market at that price level, and bidding wars over $14 million properties were practically unheard-of.

Steinberg suspected that something perverse was going on; after failing to attract any interest for months, another offer had suddenly materialized at the exact same moment as his? He raised his offer anyway, and the other bidder raised as well. Ruggiero went back to deliver the news to Steinberg, who said that he was still determined to buy the house. He told Ruggiero to call the seller's broker again and relay that he would pay $25,000 above any other competing bid, irrespective of what it was. Ruggiero was sure that would settle the matter. But when she made the new offer, the seller's agent just laughed; the other bidder had apparently told the seller's agent that he didn't care what the amount was, and that he was paying cash. He'd specifically said: "I'm standing here in Stamford with my checkbook, and I'll write out a check right now."

Ruggiero pressed the agent to tell her who the other buyer was. Then she called Steinberg back.

"It's someone named Stevie Cohen," she said. Steinberg had never heard of him.

The next day Steinberg approached the Bear Stearns salesman who was responsible for the Cohen account. "Do you know a guy named Stevie Cohen?" he asked.

"Yeah," said the salesman. He wasn't sure what the context of the question was, so he answered vaguely, "He's a client."

"What do you know about him?" Steinberg asked.

Cohen was a hedge fund manager and an important client, the sales-man said. He'd been to Cohen's wedding at the Plaza, and was acquainted with his reputation as a trader. The only hedge fund Steinberg was famil-iar with was the one run by Ivan Boesky, the arbitrageur who was shut down during the Drexel Burnham Lambert insider trading scandal. Steinberg, who was on the board of one of the most tenacious investment firms on Wall Street, was not accustomed to being prevented from doing what he wanted by day traders. "Give me his phone number," he said.

Steinberg got Cohen on the phone and introduced himself. "Listen," he said, "it's come to my attention that you're the other guy bidding against me on this house. My wife really has her heart set on it."

Cohen replied that his wife would also be devastated not to have the house, and he therefore had every intention of buying it.

"You're not going to buy it," Cohen said. "*I* am."

When Steinberg asked why, Cohen said: "Because I have more money than you."

"This is getting out of hand," Steinberg said, growing exasperated. "Here is what I'm willing to do: I'll give you a million dollars to walk away."

"What am I going to do with a million dollars?" Cohen said, then paused. "Here's what I'll do," he said, chuckling. "Let's flip a coin for it."

"What?" Steinberg said.

"I'll flip you for it," Cohen said.

Steinberg was insulted. He knew that his wife would be horrified if she found out that he had flipped a coin in order to buy their house. It was absurd. "No," he said.

Cohen hung up the phone. Then he called his real estate agent, raised his bid to $14.8 million, and bought the house with cash.

The excavators started to arrive not long after, one after the other, in a convoy. Cohen and Alex wasted no time upsetting their new neighbors with their renovation. 30 Crown Lane was located in Greenwich's "back-country," the forested area to the north of the town, where families descended from generations of wealth kept things discreet; showiness betrayed insecurity about one's money. New billionaires like Cohen and his wife were ignorant of such conventions, however, and likely would have ignored them anyway. They immediately started bulldozing the grounds and building massive new additions.

A new wing was built to accommodate an indoor basketball court and a swimming pool with a one-and-a-half-story glass dome above it. In the backyard, they constructed a six-thousand-square-foot ice-skating rink with its own Zamboni, as well as a shed for the Zamboni. They added a massage room, a gym, and a small golf course with putting greens. They built a nine-foot stone wall around the perimeter and installed a sophisticated security system. The final building was thirty-six thousand square feet, one of the largest in the area. It took 283 dump-truck loads to bring in all the dirt for the landscaping.

"I feel that it's not a home," a neighbor named Susan Hut complained to the town planning board. "It's a showplace. It could be in the Bronx Botanical Garden."

Ruggiero, who has sold real estate in Greenwich for thirty-nine years, cites the Cohen deal when she trains new realtors entering the business each year. She uses it as an example of the two different kinds of wealth that they are likely to find among buyers of high-end properties. "Strangely enough," she tells them, referring to the first type, "even if you're someone buying a $3 million, $4 million, or even $6 million house, who may seem very well-off, you're still a worker—you still have to worry about your salary."

There is a second category of rich person, however, for whom money is literally of no concern. They simply take their checkbook out and pay whatever it takes. Those people are great for the real estate business. But if you find yourself bidding against them, she tells the other realtors, it's best to just step out of their way.

"The minute you can afford $10 million, $20 million, you don't have to worry about your paycheck," Ruggiero said. "Steve Cohen didn't have to worry about his paycheck. Whatever Stevie wanted, Stevie could get."

CHAPTER 3

MURDERERS' ROW

Between 1998 and 1999, SAC reached an important marker, surpassing $1 billion a year in assets, which was achieved after five years of almost doubling their money each year. As SAC grew, though, the drawbacks of its bare-knuckled investing approach became increasingly hard for Cohen to ignore. He had hundreds of millions of dollars to invest, and, by necessity, the size of the positions the fund took were larger than they'd ever been before. But Cohen's trading method, which continued to be a form of day-trading, only worked with a smaller pool of money, where one could build more modest, but significant, positions and get out of them quickly.

New hedge funds were opening every day, with competitors moving into areas that Cohen had once claimed as his own. With so many traders pursuing the same ideas, returns were getting harder to find. When traders at other firms found out that Cohen was buying a particular stock, they tried to replicate what he was doing, driving the price up and eliminating the profits that once came so easily. As he contemplated the new demands the fund's size placed on his traders, he looked around SAC's trading floor and felt annoyed by what he saw: a room full of men with

Long Island or New Jersey accents who couldn't fit in at a proper analyst conference if they tried. They were trading in and out of microchip manufacturers and biotechnology firms every day with very little idea of what these companies actually *did*. They couldn't even be fairly characterized as stereotypical Wall Street "speculators." They were gamblers, and unsophisticated ones at that.

Cohen sensed that the industry was changing, and he needed to change with it. He also had his ego to contend with. He wanted to be known as a brilliant investor, not just a "trader," a title that didn't confer a lot of prestige. His new goal was for SAC to become a well-respected firm, one that would establish him as a legendary money manager. In order to accomplish that, he and his employees needed to learn to analyze their investments in a more sophisticated way, to understand how companies were going to perform over longer periods of time, rather than trading blindly on momentum. And to do that he needed to hire the kinds of people he had previously shunned, experts who knew something about the stocks they were buying. They would get their edge directly from companies and other sources rather than relying on research from firms like Goldman Sachs and Morgan Stanley. "We're changing the way we do things around here," Cohen announced one afternoon after the market closed.

He told his top lieutenants that, from now on, he wanted to hire only traders who had a "fundamental edge," that is, deep expertise or connections in a particular industry. He walked around SAC's own trading desk, pointing at his employees one by one and anointing them healthcare traders, consumer stock experts, energy traders. Anyone who couldn't adapt and turn himself into a specialist would be let go. The era of anti-intellectualism at SAC was over.

This shift opened the door to a new breed of person at the firm: the slick, well-connected, Ivy League–educated professional. To remake the company, Cohen began to hunt them down.

He hired a technology-stock trader named David Ganek, the son of a wealthy investment manager, who had run the risk arbitrage department at the investment bank Donaldson, Lufkin & Jenrette. He hired another trader named Larry Sapanski, from Morgan Stanley, who had a reputation as a great oil and gas investor. Cohen seated the new traders he thought were the best close to him so that he could see what they were doing. That part of the floor became known as "murderers' row," once used to describe the New York Yankees lineups of the late 1920s, when players like Babe Ruth and Lou Gehrig made the team the best in history.

One of the old SAC employees who managed to make the transition to the new style was a former college basketball player named Richard Grodin, who had worked for Cohen since 1992. When Cohen asked him which sector he wanted to specialize in, Grodin immediately picked technology—specifically, semiconductor manufacturers. Technology, to Grodin, meant growth and new products and trading opportunities galore. He believed that he could analyze the microchip industry in terms of supply chains, the interdependence of companies that created components for computer products and cellphones. If you found out that one company along the line was doing poorly, you could make inferences about everyone else on the chain. This information, however, was not easy to get. Most of the companies were based in Asia, making them hard for investors in the United States to access.

Outside of work, Grodin was known as a gregarious, goofy guy who enjoyed gambling and was quick to laugh. But those who had to interact with him during market hours dreaded it. He was "absolutely the most mercenary guy you will ever meet," one colleague said. "He would sell his grandmother to make five cents."

Grodin's microchip investing strategy was effective. He was responsible for a relatively small pool of money, typically $30 to $40 million, but his returns were 30 percent or more, the highest at the firm on a risk-adjusted basis. Still, he became a source of frustration to Cohen. Not only was he ungenerous with the information he was getting, but Cohen believed that Grodin could be making a lot more if he would make bigger trades. He was exactly the sort of person Dr. Kiev could have helped, if only Grodin would let him. The trouble was, Grodin lacked that particular genetic condition that enabled Cohen to take massive risks without being consumed with anxiety. Grodin hated the possibility of losing money.

Cohen made Grodin sit in the chair next to his so that he could watch everything he did. Grodin got in the habit of whispering his orders to his traders so that Cohen wouldn't hear them. He knew that if he tried to buy 50,000 shares of something, Cohen might try to put in a 100,000-share order before him, pushing the price up before he managed to buy anything himself. Grodin's traders were always straining to understand what he was saying, and when they asked him to repeat himself, he'd scream: "Are you fucking deaf? You're a fucking idiot!"

Grodin couldn't have done any of it without his most important collaborator, his analyst, Richard Choo-Beng Lee.

C. B. Lee was a quiet, disheveled fellow with dark eyes, a wide, flat nose, and a belly that protruded slightly over his belt. He didn't look like an experienced professional who enabled those around him to make millions of dollars in the stock market. But no one had better connections to Asian technology manufacturers. Lee was constantly in motion, traveling around the world to visit chip manufacturers and collecting valuable details about their businesses. The information he gathered was precious.

As a result, Lee was very popular around SAC's offices. Everyone, particularly Cohen, wanted access to his reports, but Grodin did not like to share them. He had recruited Lee from a brokerage firm called John Hancock Securities, where he worked as an analyst after getting an engineering degree from Duke, and cultivated him at SAC. Using Lee's "datapoints," as he called them, Grodin would methodically formulate a trade and quickly lock in a profit, often not a huge one. Cohen preferred a more aggressive approach. If a trade looked good, Cohen thought you should bet as much as you could.

There were regular conflicts about getting access to Lee's research, and shouting matches between Cohen and Grodin erupted with increasing frequency. Catching Grodin trading on Lee's information before sharing it made Cohen so crazy that he ordered his in-house programmers to design a system that would show him every trade order entered by anyone on SAC's staff before it was executed, allowing Cohen to enter his own trades ahead of them if he wanted. The new software was referred to as the "eye in the sky."

After suffering for months under Cohen's daily scrutiny, Grodin came up with a plan to get away from him. SAC maintained a satellite office in Manhattan, called Sigma Capital Management, which occupied two floors of a tower on Madison Avenue. Grodin asked to move his trading group there based on the argument that he was getting married and didn't want to commute anymore. Cohen reluctantly agreed.

Relocating to the city gave Grodin a little more freedom, but the new state of affairs wouldn't last long. Barely a year later, in January 2004, Cohen sent Grodin an instant message: "Richie, by the way—I want cb to write up ideas this year or no capital." Until that point, C. B. Lee had conveyed his market research to Grodin in informal ways, mostly over the phone or in brief emails. Now Cohen was demanding a more formal presentation, a report that he could read for himself and pass along to others. It was the only method Cohen could come up with to try to ensure that his traders were giving their most valuable information to him before anyone else.

Grodin hated the idea. "So the whole firm can IM it all over the street?" he replied.

"Than quit," Cohen wrote back, in one of his famously typo-riddled communiqués. "Rules are the same for everybody. You no like, than time to move on. Why should outside people get cb ideas and me not? It's wrong and needs to be corrected. I will be firm on this and if no happy than life goes on."

Grodin tried to negotiate, asking why Cohen was suddenly being so rigid after all of their years working together. "Cb doesn't write up ideas he has datapts and if they make sense I put them on in positions which u see," he wrote.

"Not enough," Cohen wrote. "It pisses me off that people don't feel any obligation to keep me up. That I have to guess. It is totally wrong."

"Ok," Grodin wrote back. The next day, he submitted his resignation.

The need to hire new traders and analysts at SAC became a constant, almost unmanageable challenge. Cohen approached every aspect of his life like a trader, and with his employees it was no different; many years, Cohen fired dozens of people for failing to deliver the returns he wanted. Others, like Grodin, got frustrated and quit. For traders, getting a job at SAC was like pulling the pin out of a grenade: It wasn't a question of *if* you would blow up, it was a matter of when. It was a place that made many careers—and ruined even more.

Despite the high-stress environment, there was no shortage of eager candidates. Everyone wanted to work at a hedge fund, particularly SAC. The money that could be made was magnitudes greater than anywhere else, and even at a place as volatile as SAC, you could quickly save enough money to be comfortable for the rest of your life. Responsibility for finding new candidates at SAC fell to an enterprising and aggressive group led by Solomon Kumin, the firm's director of business development. Sol was a natural salesman. He was a former Johns Hopkins lacrosse player with a taste for popsicle-hued polo shirts and had a powerful charisma that drew comparisons to Bill Clinton. He called everyone he met "buddy" and he lived flamboyantly, always flying private and betting prodigiously on sports. His nickname was "King Midas."

Kumin's job was to search for the very best traders on Wall Street; he sometimes followed their careers for years before approaching them. As more and more hedge funds sprouted up, competition for talent became intense. Two funds in particular, Citadel Investment Group, founded by Ken Griffin in Chicago, and Millennium Management, run out of New York by Israel "Izzy" Englander, were often trying to hire the same traders as SAC. Both funds had models similar to SAC's, with hundreds of traders making short-term investments that were expected to be influenced by some kind of event.

One of the things SAC looked for in new traders was personal connections the trader had with people working at public companies that might yield valuable intelligence. If a potential hire had a summer rental in the Hamptons with a corporate executive at an Internet company, for example, this was noted with approval in the file. Friends, fraternity brothers, fathers-in-law, and wives: They could all prove valuable when it came to getting information.

In late 2004, an ambitious young employee approached Cohen with an idea: What if they developed an exclusive new unit at SAC, a trading group that was driven by in-depth research? The concept was to have traders who were focused on developing industry expertise, in the mold of the famous investor Warren Buffett, who took large stakes in companies and held them for decades through his wildly successful firm Berkshire Hathaway. They wouldn't be concerned with tiny stock price movements when companies announced their earnings each quarter, for example, and as a result, the firm would be less dependent on Cohen and his intuition for those kinds of trades. These new traders and analysts would become authorities on the companies they were researching. Over a series of meetings, the employee, a manager in his twenties named Matthew Grossman, outlined his vision for Cohen. He referred to it as SAC's "top gun." Part of the purpose of the new unit, Grossman explained, would be to manage Cohen's own portfolio, which deserved to be handled by the best people at the firm. They would hire a bunch of new analysts and traders to staff it, and it would become the firm's equivalent of the Navy SEALs.

Cohen was intrigued. It was really an extension of what he was trying to do already. The concept appealed to his sense of vanity in that it made him sound more like a visionary than a profiteer. Even people who disapproved of Wall Street generally admired Warren Buffett, who got calls from bank presidents and Treasury secretaries seeking his counsel. But the research unit also made business sense. SAC was now managing billions of dollars; a more studious, longer-term approach was wise. Cohen liked Grossman, who was privileged and precocious. He'd attended Deerfield Academy, an elite boarding school in Massachusetts, and gone to college at Columbia, and then finagled himself a job as the first-ever college intern at Julian Robertson's trailblazing hedge fund Tiger Management. Grossman had been with SAC since 2002.

Before his boss could get too excited, Grossman told Cohen that he had three conditions before he would agree to help build the new group:

that if the new unit didn't work out, he would be given a job as a portfolio manager; that he would be paid a percentage of the new unit's overall performance; and that he would command the same level of authority within SAC as Cohen—specifically, that everyone at SAC had to know that a directive from Grossman was as important as one from Cohen himself. Much to the surprise of many at SAC, Cohen told Grossman to go ahead.

Grossman's colleagues were stunned to observe Cohen practically taking orders from his young upstart. SAC employees had never seen anything like it.

While Cohen seemed infatuated with Grossman, most of the people at SAC disliked him. His nickname around the office was "Milhouse," after Bart Simpson's nerdy sidekick on *The Simpsons*—although this Milhouse was a perfectionist who badgered other employees over tiny mistakes or missed opportunities, much the way Cohen did. Grossman knew that he wasn't liked, and it bothered him. He told the few colleagues with whom he did get along that his "lack of people skills" came from the fact that he'd been picked on in middle school and had suffered through his parents' traumatic divorce. Still, for whatever reason, he seemed powerless to change the way he treated those working under him. When Grossman walked into a room full of people, they would fall instantly silent. He was soon making more than $10 million a year, before he even turned thirty. He moved to Greenwich and bought a blue Aston Martin, a $269,000 updated version of the British sports car featured in the James Bond movie *Goldfinger*. He sometimes offered to drive traders SAC was trying to hire around in it as a way to entice them to join the firm.

After Cohen told him to go forward, Grossman disappeared from the office for an entire day without telling anyone where he was. He reemerged with a business plan for his new investment unit. It would be called "CR Intrinsic." The "CR" stood for "Cumulative Return."

The art market offered a way to transform wealth into an alluring form of influence and power. "It is not even cool to be a billionaire anymore—

there are, like, two hundred of them," as Loïc Gouzer, a specialist in contemporary art at Christie's New York, put it. "But, if that same guy buys a painting, suddenly it puts you in a whole circle.... They enter a whole circuit. You are going to meet artists, you are going to meet tech guys. It is the fastest way to become an international name." Cohen watched as some of his employees transformed their reputations by amassing extravagant art collections, as each new museum endowment was covered in the society pages.

His trader David Ganek had been collecting art since college, when he and his wife started visiting small galleries and the studios of artists who weren't well-known. Ganek made a fortune after the technology market crashed in 2000: He had been almost entirely short in his portfolio, and he directed much of his new capital into art collecting of a different order. By the time he became one of Cohen's most successful traders, it seemed as if Ganek was spending all of his free time bidding on contemporary pieces by world-famous artists like Jeff Koons and Cindy Sherman. If he was busy, he had his secretary hold his place on the phone during auctions at Christie's and place bids on his behalf.

"Don't spend more than $750,000 on this one," Ganek would tell her, before disappearing to make a trade.

Cohen was impressed, and envious. People admired Ganek for his taste in art. Though Cohen had acquired a handful of paintings over the years, he had never thought of himself as a "collector." He knew that for a smart trader there was potential not just to enhance his reputation by buying and selling art but to make a lot of money.

Art dealers and galleries in New York operated under their own restrictive code, and they wouldn't deal with just anyone, no matter how much money he or she had. You couldn't simply walk into a gallery and write a check for a Monet to hang on your penthouse wall. The gatekeepers of the art world understood that the exclusivity of their product depended on not allowing rich hedge fund managers from Greenwich to buy whatever they wanted. It was a form of discrimination, in a sense, but it was also simple market economics: In order to generate demand, you needed to control the supply. In response, Wall Street collectors needed to hire the right people to make the introductions that would move them to the front of the line.

For Cohen, that person was Sandy Heller, a childhood friend of Michael Steinberg, one of Cohen's longtime traders. Many in the art world privately regarded Heller as something of an opportunist, but there was no denying that he had access to art buyers who occupied the top of the economic scale. He specialized in working with clients like Cohen, rich men who didn't yet understand the intricacies of the art world. He started visiting galleries with Cohen, suggesting ways for him to build a collection, patiently developing him into a connoisseur. For Cohen, it was intoxicating. When he spent millions of dollars on a piece—paying $8 million for a shark suspended in 4,360 gallons of formaldehyde by Damien Hirst, for example—it made news. But it wasn't just vanity. Cohen also developed a genuine love for many of the pieces he bought. He prided himself on buying only the best, highest-quality work.

When a painting by Picasso called *Le Rêve* (The Dream) became available in the fall of 2006, it was an opportunity to take his collecting to a whole new level. Cohen was overcome with the desire to own *Le Rêve* as soon as he saw it. A highly erotic portrait of Picasso's young mistress Marie-Thérèse Walter asleep in an armchair, it was painted in 1932 when Picasso was fifty years old, a form of soft porn in jewel tones. In 2001, the casino magnate Steve Wynn had bought it from another collector who had paid $48.4 million for it in 1997. Then, five years later, he decided that he wanted to sell it. As soon as Cohen heard, he flew an art advisor out to California to look at the piece and evaluate its condition.

Cohen's advisor inspected the painting closely and wrote a report confirming that it was in fine condition. A deal was made, with Cohen agreeing to pay $139 million for the painting. Then, the next weekend, Wynn hosted a celebratory cocktail party.

Wynn and his wife, Elaine, had a group of celebrity friends visiting from New York, among them Nora Ephron, Nicholas Pileggi, Barbara Walters, and the power lawyer couple David and Mary Boies. Wynn couldn't help but brag about the record-setting deal he had just struck with Cohen. "This is the most money ever paid for a painting," Wynn told them, noting that it surpassed the prior record of $135 million that Ronald Lauder had paid for *Portrait of Adele Bloch-Bauer I* by Gustav Klimt.

Wynn invited his friends to come see the Picasso in his office, before it disappeared forever into Cohen's mansion in Greenwich. The piece shared a wall with a Matisse and a Renoir. Wynn began to entertain his guests with explications about the eroticism of *Le Rêve* and how part of Marie-Thérèse's head actually made the shape of a penis and how the piece had once belonged to the collectors Victor and Sally Ganz, who had accumulated a celebrated art collection in their Manhattan apartment in the 1940s and 1950s. As Wynn spoke, he suddenly backed up and jammed his elbow right through the canvas. There was a "terrible" ripping sound, as Ephron later recalled. The room suddenly got very quiet.

"I can't believe I just did that," Wynn said as his guests looked on in horror. "Oh, shit. Oh, man."

Wynn tried to make the best of the situation. "Well, I'm glad I did it and not you," he told his friends. "It's a picture, it's my picture, we'll fix it. Nobody got sick or died. It's a picture. It took Picasso five hours to paint it."

The next day, he called William Acquavella, his art dealer in New York, who reacted almost as if he'd been told someone he cared about had been murdered. "Noooo!" he cried. Soon, Wynn's wife, Elaine, was on a private jet to New York along with the damaged painting. An armored truck met them at the airport and transported them to Acquavella's gallery, located in a townhouse on East Seventy-ninth Street. Cohen met them there. He wanted to see the damage for himself. Although Wynn harbored some hope that the piece could be restored, they agreed that for the time being the sale was off.

Cohen was bitterly disappointed. *Le Rêve* would have to wait.

Finding people to work at CR Intrinsic, SAC's new division, was the focus of Sol Kumin's job. The new traders had to have more than a track record; they had to be brilliant and have industry expertise, and they weren't easy to find.

He heard about one portfolio manager who sounded promising, a biotechnology specialist at a small hedge fund called Sirios Capital Management, in Boston. The biotechnology industry was booming, with dozens of companies competing to produce new drugs with enormous economic potential. Understanding what they all did was not easy. The young man projected a serious, inscrutable eggheadedness, as if he were a surgeon or medical researcher rather than a mere investor in medical companies. He had recently gotten an MBA from the Stanford Graduate School of Business, one of the top business schools in the country. His name was Mathew Martoma.

"Would you be open to considering a job at SAC?" Kumin asked him.

Martoma wasn't sure. Like everyone in his industry, he had heard stories about SAC, and he wasn't sure if he was suited to the intense culture. He was quiet and courteous, not someone who handled open conflict well. Still, one aspect of the job was very interesting—the money.

Kumin explained the details. Martoma would have a portfolio of about $400 million to invest, putting it in the middle in terms of relative size at the firm. He would also have a guarantee that he'd take home more than 17 percent of the profits he made in his portfolio, as well as a portion of any profit Cohen made based on the ideas Martoma supplied. If he returned just 15 percent at the end of the year, he'd make more than $10 million. Almost no other hedge fund offered such a generous arrangement. Plus, he would be part of SAC's new research team, working with the most talented people at the company.

At home that night, Martoma debated the job offer with his wife, Rosemary. She was a doctor, and she was involved in every decision he made. They concluded, based on the compensation and the prestige of working at one of the best-known hedge funds in the industry, that it was worth pursuing the job. On June 2, 2006, SAC sent him an official job offer. It included a base salary of $200,000 and a signing bonus of $2 million. Kumin noted in an internal report that Martoma had great sources of information in the biotechnology world, including a network of doctors "in the field." Martoma signed the offer letter and sent it back. If he was smart about it, no one in his family would ever have to work again.

Martoma was a first-generation American, a son of immigrants from India who had been raised to respect and fear his parents. Status, conferred through educational achievement at name-brand institutions, was a family obsession, along with the conviction that, as newcomers to America, they had to work harder than other Americans to find financial security. Theirs was a culture in which people were introduced with a lengthy summary of their achievements and credentials, including the number of school prizes they'd won going all the way back to second grade. In addition to making him rich, SAC would add another line to his sparkling résumé.

That summer, Martoma moved with his family into an apartment in Stamford, Connecticut, and began acclimating himself to his competitive new work environment. Rosemary, pregnant with their second child, decided to devote herself to being a mother and a partner to Martoma rather than practice as a pediatrician. She was an overachiever, like her husband, and she took his work as seriously as if it were her own, giving him constant advice. Martoma was determined to do well. He fit the new SAC image Grossman had envisaged perfectly. He was a thinker, not a yeller, with all the right credentials.

In a way, Martoma was re-creating his childhood dynamic at his new firm, trying to please his demanding fathers, Cohen and Grossman. He fell into the same work habits he'd developed back when he was in high school, trying for the highest grades in the class. He started working at 4 A.M. to focus on the European stock markets and went home after the U.S. market closed to help Rosemary get the children bathed and put to bed. Then he stayed up late working another shift, reading research reports while his wife slept beside him. There was a sense of urgency to his work. He was in a hurry to find a winning trade.

Healthcare was one of the most exciting, unpredictable, and, at times, profitable areas of the stock market, where companies in heavily regulated industries were trying to create and market products to save people's lives. Drug development and other healthcare research consumed billions in resources. Every new drug trial was a gamble, making for a volatile market in the companies' stocks. It was one of Cohen's favorite sectors to trade.

By the time he started at SAC, Martoma was already paying close attention to two companies, Elan Corporation and Wyeth, which were testing a new Alzheimer's drug called bapineuzumab, or "bapi" for short. Drug development was so expensive that the two companies had teamed up to help defray the costs of years of research and drug trials. Alzheimer's was a long-standing interest of Martoma's, dating back to his time as an undergraduate at Duke, when he volunteered in the Alzheimer's wing of the university medical center, and he felt that this particular drug had considerable potential. Reduced to its simplest terms, bapi had been designed to improve upon a precursor Alzheimer's drug, AN-1792, which had had to be withdrawn from testing after it was shown to cause severe brain swelling in patients. Bapi had a less complex structure and had shown some effectiveness in animal studies. Martoma thought that it might prove to be a huge commercial success, and he wanted to learn everything he could about the science behind it and the logistics of the trials.

To do so, he planned to make use of every resource he had access to, which at SAC included several high-priced research services. One in particular was of great interest to him, the Gerson Lehrman Group, which was an "expert network" or "matchmaking" firm. The matches it made were between Wall Street investors like Martoma and people who worked inside hundreds of different publicly traded companies, people responsible for ordering new truck parts or buyers for retail chains who could provide insight on their industries, their competitors, or even their own firms. The investors paid GLG a fee to connect them with these company employees, who in turn were paid handsomely—sometimes as much as $1,000 an hour or more—to talk to the investors. The company employees were supposed to share only information that was publicly available, to avoid breaking any laws. Or at least that was the idea.

By the 2000s, after years of regulatory scrutiny, most traders had become more careful about sensitive mergers and acquisitions information.

The Michael Milken case had taught traders to avoid buying shares of companies right before takeovers were announced; big price movements in stocks right before takeovers were announced often drew the attention of the SEC. Still, investors were desperate for information that might provide them with an advantage, and they went to a lot of effort to get it. Hedge fund analysts monitored shopping mall parking lots and sent spotters to China to watch trucks driving in and out of factory loading bays, searching for unique insights into how companies were doing. It was understood that information already in the public domain, like a company's SEC filings or earnings releases, was essentially worthless for trading purposes.

In the years since the Milken case, short-term investors had turned their attention to quarterly earnings announcements instead, particularly of companies in the technology and science sectors, where the stocks could move dramatically after the results were made public. Setting up the right trade anticipating a company's earnings release became an incredibly profitable strategy, but it only worked if you got good information about the earnings *before* they were announced.

Getting earnings intelligence, then, was what hedge fund traders became focused on. They badgered corporate executives for hints about what might happen. Would the third-quarter results be disappointing? Was a big announcement about next year's growth plan coming up? The traders used whatever crumbs they gathered from these interactions—from the "body language" of the CFO to explicit details provided by investor relations staff—to trade in and out of the stock. In 2000, the SEC, deciding that such shenanigans were bad for the market, passed a rule called Regulation Fair Disclosure, often called "Regulation FD." It prohibited public companies from offering important information about their businesses to some investors and not others. After the rule passed, companies had to tell everyone everything at the same time through public announcements and press releases. This made it much easier to get the information, but it also made the information much less useful, because everyone else had it as well. Traders had to find some other way to gain an advantage in the market.

Companies like GLG rose up to help provide it, by offering access to the heart of a company's operations. Hedge fund traders saw the expert network firms as a way to fill the information gap. "We thought it was kind of ridiculous that the hedge fund business got so much information by asking for favors—'Could I please have 15 minutes of your time?'— when they would certainly pay for that information," Mark Gerson, one of GLG's founders, said shortly after starting the company. "We just thought there should be a way to get the two connected."

Of course, GLG told the company employees it signed up as consultants not to share material nonpublic information with their Wall Street clients. But the employees often had only a fuzzy understanding of where that line was. The hedge fund investors, on the other hand, knew exactly what they were after and would do whatever they could to get it. SAC traders loved the service and had a $1.2 million annual subscription. It enabled them to have conversations with employees who worked at all levels of companies in healthcare, telecommunications, energy, and countless other industries, people they never could have found or persuaded to talk to them on their own. SAC was one of GLG's best customers.

On August 30, 2006, Martoma sent GLG a list of twenty-two medical experts he might want to talk with, all of whom were involved in the clinical trials for bapineuzumab. "Are any of these docs in your database?" he wrote. "I would like to seek consultations with all of them on Alzheimer's Disease and AAB-001. For those not available, can we recruit?"

One physician in GLG's network replied to him.

"I am Chair of the Safety Monitoring Committee for this trial," the doctor wrote in response to Martoma's request. "Although I know more than is publicly available, I have a confidentiality agreement and will share only information that is openly available, of course."

The doctor was a respected neurologist in his seventies, a leading expert in Alzheimer's research who held an endowed chair at the University of Michigan medical school. His name was Sid Gilman.

PART

TWO

CHAPTER 4

IT'S LIKE GAMBLING
AT RICK'S

Twenty-six Federal Plaza is a blunt rectangular tower surrounded by security barricades in lower Manhattan, located near the courthouses and City Hall. Michael Bowe took a deep breath as he pushed through the revolving doors, dropped his bag on the security belt, and told the guard he was visiting the New York field office of the FBI. Then he passed through the full body scanner that led to the elevators.

A partner at Kasowitz Benson Torres & Friedman, a law firm that specializes in commercial litigation, Bowe was known for his expertise in financial fraud cases. He was a broad-shouldered Irishman with ruddy skin and bright blue eyes and had the look of someone who had gotten into his share of bar fights as a young man but had since developed a taste for loafers and cashmere sweaters. It was November 2006, and Bowe was in the middle of two nasty lawsuits representing companies suing SAC Capital and a handful of other hedge funds for allegedly manipulating their stock prices. Things had gotten so ugly that there were accusations of each side rifling through the other's garbage. Bowe had been investigating SAC and its founder for two years.

One of the cases Bowe was working on had been initiated by Biovail, a

Canadian drug manufacturer. Biovail's stock price had been lurching up and down as rumors swirled in the market that it was engaged in some sort of accounting fraud. The company's CEO said he believed that short sellers at a group of hedge funds were colluding with each other and with stock research analysts to publish negative reports about certain companies, including Biovail, in order to drive the share prices down.

Short sellers have an unsavory reputation in the market, as something akin to trolls who rejoice at the misfortune of others. Their livelihood depends on stocks going down, making them the natural enemies of most investors. Shorting is so risky, with potentially unlimited losses if a stock keeps going up, that only the most sophisticated investors, such as hedge funds, generally engage in it. Naturally, most corporate executives see the shorts as enemies of the happy stories they're trying to tell about their companies, which tend to be full of puffery. For that reason, short sellers play a crucial role in the market, as the only actors who are motivated to look for problems at publicly traded companies—such as accounting fraud—which can be covered up for years. Short sellers were the first ones to point out problems with Enron.

But the field is also filled with opportunities for abuse.

When Bowe first sat down with Biovail's CEO, Eugene Melnyk, two years earlier, in 2004, he was skeptical of Melnyk's contention that his company was being targeted by groups of short sellers bent on driving its stock down. But he billed by the hour, so he listened to what Melnyk had to say. Melnyk thought that SAC Capital Advisors was spreading negative information about Biovail in the market, and he wanted Bowe to investigate how the fund worked. The name SAC meant almost nothing to the lawyer. He was well aware of the burgeoning hedge fund industry, but his understanding of SAC's reputation or how it operated was close to zero. He was surprised by the idea that a private investment fund could terrorize a billionaire CEO.

A little preliminary research brought up the only substantive article that had ever been written about SAC and Steven Cohen, a piece in *Business Week* published in 2003 called "The Most Powerful Trader on Wall Street You've Never Heard Of." The article described Cohen as an aggressive day trader running a $4 billion fund, someone who paid out over $150 million a year in trading commissions in order to gain access to information before anyone else. As evidence of how close SAC seemed to be to nearly every Wall Street controversy, the article reported that the day after Sam Waksal, the chairman of the biotechnology company ImClone Systems, had found out that his company's application for approval of a cancer drug had been rejected, a full twenty-four hours before the news became public, he got a call from an SAC trader who had allegedly noticed a movement in the stock that no one else had picked up on. (The SAC call came a few minutes before Martha Stewart tried to reach Waksal, leading to her infamous insider trading and perjury case; no one ever returned the SAC call.) The article said that Cohen was one of Wall Street's ten largest customers in terms of trading commissions, and quoted someone saying that he was "almost as secretive as Howard Hughes."

"Who the hell is this Cohen guy?" Bowe wondered.

Intrigued, Bowe and an investigator at his law firm started to look into Melnyk's conspiracy theories. When Bowe asked people on Wall Street who the most important figures were in the hedge fund business, the name SAC kept coming up. Their business model was described as: They pay to know first.

Bowe put Cohen under surveillance, having him followed on his way to work and monitoring who he had lunch with. His investigator noticed that Cohen always seemed to be surrounded by bodyguards.

On February 23, 2006, Biovail filed a lawsuit against SAC, naming Cohen and a few of his employees and accusing them of manipulating Biovail's stock. The list of defendants also included Gerson Lehrman Group. The lawsuit accused the SAC traders of working together to drive Biovail's share price down, from close to $50 to $18 in Canadian dollars. The allegations were based on the idea that Cohen was so powerful, and SAC was such a force in the market, that they were able to demand that the big banks SAC traded with each day give them early access to information that was supposed to be released to everyone at the same time. "To maximize the use of SAC's substantial market influence," the complaint read, "under Steven Cohen's direction, SAC places extreme pressure on its traders, managers, employees and agents to produce at all costs."

SAC and the other defendants vigorously denied the accusations and argued that the drop in Biovail's stock price was the result of real problems with its business, which was not an unreasonable assertion. Still, the case gathered momentum, and the SEC launched its own investigation. Then came the kind of publicity that, from the perspective of Kasowitz Benson, was more valuable than anything Bowe could have generated himself: A month after Biovail's lawsuit was filed, *60 Minutes* aired a segment about the litigation, called "Betting on a Fall," which analyzed Biovail's case in depth. It also took a highly skeptical view of SAC's business.

At the time it aired, the stock market was setting record highs every day, while real estate inflated even faster. As the pensions enjoyed by previous generations were phased out, working Americans were pouring their life savings into the stock market with the hope that it would eventually provide for their retirements. Watching the Dow Jones Industrial Average go up became a national obsession.

60 Minutes made it clear that, in spite of the pervasive sense of affluence among many investors, there was something menacing out there. It was not the dangerous bubble that was developing in the real estate market, however; the threat was short sellers at hedge funds. The segment depicted Cohen as a powerful fund manager who sat atop a vast financial network that most Americans didn't even know existed. Cohen was so private that CBS couldn't find a photograph of him anywhere that it could use, so instead they broadcast a grainy video that Kasowitz Benson's investigator had surreptitiously taken of Cohen walking to his car after attending a mixed martial arts fight in Las Vegas. The episode included an extensive interview with Eugene Melnyk. "When you see a tidal wave coming, a tidal wave of negative publicity, a tidal wave of misinformation, and word gets out that the gorilla is about to stomp on you, a lot of people run for the hills," he said. "We're lucky we survived."

On the night the *60 Minutes* report aired, miles away from the CBS television studio, a woman sat transfixed in front of a TV, smoking one cigarette after another. As she watched the exposé on Steve Cohen and his hedge fund, Patricia Cohen drew her breath in sharply. She could not believe the way her former husband was being portrayed.

Ever since she and Cohen had finalized their divorce in 1990, she had been unhappy about the settlement, which left her with $1 million in cash, their Manhattan apartment, and child support, which, as she saw it, was not enough to live on. It never seemed fair, considering the millions she imagined her husband was earning trading at the time. It didn't help matters when the real estate market crashed almost immediately after the agreement was signed, and Patricia was unable to sell the apartment as she had planned. She ran out of money and asked Cohen for more, $100,000 a week. It was a war, but one whose front line might have seemed absurd to some people: Patricia's lawyer wrote in a petition to the court that she and their children, aged ten and six at the time, "are on the verge of being put out on the street because [Cohen's] wife . . . is virtually penniless." Cohen reluctantly increased the child support payments to $5,200 a month and then to $10,400, although they dropped again when Robert, their youngest, left for college at Brown. Cohen complained that his ex-wife was on a "never ending quest to poison my relationship with our children" and accused her of having a "vendetta" against him and his second wife. When Patricia said that she was out of money again, Cohen told her to get a job.

After the *60 Minutes* segment ended, Patricia started to wonder: Was it possible that her ex-husband was a truly dishonest person? Could he have hidden money or lied to her during their divorce? While they were married, she paid very little attention to the details of his business affairs. If he asked her to sign papers for an insurance policy or a checking account, she signed them without asking questions, as many wives of her generation did. Now, fifteen years later, she had only a foggy sense of his wealth or how it was achieved.

She went to her computer and typed Cohen's name into a search engine. An article that she'd never seen before popped up, a lengthy piece in

Fortune from 2003 titled "Shabby Side of the Street." It was about Gruntal, the brokerage where Cohen had worked when they were married. The article depicted the company as a sleazy place, to say the least. During the 1980s and 1990s, it claimed, Gruntal brokers were charged with insider trading and securities fraud; the company paid $750,000 to settle a sexual harassment lawsuit; and a group of employees was indicted for embezzling $14 million over a period of ten years by siphoning money from the dormant accounts of dead customers. And that was only a partial list. But it gave Patricia a sense of the environment her ex-husband was operating in as he started on the path to building his hedge fund empire. She remembered the SEC investigation that Steve had been so upset about in 1986, when the agency questioned whether he had traded RCA shares based on inside information. He had cried on her shoulder every night.

The next day, Patricia picked up the phone and dialed the number for Kasowitz Benson.

Michael Bowe was sitting with his feet up on his desk when his phone rang. His office looked like a high wind had just passed through, with baseball jerseys hanging off the chairs, his son's chess trophies crowded in a corner, cups and papers and folders all over the place in little piles. The desk didn't have any clear space on it.

"My name is Patricia, and I used to be married to Steve Cohen," a woman's voice said. "I have some information that may be of interest to you."

Bowe took his feet down and sat up.

"How can I help you?" he said.

She needed advice, she told Bowe. She felt that she'd gotten an unfair divorce settlement and she didn't know what to do. She was out of money and was living in a three-bedroom apartment on Central Park West that Cohen held under his own name, so she could get kicked out onto the street at any moment. Cohen's wife, Alex, wrote the maintenance check every month. She also believed that she had information about Cohen that she thought Bowe should know, information she'd kept secret for years.

She never felt comfortable coming forward with it, because everyone she talked to was afraid of Cohen. But Bowe didn't seem scared of him.

She met with Bowe in his office and told him about her relationship with her ex-husband and his time at Gruntal. In their private conversations, he had admitted to receiving information about the RCA takeover by General Electric in the 1980s, she said. He had panicked when the SEC investigated him and was afraid that he would end up in prison. After that investigation ended without any charges, she said, Cohen became extremely careful, almost paranoid, about his trading. He was moody and had an uncontrollable temper. He kept a shrink on retainer at his office, whom she thought was incompetent. She believed their children were frightened of him.

Bowe wasn't sure what to do. Matrimonial law wasn't his area of expertise. Patricia was clearly, at a minimum, extremely biased. But Bowe was also disgusted by what he was hearing. It reminded him of Cohen's reputation on the trading floor, where he went out of his way to abuse people and belittle them. Here was a damaged woman, suffering from serious emotional and financial distress. Bowe couldn't believe that Cohen, who made close to a billion dollars that year, wouldn't find a way to pay some amount of money to resolve his issues with his ex-wife. Instead, he had a team of lawyers fighting with her over every expense and his wife looking through her dry-cleaning bills.

The first thing he did was introduce Patricia to one of the lawyers in Kasowitz Benson's divorce group. Then Patricia asked Bowe whether he thought she should go to the FBI.

"No," Bowe told her. He knew that what he was telling her was partly out of self-interest, because he wanted to keep her as a possible source for his own cases. "I know it feels empowering and all that," he said, "but you have to know where talking to the Feds would lead. It'd be like sticking your neck into a buzz saw."

A few months went by, and Bowe didn't hear from Patricia. Then she surprised him one afternoon with a phone call. "I just finished a long meeting with an FBI agent," she told him.

Bowe tried not to seem too interested, but he was curious. "Oh yeah?" he said. "Who?"

"His name was B. J. Kang."

A few weeks after the *60 Minutes* broadcast, Bowe received another odd phone call. It was an executive with a Canadian insurance company called Fairfax Financial Holdings. The executive had been following the Biovail case closely, largely because the accusations Biovail had made sounded familiar. The Fairfax executive said that they, too, had been targeted by short sellers at a group of hedge funds who had been generating negative research about their company and even harassing Fairfax's executives. The difference was that while the Biovail case mostly dealt with events that had already happened, the Fairfax situation was still unfolding. Internet chat rooms were buzzing every day with talk about how Fairfax was going to collapse. Bowe watched one day as Fairfax's stock fell after message boards were flooded with rumors that the company's CEO had fled the country and that its offices were being raided by the Royal Canadian Mounted Police.

Fairfax was founded by Prem Watsa, a Canadian billionaire frequently described as "Canada's Warren Buffett" in the press. Watsa alleged that an analyst at an independent research and trading shop based in Memphis called Morgan Keegan was working in partnership with a handful of hedge funds to spread false information about Fairfax. It turned out that one of the funds was SAC Capital. Through its investigation, Bowe uncovered emails that he believed showed that a Morgan Keegan analyst had sent a draft of his Fairfax report to SAC and other funds before publishing it. Bowe hoped to prove that the hedge funds were insider trading on company research they were helping generate themselves.

Anonymous websites had been created comparing Fairfax to Enron, and Fairfax employees reported getting prank phone calls in the middle of the night: "Fairfax is a fraudulent company," a voice would say. "Save yourself!" Traders shorting the stock lobbied the FBI and the SEC to start an investigation into possible accounting fraud at the company. The

Manhattan U.S. Attorney's Office also opened an investigation. Fairfax had an incredibly complex structure that made it seem like it could easily be designed to conceal accounting issues. Traders at various hedge funds shorted the stock, making money each time it went down, dropping from $150 to below $110.

On July 26, 2006, Bowe filed a lawsuit in New Jersey State Court, accusing SAC and a group of other funds of spreading false rumors about Fairfax in the market. The lawsuit accused the hedge funds of violating the Racketeer Influenced and Corrupt Organizations Act, or RICO, a criminal statute designed to target the Mafia by holding the leaders of a criminal syndicate responsible for the actions of its lower-level employees. Fairfax asked for $5 billion in damages. SAC and the other defendants denied the charge.*

Just hours after Fairfax filed its case, Bowe got a call from the U.S. Attorney's Office in Manhattan. It was a prosecutor from the securities unit named Helen Cantwell.

"Can you come down here?" she said, sounding irritated. "We need to talk to you." She was in the midst of a criminal investigation involving Fairfax, working with an FBI Special Agent named B. J. Kang. The government was looking into possible fraud at Fairfax, *not* misconduct of hedge funds—basically the opposite of what Bowe's case alleged. Fairfax's complaint was full of all sorts of information that came as a surprise to the government, suggesting that it was on the completely wrong track. Cantwell and everyone else at the U.S. Attorney's Office seemed upset. They wanted Bowe there the next day.

The next morning, Bowe strolled into a conference room inside 1 St. Andrew's Plaza in downtown Manhattan. Kang was at one end of the table and an investigator from the SEC was at the other. Cantwell was in the middle. She pointed toward a chair and Bowe sat down. None of them looked happy.

"What would you like to know?" he asked.

---

* SAC and the other hedge funds won dismissal of the case. The court found that SAC had no economic interest in the scheme. Fairfax appealed in 2013.

Cantwell said that the U.S. Attorney's Office was investigating Fairfax for possible fraud. She said that Fairfax, and Bowe, should have waited to file Fairfax's lawsuit until their criminal investigation was resolved. The lawsuit had just created major problems for their case. Was the government supposed to be looking into possible allegations of fraud at Fairfax or criminal activity of short sellers at hedge funds who were shorting Fairfax stock? Cantwell wanted Bowe to explain every aspect of Fairfax's 160-page complaint.

Bowe spent the next three hours describing the charges and the evidence behind them, telling them about SAC and the other hedge funds Fairfax believed were targeting them, the false rumors and prank phone calls, the short selling and the allegations of insider trading. While he spoke, Kang took notes.

The atmosphere was chilly, but Cantwell said that they would look into Fairfax's claims against the hedge funds. She thanked him and said goodbye.

Michael Bowe was not raised to avoid conflict. In some ways he sought it out. Most everything he knew about life he'd learned growing up in Pearl River, a town an hour north of Manhattan crammed with Irish bars and knickknack shops. At recess, eight hundred children of New York City cops and firefighters would extrude from the Catholic elementary school in town into an asphalt schoolyard where a teacher looked the other way as the kids took turns picking on one another and concocting cruel games.

After school, they roamed the streets in packs, getting into fistfights and trying to make each other cry. It was there that Bowe developed some crucial skills: how to deal with people who had it in for you, how to be the big guy in a situation as well as the little guy, how to overcome adversity. Bowe's father had been a fireman with Ladder 36 in Inwood, in northern Manhattan, until he was badly burned in a fire and retired. His petite Irish American mom would hoist her young son up onto the kitchen counter after he came home crying from a neighborhood beating. "Michael," she'd say, "you need to learn to take care of yourself." He did not go on to get an Ivy League degree like most of the federal prosecutors in the U.S. Attorney's Office in Manhattan. Bowe was a proud product of Fordham and New York Law School, and conflict didn't faze him.

By the time B. J. Kang called him again to follow up on the hedge fund allegations, four months after their initial meeting, Bowe had become the world's living expert on SAC Capital Advisors.

"We were wondering if you could come down and walk us through what you've learned about SAC and other hedge funds and the insider trading you see out there," Kang said. He especially wanted to know about what Bowe had referred to as the "insider trading business model" he believed many hedge funds employed. Would he let the FBI agent ask him questions for a couple of hours?

Sure, Bowe said, he'd be happy to.

Kang was still new at the FBI's securities fraud unit. Until then he had been assigned mostly to cases involving small brokerage firms, many of them located outside of New York City in strip malls, where salesmen pitched worthless penny stocks to people who didn't know enough not to take stock tips from strangers over the phone. The amounts of money involved were negligible, and each time the FBI shut one down, another one popped up in its place. Kang's boss, Pat Carroll, had a feeling that there was more going on, bigger cases involving significant frauds they should be pursuing. He had recently called Kang into his office to tell him about it.

"The pyramid schemes and pump and dump cases are all fine," Carroll told him, by way of a pep talk. "But we need to start looking at hedge funds. The industry is not very transparent, and we haven't really looked at them before."

Kang nodded, not quite sure that he understood.

"If you follow the money, hedge funds are where it leads," Carroll explained. He wasn't saying that all hedge funds were breaking the law, but he was concerned that the FBI didn't have a clue as to what these funds were doing and how they were making so much money. New ones were opening for business every day, and billions of investor dollars were flowing into them. "We need to start thinking big," Carroll said.

Kang had wanted to work in law enforcement since he was a kid in suburban Maryland playing cops and robbers. He had fused this good guy–bad guy obsession with a practice his parents had drilled into him growing up, to work harder than anyone else until he succeeded. If the guy at the desk next to him showed up at 7 A.M., Kang would come in at 6; if the other guy started coming in at 6, Kang would show up at 5:30. When he graduated from the FBI Academy, he asked for a placement in New York, which was where the most important cases happened.

The first thing Kang did after Carroll's speech was try to educate himself about the hedge fund industry. He was familiar with the most prominent fund managers and the incredible amount of money they seemed to be making. He was vaguely aware of Galleon, Raj Rajaratnam's fund, which was one of the top performers in the industry. But there was a lot more he still had to learn.

During interviews with informants and witnesses from the financial world, Kang always asked the same questions: Who are the most successful hedge fund traders? How do they make their money? Do people think they're clean? One name came up over and over again: SAC Capital.

SAC, according to Kang's sources on Wall Street, was the most profitable, and aggressive, fund out there. Its competitors couldn't understand how SAC was able to make 30, 40, 50 percent year after year, apparently without ever suffering a loss. It seemed too good to be true. Kang wanted to know more.

He and Bowe spent most of the afternoon alone in a conference room, as Bowe explained how he thought the hedge fund world worked.

The way Bowe saw it, Wall Street had undergone an enormous shift over the previous five or six years, unbeknownst to the people responsible for policing and regulating it. The capital markets system existed to help channel capital that people had to invest to businesses that needed it to build bigger plants and develop new products and hire more workers. This system was the engine for economic growth. Banks made loans, while investment banks made the engine run by facilitating stock and bond trading, IPOs, and mergers and takeovers. Up until 2000 or so, the market was dominated by a handful of these large firms, with names like Goldman Sachs and Morgan Stanley, as well as mutual fund companies that managed people's retirement accounts. And all of them operated under an umbrella of rules and regulations that had been in place for almost seventy years. There were, of course, regulatory violations and even criminal activity taking place, but it was mostly happening in well-defined, predictable ways. The big banks, for the most part, understood what was legal and what wasn't and had compliance departments in place to make sure they didn't run too far afoul of the law. The SEC knew what it was supposed to be looking for when it monitored them.

Over the previous ten years, however, billions of dollars had moved out of the heavily regulated big banks and into hedge funds, which were aggressive investment vehicles promising enormous returns. Hedge funds were subject to only light regulation, and most operated behind a veil of secrecy. "When you look at the nature of the regulatory cases that have been brought against the big banks—I'm not saying the conduct wasn't bad," Bowe told Kang. "But a lot of the cases involved stepping over a line that was far away from the type of stuff going on at the hedge funds."

Look at it in practical terms, Bowe said. Many of the people working at these funds had unconventional backgrounds; their main qualification might be that they were buddies with the fund manager, and they couldn't have gotten a job at Goldman Sachs if they'd tried. These hedge funds weren't under the big regulatory umbrella, they didn't always have real compliance departments, and the philosophy was to hire anyone who could make money trading, regardless of how they did it. The SEC had only minimal information about them. Given all this, what did Kang think was going to happen?

In the course of investigating the industry on behalf of Biovail and Fairfax, Bowe had become convinced that hedge funds were incubating a new and virulent form of corruption. At the same time that high finance was inventing a nearly incomprehensible new array of financial products and instruments, collateralizing mortgages and other debt and turning it into securities, traders were finding new ways to cheat. When it came to innovating financial crime, hedge funds were like Silicon Valley.

Government intervention had made matters worse, in a classic example of unintended consequences. In 2000, New York attorney general Eliot Spitzer launched an investigation of research departments at Wall Street investment banks, ultimately charging them three years later with manipulating their buy and sell ratings on stocks, the same ratings that many investors in the market turned to as guides when evaluating the health of various companies. Spitzer accused the banks of using their analyst reports as sales tools to generate investment banking business for their firms. At the time, underwriting initial public offerings and advising on mergers and takeovers provided the bulk of most big firms' profits. Promising a positive report on a particular company was an effective way of paving the way for more advisory fees on deals.

The classic case was Henry Blodget, the star Internet analyst at Merrill Lynch who said in 1998 that he believed shares of Amazon were worth $400. He publicly praised companies like Pets.com and eToys.com while his firm courted business from them. In private emails to colleagues, however, he said that he really thought the companies were overhyped, calling Excite@Home "a piece of crap" and other dotcom companies "dogs."

When the attorney general's office exposed these conflicts of interest and settled with Merrill Lynch, Goldman Sachs, Lehman Brothers, J. P. Morgan, and the six other top Wall Street firms at the end of 2002, it extracted billions of dollars in fines and restitution as well as promises from the banks to abide by a new set of tighter rules. Investment banking and research departments had to be completely separate from one another, and analysts could no longer be paid in relation to how much banking business they generated for their firms. Almost overnight, the job of being a Morgan Stanley or Goldman Sachs technology analyst went from being one of the most desirable positions in the financial industry to that of a glorified librarian.

As this was happening, hedge funds were becoming increasingly important to the big banks because of the volume of trading they did. Their commissions became a major source of profit. The hedge funds demanded service in return for the hundreds of millions in fees that they paid, and the big firms started to do whatever they had to to keep them happy. The most aggressive hedge funds wanted to know if an analyst was going to downgrade or upgrade a stock before anyone else. A skilled trader—and even a not-so-skilled one—could turn that information into instant profits.

Meanwhile, in response to calls from Spitzer and others for independent stock research, boutique research firms started up, promising unbiased opinions about whether investors should buy or sell stock in certain companies. At first, this seemed like a good idea. But these little research shops didn't have big compliance departments, either, or much in the way of a reputation to protect. Some employed analysts who were barely qualified for the job. What was to stop a powerful hedge fund from coming along and saying it was going to buy the little firm's research reports and then suggesting which companies it wanted to read about, even what it wanted the research reports to say? Bowe believed that hedge funds could easily manipulate the market by commissioning negative reports on companies whose shares they were already short and then making a profit when the negative research drove the stock price down.

Finally, Bowe told Kang about expert networks like Gerson Lehrman Group, the matchmaking company that helped connect investors with executives at publicly traded companies. Hundreds of doctors involved in drug research and middle managers at technology companies were moonlighting for these expert network firms, taking money to have "consultations" with hedge fund traders. The consultants weren't supposed to disclose confidential information, but there was little in place to prevent that from happening. Hedge funds were paying millions of dollars in fees to these consultants. Why would they do that for information that anybody could get? This in particular struck Bowe as an arrangement that could easily be misused.

They talked for four hours. For Kang, it was like learning a new language. He scribbled on a legal pad and interrupted Bowe to ask questions, saying, "Hold on," "Back up," and "Could you please repeat that?"

He was astonished at just how unethical the business seemed to be.

"We both know that if you have tons of money at stake and nobody is watching, you will find bad conduct," Bowe said. On Wall Street, he argued, you were likely to find a range of misdeeds: some close to the line, some over it, and a few that went way beyond. The worst stuff, Bowe was convinced, was happening at hedge funds.

"You don't have to believe me, you just have to go and look, start talking to people," he said. "This is like gambling at Rick's. If you start picking up rocks and looking under them, particularly with respect to SAC, you're going to find it."

CHAPTER 5

EDGY, PROPRIETARY INFORMATION

There were many advantages to working at one of the most envied firms on Wall Street, as SAC was, but its employees often felt like they were part of an experiment looking at the effects of prolonged stress and uncertainty. There was continuous scrambling and reshuffling of the computer terminals and the seating chart, and the hierarchy that accompanied it, which meant that no one ever felt secure. The possibility of a career-ending loss constantly hung over a portfolio manager's head. People who visited the offices regularly were startled to find that entire desks or departments had disappeared without explanation. But all that change created opportunity, and Michael Steinberg intended to make it work for him.

Steinberg had started working at SAC in 1996 as a clerk to Richard Grodin, Cohen's treasured technology trader. Tall and broad-shouldered, with the preppy affect of a college lacrosse player, Steinberg could be seen bent over the trading desk, writing Grodin's trade tickets, jumping on the phone with brokers if there were problems with trades, and generally doing whatever the guys above him wanted, no matter how small. Steinberg's parents were worried when he majored in philosophy in college because it seemed so impractical, and he was determined to show them that he could become a success at something that would bring financial security. Gradually, he was promoted at SAC, and by 2004 he was running the portfolio alongside Grodin. Once Grodin quit, after his dispute with Cohen over sharing C. B. Lee's research, Steinberg was put in charge of the portfolio on his own.

He set about trying to find good people to work with. As a portfolio manager, Steinberg was responsible for assembling his own team of analysts and traders, who would help him manage his allotted pool of capital. In September 2006, a thirty-six-year-old analyst named Jon Horvath joined his group, hired to research computer-related stocks like Dell, Apple, Intel, Microsoft, and IBM. The hiring process had lasted six months and involved at least a dozen interviews with ten different people. Horvath went stoically through it, knowing that if he got the job, he could work for a few years and then spend the rest of his life skiing.

Horvath looked like he was stoned half the time, but he was a hard worker. His job was to propose trading ideas to Steinberg—but not just any trading ideas. The SAC approach, he quickly learned, was to seek out investment opportunities where a specific event like an earnings announcement would move the price of a stock up or down. The trick was to figure out what that event was and how to set up a long or short position to benefit from it. Horvath built elaborate spreadsheets and earnings models. He had an apartment in San Francisco, near Silicon Valley, and he traveled back and forth between New York and the West Coast as well as to investment conferences and technology companies all over the world, trying to learn everything he could about his companies.

Horvath had been at SAC for only a few months when, in early 2007, there were stirrings of trouble in the economy. Real estate values across the country had started to decline and mortgage delinquencies were spiking, imperiling the banks and other investors that had bought up large amounts of mortgage debt on the assumption that housing prices could only go up. Most investors chose to ignore the signs of impending disaster, however. Rather, they were acknowledged only by those who were open to the possibility that their rapid accumulations of wealth hadn't made them infallibly brilliant. In May, two hedge funds owned by Bear Stearns that were heavily invested in subprime mortgage bonds started to plummet in value. Each had been worth more than $20 billion—and then, in a matter of weeks, no one in the market wanted anything to do with the mortgage securities they owned. Bear Stearns management tried to support the funds, but the value of the securities continued to plunge. On July 18, Bear announced that the hedge funds were essentially worthless and that it was shutting them down, leading to billions of dollars in losses.

Thousands of investors struggled to figure out what the funds' collapse meant. Was this just a small setback, or the sign of a coming economic crisis? Horvath hoped it was the former. He continued to do his job as if everything was stable, bringing ideas to Steinberg. When Network Appliance, a data storage company that Horvath had been researching, announced at the beginning of August that it was going to miss the next quarter's earnings estimates by a large amount, the stock dropped $5. Horvath liked the company, and, figuring that the worst was over, he urged Steinberg to buy. Steinberg bought up NetApp shares based on Horvath's recommendation. The stock recovered a little, but when NetApp released its earnings later in the month, it sank again, causing $2 million in losses. Steinberg was infuriated.

A couple of days later, after the office had emptied out, Steinberg called Horvath over to his desk. "I can day-trade these stocks and make money by myself, I don't need your help to do that," Steinberg told him, speaking slowly. "What I need you to do is go out and get me edgy, proprietary information that we can use to make money in these stocks." Steinberg paused. "You need to talk to your contacts and the companies, bankers, consultants, and leverage your peer network to *get* that information." He looked hard at Horvath, seemingly to make sure that he understood.

To Horvath, it was clear what his boss wanted him to do: get inside information. Something guaranteed to make money.

Two blocks from Central Park and the Metropolitan Museum of Art, 925 Park Avenue sits squarely in the most expensive zip code in Manhattan. A prewar limestone cooperative, the building's apartments feature crown moldings, wood-burning fireplaces, and Juliet balconies peeking over the street. One day in June 2007, FBI Special Agent David Makol crossed the building's gleaming art deco lobby and stepped into the elevator, which he rode to the ninth floor. He approached apartment 9A and knocked on the door. Makol was hoping that the person who answered would help him bring down a Wall Street titan.

For the previous year, Makol had been investigating an insider trading ring that was separate from the ongoing Raj Rajaratnam case. An analyst at a hedge fund called Chelsey Capital was allegedly getting inside information from a friend who worked on the investment review committee at the Swiss bank UBS. The friend was telling the hedge fund analyst about changes UBS analysts were making to their stock and bond ratings before the bank made them public, and the analyst, Makol believed, was trading on the information. The FBI was set to arrest him when the analyst flipped and agreed to give up the names of others he knew on Wall Street who were breaking the law. One of those he turned in was his colleague from Chelsey, a former Galleon trader named David Slaine.

When Slaine came to the door, Makol held out his badge. "I'm here to talk about insider trading," he said. Makol described the evidence the FBI had against him and raised the threat of a long prison term. "You might never see your daughter again if you don't cooperate," he told Slaine, who was married with one child. By the time Makol was done, Slaine was badly shaken. After consulting with several lawyers, he agreed to cooperate.

Cooperation consisted of dozens of interview sessions with Makol, who questioned Slaine for hours about everyone he'd ever worked with and any criminal activity he might have seen. In order to avoid prosecution, Slaine had to prove to Makol that he wasn't holding anything back. No one could be spared, not even the people closest to him.

Slaine seemed to be surrounded by people who were trading on inside information, some of it obtained from corporate lawyers, some from other traders. The FBI wanted to go after all of them. Slaine agreed to make recordings of his conversations, placing phone calls to his Wall Street friends and sources as Makol directed. Still, even after his efforts, the evidence felt anecdotal, not necessarily enough for criminal cases. In order to expand the investigation, the FBI agents and the prosecutors they worked with needed overwhelming evidence that couldn't be beaten in court. How could they get it? Makol puzzled over this question during a meeting with his supervisor, David Chaves, and Reed Brodsky, the prosecutor who had taken the lead on the Slaine case.

"We need to take this to the next level," Brodsky said.

Brodsky went to his boss, Raymond Lohier, the head of the securities unit at the Manhattan U.S. Attorney's Office. He complained that they were having trouble moving the cases forward.

"Have you thought about getting up on a wire?" Lohier asked. "You need to find someone to 'tickle' the phone and get it dirty. You need to bring up fresh information to get permission."

To persuade a judge to authorize a wiretap, prosecutors couldn't just go on hunches or educated guesses. They essentially had to show that criminal activity was being discussed over a specific phone line—i.e., that it was "dirty." Wiretaps hadn't been used in insider trading cases before, but the insider trading rings were in many ways similar to organized crime. And like crime syndicates, many of the hedge funds the FBI was looking at were secretive and hierarchical, with the lower-level workers doing questionable things while the bosses at the top maintained intentional ignorance and reaped most of the benefits. The FBI felt that it needed the same tools it had used to investigate the Mob. Makol helped Slaine make a recording of a call with one of his best friends, a Galleon trader named Zvi Goffer, in which they discussed illegal information. Using this as evidence, the government got permission to wiretap Goffer's phone. Soon, the FBI's wire room came to life.

In spite of the dismal performance of the stock market that year, 2007 was a profitable one at SAC. Michael Steinberg's group alone made more than

$27 million, even after the losses in NetApp. Steinberg's payout—the amount of the profit he got to keep—was 31 percent. It was his responsibility to pay bonuses to the analysts and traders in his group out of that based on how much he felt they contributed. Money was how a person's value was articulated at SAC, and Steinberg sent a strong message to Horvath by giving him a relatively modest $416,084 bonus, compared to the $1.5 million that went to another analyst in Steinberg's group. Horvath could tell that he was at risk of being fired. He rang in the New Year with a commitment to do better.

He thought about everyone he knew, trying to figure out who might be in a position to help him get the kind of information his bosses at SAC wanted. All sorts of relationships could potentially be useful—his parents, his friends' parents, neighbors, doctors, ski partners, anyone he came into contact with might have access to valuable corporate information, even if they didn't know it. In some cases it might come from an obvious place, like an analyst at another hedge fund who was out looking for edge himself. One friend of Horvath's in particular, an analyst named Jesse Tortora, seemed eager to share.

Tortora was the opposite of Horvath—polished, confident, connected, or at least he seemed so on the outside. He had followed a common route into the hedge fund world. After getting an engineering degree, he worked at Intel for three years before becoming a technology analyst at Prudential Securities. From there, he was able to use his former Intel colleagues as sources of information about the semiconductor industry, information he then passed on to analysts at a bunch of mutual funds and hedge funds, including Galleon and SAC, which were clients of Prudential. When Prudential shut down its stock research division, Tortora lost his job. He relocated to the East Coast and interviewed for an analyst position at a hedge fund called Diamondback Capital. His connections at technology companies helped get him hired.

Tortora sensed instinctively that you needed inside information to make money at a hedge fund. Good information wasn't easy to get, though; securing it took months of building trust and relationships with employees who had access to the internal goings-on at big companies.

Tortora had some of those contacts in place already, but he was always on the hunt for more. He figured that he and his friends could make the most of the intelligence they got if they shared it with each other, a sort of "fight club" of inside information. He suggested the idea to Horvath, who readily signed on. Then Tortora invited a few others to join, people he knew and trusted, including Sam Adondakis, an analyst at a hedge fund called Level Global Investors with whom he'd worked at Prudential, and Ron Dennis, another SAC analyst who was a former client from Tortora's Prudential days. Dennis said yes, on one condition: He told Tortora never to email him the information, he only wanted to communicate by phone.

The caution expressed by Dennis about using email should have given Tortora a reason to stop and question what he was doing, but it didn't. Instead, he went ahead, putting everything down in writing. "Rule number one about email list," Tortora wrote to Horvath, Adondakis, and three others when he introduced them to one another. "There is no email list (fight club reference)." He added: "Enjoy. Your perf will now go up by 100% . . . and your boss will love you."

The economy was officially in a recession by early 2008, and real estate prices across the country were collapsing. The drops were most extreme in places like Las Vegas and Miami, where speculators had flooded the market, but the rest of the country was suffering, too. For the first time since 2000, home prices in ten major U.S. cities fell more steeply than they had at any time since 1987. All the banks that owned those home loans were in trouble. On January 11, Bank of America announced that it was buying Countrywide Financial, saving the huge mortgage company from bankruptcy. That was just the beginning of a series of rescues and bailouts of financial institutions whose insolvency threatened the financial system.

Just as the financial crisis hit, SAC reached its peak, with close to 1,200 employees and almost $17 billion in assets, half of which belonged to Cohen and his employees. Since its founding in 1992, the firm had gone through several reinventions: first a day-trading shop staffed with Cohen's college friends; then a more professional operation with Ivy League types; and finally a research and intelligence-gathering machine filled with analysts who specialized in different industries. Its final expansion had been the most ambitious. Cohen had pushed the company into every corner of the market, opening offices in Asia and Europe, launching a private equity unit to take stakes in private companies, and starting a bond trading group, an area he knew little about but that now accounted for a quarter of his fund. SAC's returns had averaged 30 percent over the previous eighteen years, an impossibly high level of performance that was several times greater than the average market return. Cohen was one of the richest men in the world, worth nearly $10 billion.

He and his traders made little effort to conceal their good fortune. For evidence of the firm's success, you didn't need to look any farther than the SAC parking lot in Stamford. One portfolio manager drove a Mercedes with gull-wing doors, another had a Maserati, while still another, who had started as an intern not long before, drove a brown Bentley Continental. The president of the firm, Tom Conheeney, commuted to work on a Ducati motorcycle and sometimes parked his cigarette boat in the lot. SAC traders were known to travel to weekend golf games by helicopter.

One day a consultant trying to leave after a company visit accidentally put his car into the wrong gear in the parking lot and backed into a $150,000 Mercedes, a Series 7 BMW, and a Ferrari owned by an SAC trader. The consultant was aghast and started apologizing, certain he'd be fired or worse. Although the owner of the BMW, a woman, screamed at him, the men whose expensive toys were affected remained calm. The trader who owned the damaged Ferrari shrugged and said, "I'll just drive the other Ferrari." Even by the money-obsessed standards of Wall Street, SAC's extravagance stood out.

Between 2006 and 2008, SAC had doubled in size, and the firm's top traders and analysts were pampered like Thoroughbreds. Three masseuses were on the payroll to work on their tense muscles. Crystal was their favorite; she was a specialist in Thai massage who walked on traders' backs, working their IT bands with her heels. Masterpieces from Cohen's personal art collection, which by then was valued at $1 billion, adorned the walls. In his office he showcased a quirky piece titled *Self,* by the conceptual artist Marc Quinn, which prompted a few snickers around the office. It was a sculpture of the artist's own head, made from eight pints of his blood that had been poured into a mold and frozen. Cohen had a custom refrigeration system installed to keep the sculpture at the necessary temperature. He had purchased the work in 2005 from Charles Saatchi for $2.8 million, a few months after he'd paid $8 million for another flashy showpiece from Saatchi's collection, Damien Hirst's shark suspended in formaldehyde, called *The Physical Impossibility of Death in the Mind of Someone Living.* People made jokes about the shark, an ironic ode to Cohen himself, the ultimate predator.

There was almost no time in a twenty-four-hour day Cohen didn't use for a moneymaking purpose, and he attributed much of SAC's success to this work ethic. Cohen got up early and studied the market at home before being driven to the office by 8 A.M. by a bodyguard in a gray Maybach. He arrived to find a bowl of hot oatmeal wrapped in cellophane waiting on his desk. His station at the center of the trading floor resembled a cockpit, with twelve monitors mounted in front of him. Because Cohen's time was so valuable, most activities—from haircuts to meetings—were scheduled so as to not distract him from his screens between 9:30 A.M. and 4 P.M. "Everything happened at his desk," said one trader who sat at his elbow for years. "Everything."

Cohen was so focused on making sure that he had access to every piece of available information that he hired research traders to filter through his messages and make sure that he saw the important ones. Any time he traveled to Las Vegas to visit his parents, or to Brown University, where Cohen was on the board of trustees, or on his yearly summer vacation with Alex, an advance team of consultants made the journey ahead of him. He rented an extra room wherever he was staying and used it as a staging area where his staff re-created his trading station in such detail that he could hardly tell he was away from his office.

Every Sunday around noon, Cohen sat down at his desk in his home office with a yellow notepad in hand. His portfolio managers called in one by one to pitch their best trade ideas for the upcoming week. It was called the Sunday Ideas Meeting, and it was a source of constant anxiety among SAC's employees. Each conversation typically lasted five minutes, with Cohen's research trader also joining them on the line to take notes. Portfolio managers were expected to have a moneymaking idea to pitch him and an accompanying "conviction rating"—a way of conveying how sure they were that the investment would pay off.

The traders who worked directly for Cohen, executing the trades in his own book, were called "execution traders," and they, much like actual executioners, did what they were told and did not ask questions. They were known around Wall Street as Cohen's "henchmen," because they had the thankless task of burning other people in the market each day on behalf of their boss. At the same time, they had to try to maintain good relationships with those same people so that they could get access to information and the flow of trading activity each day. It was an awkward job.

A typical weekday morning in the life of a henchman might hypothetically go as follows: After the oatmeal was consumed and the market opened, Cohen would shut off the "Steve-cam," an audio and video feed that broadcast his movements and his conversations to everyone on the trading floor, and take a phone call. After a few minutes he would hang up. Because he was in "private" mode, his staff could only guess what was being said. Then he might turn to one of his execution traders with an order: "Short 500,000 Nextel."

The trader would turn to the guy in charge of stock-loan, the department responsible for borrowing shares of a stock from another firm so that SAC could sell them short: "Get me a borrow on 500 Nextel."

The trader would then make a call to, say, his Bear Stearns broker with an order to short the stock. "I'm a seller of 500 Nextel."

The Bear broker would know that the order was coming from Cohen and, for self-preservation reasons, would try to find out as much as he could about the motives behind it before responding. "What are you thinking?" the Bear guy might ask.

"You know where it's coming from," Cohen's trader might reply. Translation: "Stevie is selling, that's all you need to know."

The Bear broker then had a decision to make: Either take the 500,000 shares off of Cohen's hands and try to get rid of them, knowing full well that the greatest trader on Wall Street, Stevie Cohen, was selling them short for a reason. Or refuse what was certainly the crappy end of a transaction—taking the opposite side of a trade with Cohen—and risk alienating one of the firm's most valuable customers.

In all likelihood, Bear Stearns would buy the stock, and Cohen's trader would report back to his boss: "Sold 500 Nextel."

"You get the best price you could get?" Cohen would ask. Yes, the trader would say, he got the best price. Great, Cohen would say, now go short 500,000 more.

Then Cohen's trader had a dilemma. "Do you call Bear Stearns again?" said a trader at a rival fund who was familiar with the strategy. "No, 'cause they're going to ask what the fuck you're doing. So you call Morgan Stanley."

So Cohen's trader would call Morgan Stanley and say, "I'm a seller of 500 Nextel. It's gotta be tight," meaning, it's got to be for the best possible price. Morgan Stanley might offer to buy it at $21¾. The trader would say, No, it's got to be $22. Morgan would go through the same calculus Bear had, take the shares, and then turn around and try to sell them in the open market, and that would push the price down even more.

Suddenly Bear Stearns, which had managed to sell only 200,000 shares out of the 500,000 it just bought from SAC, would want to know what the hell was going on. The SAC trader would stall—he didn't fucking know, he was the execution trader and he was doing his job: executing. Then the SAC trader would have to go to his other brokers and keep selling Nextel, shorting more shares until Cohen said he didn't want to sell any more.

After the market closed, Nextel might preannounce negative earnings, warning Wall Street that its next quarter would be a disappointment. The stock would dive $3. Cohen would have made $3 million, while the Bear trader lost $900,000, Morgan $1.5 million. Cohen's trader promised to pay them back with future commissions.

Every day it was "I'm going to destroy you today and make it up to you later." Year after year, Cohen's employees would watch in astonishment as this same scenario played out again and again with different stocks and different situations. No one ever got the better end of a deal with Stevie Cohen.

As the financial crisis gathered strength, even some of the richest people in the world started to worry about whether their fortunes were secure. Cohen, who was normally impervious to feelings of panic, started warning his traders and portfolio managers against taking too much risk in the market. For years, Wall Street had made billions of dollars off the booming housing market and the baffling array of mortgage products and derivatives that emanated from it. Certain that the value of their homes would only go up, millions of Americans borrowed recklessly against them, aided and abetted at every step by the financial industry. Between 2000 and 2007, Wall Street had made more than $1.8 trillion worth of securities out of subprime mortgages. Now all of that looked suspect.

By 2009, three powerful forces began to converge on SAC. One was the larger economic climate, which was looking more unpredictable with each passing day, making traders desperate for a sure way to make money. The second was Cohen's own personal ambition, as strong as ever but morphing in nature. His days as a cowboy investor were over. He wanted more substantial investment ideas, produced by the kind of research and connections that smaller, less sophisticated rivals couldn't mimic. Finally, there was the government. Wall Street regulators were beginning to understand that if they wanted to bring order to the financial industry, funds like SAC would have to come under far more intensive scrutiny.

Into the midst of this tumultuous environment stumbled Mathew Martoma, the new healthcare portfolio manager at SAC's CR Intrinsic unit. Martoma wanted to prove himself. On June 25, 2008, he instructed his trader, Timothy Jandovitz, to start accumulating shares of the pharmaceutical companies Elan and Wyeth. It was the worst June the stock market had experienced since the Great Depression, and most traders were anxious about holding shares of anything. Martoma was, however, determined.

"I want to buy 750,000 to 1 million Elan over the course of the day," Martoma told Jandovitz an hour before the market opened. That was just the beginning.

CHAPTER 6

CONFLICT OF INTEREST

Alzheimer's disease afflicts roughly five million people in the United States, a progressive assault on the brain that causes memory loss and changes in behavior. It's agonizing for family members to watch their loved ones become more and more confused, unable to balance a checkbook, drive a car, or even brush their teeth as their minds deteriorate to the point that they don't recognize their own children. The disease has proven to be a particularly stubborn adversary for scientists. Nothing has been shown to stop its effects, but scientists had hopes that the new drug bapineuzumab might be different. Elan, which was based in Ireland but traded on the New York Stock Exchange, and Wyeth, a midsized drug company founded in Philadelphia, had teamed up for the development of bapi, known also as AAB-001, in part to share the formidable costs of bringing a new pharmaceutical treatment to the market. If the companies were able to navigate the gauntlet of drug trials and regulatory permissions and come out with a safe and effective drug, they stood to make billions of dollars.

Alleviating suffering was beside the point for the Wall Street investors, like Mathew Martoma, who were monitoring bapi's long journey through the regulatory approval process. Each week, Cohen's portfolio managers were supposed to send him written updates on the investment ideas they were following and offer recommendations for trades. The SAC compliance department had set up a special email address for these writeups, steveideas@sac.com, so that they could keep an eye on what was in there. Martoma used it to push bapi hard.

The writeups followed a prescribed format, with the name of the stock at the top, followed by "Target Price"—where the portfolio manager thought the stock might go—and the timing that was suggested for the trade. The most important part of the memo was the "Conviction" rating, a number on a scale of 1 to 10 that conveyed how certain the portfolio manager was about what he was suggesting. Martoma sent a memo to Cohen on June 29, 2008, recommending Elan with a target price of $40 to $50. The stock was trading in the $26 range, so the increase he was predicting based on the research he had done so far was huge. Under "Catalysts," which were the events he expected to move the stock price higher, Martoma wrote that there was an upcoming Phase II Alzheimer's drug trial presentation at ICAD, an industry conference, at the end of July. For "Conviction" he wrote "9." He sent a similar note for Wyeth, with a "9" attached to it as well.

A conviction rating of 10 was reserved for "absolute certainty," a level that would seem to be impossible to achieve through conventional research methods. How could a person be 100 percent certain about any event in the future, let alone the performance of a stock? The rating was how the traders communicated the value of their information to Cohen without exposing him to the details of how they knew something. Cohen relied on it to decide whether to buy for his own account. The rating system had been the idea of the compliance department, which was always trying to find ways to protect Cohen and keep him from explicitly receiving material nonpublic information—it was like a moat around the company's most valuable asset.

As SAC's main healthcare trader, Tim Jandovitz was responsible for buying the shares of Elan and Wyeth that Martoma was recommending. Jandovitz was well suited to the job, with a brain that could execute complex calculations in seconds. He arrived most mornings by 7 A.M. and started the daily ritual of culling through dozens of research notes from Wall Street firms, making sure to forward the ones that were relevant to Martoma. He and Martoma usually huddled around 9:15 A.M., just before the market opened, to strategize on their trades for the day. By closely monitoring the market and striking at opportune moments, he helped Martoma build a bigger and bigger position in the two drug companies Elan and Wyeth, while Martoma also pushed Cohen to do the same. "I spoke to Steve about it," Martoma would say after giving Jandovitz another buy order. He wanted to make it clear that their boss approved.

Jandovitz wondered what it would take for a portfolio manager to label something a 10, indicating 100 percent conviction about a stock they were recommending. For that matter, he could hardly recall seeing a 9 before. It seemed strange to him, but it wasn't his job to worry about it.

Martoma had been working for more than two years to learn everything he could about bapi. He had spoken to hundreds of doctors and medical researchers, and he was optimistic that bapi would work out. And he hoped to make a lot of money when it did.

The immense confidence Martoma had in bapi came partly from the special source he had been developing. If you wanted Alzheimer's drug expertise, Dr. Sidney Gilman was the best person available. He was affiliated with the University of Michigan Medical School and lived with his wife in Ann Arbor, Michigan. Gilman was considered a leading expert on Alzheimer's disease and its treatments. Helping find a cure was his life's mission.

His many accomplishments concealed a troubled life. Gilman grew up poor in East Los Angeles, the son of struggling Russian immigrants. His father, who did odd jobs for a living, left the family when Sid was ten, leaving his mother to raise three boys on her own. Still, Gilman became an exemplary student, attending medical school at UCLA before going on to teach medicine at Harvard and Columbia University. He and his first wife, Linda, moved to Ann Arbor with their two sons in 1977 to run the University of Michigan's neurology department. When their elder son, Jeff, revealed that he was gay, Gilman had trouble accepting it, and the two became estranged. Jeff had struggled with depression since childhood, and, after moving out of the house and dropping out of school, he committed suicide in 1983. It was a terrible echo of what had happened to Gilman's mother, who had taken her own life at age sixty-seven.

After they lost their son, Sid and Linda's marriage deteriorated, eventually ending in divorce. In 1984, Gilman got remarried, to a psychoanalyst named Carol Barbour. He and Barbour didn't have children of their own, and Gilman's relationship with his surviving son, Todd, was not smooth. After Todd revealed to his father that he was gay, like his brother, he and his father stopped speaking. Thereafter, Gilman spent almost all of his time absorbed in his research, to the exclusion of any personal life. "The man worked himself to distraction," one of his protégées at Michigan, Anne Young, the eventual chief of neurology at Massachusetts General Hospital, said. Seven days a week, Gilman could be found in his lab.

Much of Gilman's work outside of teaching and research was prestigious but unpaid. He served on national advisory panels and wrote hundreds of scholarly articles about dementia and diseases affecting the brain and central nervous system. He led research projects funded by $3 million in grants and wrote or edited nine books, all of which made him famous in his field.

He barely knew what a hedge fund was, but when a manager from Gerson Lehrman Group approached Gilman in 2001 about becoming a consultant, he was intrigued. He could make the time, he figured, and the money was good. He soon found himself having hundreds of conversations a year with people he normally wouldn't have had any contact with, cunning traders and analysts interested in different aspects of healthcare, from Parkinson's disease to multiple system atrophy to Alzheimer's. They were polite and well-informed, and the questions they asked were flattering to Gilman's ego, always laced with compliments about the depth of his knowledge. They begged him to elaborate on obscure details of protein reactions or dose modifications that would have made most dinner party guests plead for mercy.

Gerson Lehrman Group called itself a "knowledge broker," a description that carried a certain irony. In reality, it was a vehicle for delivering superior information to sophisticated investors who were willing to pay for it. Gilman didn't find his role as an actor in this small market injustice to be unpleasant, however. Quite the opposite. "It was a chance to talk with people with a totally different perspective than the students I dealt with day to day," Gilman said of the work. "It paid well. It was a diversion. It was enjoyable." He didn't need the money—the university paid him $310,000 a year, a generous living in the frugal Midwest—but it didn't hurt that he was seeing his bank account balance grow every month. For a thirty-minute phone call with a hedge fund trader, GLG paid him $1,000, around twice what top corporate lawyers billed. In-person meetings were charged at $2,000 each.

Gilman was soon earning hundreds of thousands of dollars a year consulting, simply by talking about the work he loved. His lifestyle didn't change dramatically—as one former student put it: "He was not a flashy guy who reveled in expensive toys." But he started to allow himself certain luxuries, such as first-class flights and a car service.

The hedge fund work consumed more and more of his time, and it was all conducted out of view of his colleagues in the scientific community. Increasingly, Gilman was leading a secret life.

He made it a point never to invest in pharmaceutical stocks, as he worried about potential conflicts of interest. But he soon found himself prioritizing his consulting work over other things he used to do, such as serving on advisory panels and authoring articles that paid little or nothing. He wasn't the only one. Many of his friends and colleagues were doing it, too. In fact, the medical profession was being infiltrated by Wall Street, as more and more physicians were drawn into the web of high finance as paid sources for money managers. In 2005, *Journal of the American Medical Association* published a study finding that almost 10 percent of the doctors in the United States had paid ties to Wall Street investors, an increase of 750 percent since 1996. The unofficial number was probably much higher. The rapid coopting of the medical profession, according to the article, was "likely unprecedented in the history of professional-professional relationships."

The process of developing a new drug was long and expensive; pharmaceutical companies increasingly avoided it in favor of marketing or repurposing drugs that were already in circulation. When they did choose to embark on such a costly journey, it culminated with the human testing phase, the final stretch before a new drug could receive FDA approval and be sold to consumers. Testing began with Phase I, which was the first time a drug was tried out on a small sample of humans. If the drug proved safe and effective on that smaller first group of volunteers, it moved on to Phase II, where it was tested on a larger group of two hundred or so patients. If the drug was shown at that point to be safe and effective, it entered Phase III. There, two independent studies would be done to confirm what had been observed before: that it was safe and that it worked. In 2004, Gilman was recruited by Elan to serve as the chair of the bapi safety monitoring committee, a group of independent clinicians responsible for tracking the progress of the study, to ensure that none of the patients suffered any serious adverse effects.

Everyone involved in the bapi trial was asked to sign a confidentiality agreement covering every aspect of the program. "You and your staff should refrain from commenting to third parties on the clinical trial or AAB-001 until the final analysis and trial results have been released to the public," read one directive from the company sent to participants. "Analysts, hedge fund employees, investors, newspaper reporters and even other pharmaceutical representatives may contact you seeking trial-related information or your opinion about the expected results of the clinical trial." Another warned: "Trading in Elan or Wyeth securities while in possession of material non-public information may subject you personally to civil or criminal liability under the state and federal trading laws."

At first, Gilman did his best to follow the rules. He knew that his reputation depended on it.

Almost immediately after the trial began, the bapi safety monitoring committee started receiving reports of a worrisome side effect. It was called vasogenic edema, a type of swelling in the back of the brain that was detected through regular brain scans. Gilman was concerned. He had observed brain swelling in the trial of a previous Alzheimer's drug called AN-1792. In that instance, the drug companies had to halt the trial in 2002 as a result of severe cases of encephalitis among patients, which indicated that the drug was toxic. This time seemed like it might be different. Researchers believed that Alzheimer's was caused by a buildup in the brain of "sticky protein," or plaque, called "beta amyloid," that interfered with communication between nerve cells. Bapi was designed to attack that plaque. Gilman hoped that the swelling in the patients' brains was a sign that bapi was actually working, by burrowing itself into the patient's blood vessels and wiping out the plaque.

Over the following months, Gilman and Martoma spoke about bapi often on the phone, sometimes for hours at a time. They met for coffee at medical conferences, where Martoma usually traveled with Rosemary and the kids. Rosemary continued to be deeply involved in every aspect of his work. "Mathew didn't just do that job by himself," she later said. "It was heads-down, tails-up, twenty-four-seven kind of work." They discussed his research and investment ideas at length and debated how much money he should invest in each one. She took full responsibility for their home and children so that he could do his job without distraction. The subject of bapi became an ongoing joke in the household. She and Martoma peppered their conversations with a new exclamation: "Bapsolutely!"

Although Gilman spoke to dozens of other hedge fund traders, Martoma was his top consulting client. During their conversations, Martoma confided in him, sharing details about his relationship with his wife and the challenges of having children so close together. Although Gilman initially resisted Martoma's push to be friends, because it seemed inappropriate, he felt genuinely, perhaps inexplicably, concerned for Martoma's well-being. Gilman wanted him to succeed and felt invested in that success. The truth was, Martoma reminded him of his first son, Jeff. In turn,

Martoma treated Gilman as something of a father figure. Their relationship became so close that Gilman barely noticed when Martoma started nudging him into areas of discussion that were explicitly forbidden. Gradually, Martoma began asking more direct questions. He seemed especially focused on the side effects Gilman was observing among the patients taking bapi, which could indicate whether there was a problem with the drug. "What side effects might one expect to see?" Martoma kept asking. Through his exhaustive research, he understood that vasogenic edema, or brain swelling, was a possibility, and he pressed Gilman about it. A side effect like that had the potential to derail the drug's approval.

One day, under intense questioning from Martoma, Gilman grew uncomfortable. He tried answering in theoretical terms, keeping his responses vague and far removed from what was actually occurring. "For example," Gilman told him, "in diseases in which there are large doses of antibody, like lupus, rheumatoid arthritis, you get pain, you get headache, you get pain in the back, pain in the joints. . . ."

"Well, that's very interesting," Martoma said. He was silent for a moment, trying to nudge the conversation back toward the bapi trial. "What did you *actually* see?"

Gilman knew that Martoma was asking for details that he was forbidden to share. "I can't tell you that," he said.

Martoma kept pushing, asking to know what had been observed with bapi.

"With multiple antibodies, one might expect to see some nonspecific effects, primarily on joints, so that low back pain or headache or joint pain or other kinds of rheumatological consequences may occur," Gilman said.

"*Did* they occur?" Martoma asked.

"Yes, they did," Dr. Gilman finally said. He felt sick to his stomach. The safety monitoring committee was fielding multiple reports of vasogenic edema in patients. Although it was a secret, Martoma seemed, somehow, to be aware of it and was looking for confirmation, and Gilman had just given it to him. The trial clinicians were still debating whether the side effect was a sign of potential toxicity, of bapi's effectiveness, or both. Gilman knew that he had crossed a line by disclosing it to Martoma. But he felt powerless to say no.

He started sharing secret details of the bapi study with Martoma on a regular basis. He told him about how the brain swelling could be a sign that the drug was working, how different doses appeared to be affecting the patients, how carriers of a specific gene tied to Alzheimer's were responding. Martoma took it all in and pressed for more. He was especially interested in the number of patients showing side effects, the more specific the better. Gilman tried not to think about what Martoma was doing with the information he gave him.

Loud arguments were not uncommon on the trading floor at SAC. Cohen liked to position analysts and portfolio managers with different opinions against one another and watch them try to defend their points of view. Even in such an environment, the Elan and Wyeth trades were controversial. Though Martoma was relatively junior, he had somehow convinced Cohen to build up enormous positions in both securities. Most other traders at the firm were confused about why. People started to ask questions.

Another group of healthcare traders, led by Jason Karp, had been studying the bapi trial, too, and they had come to a different conclusion: They thought the drug was going to fail. Part of Karp's job was teaching the other analysts at the firm how to build models for estimating the value of different stocks. He was popular with his colleagues and, even though he was only in his early thirties, he thought of himself as a mentor. He loved to dispense advice. But he also knew how to navigate office politics.

Karp and his two analysts, David Munno and Benjamin Slate, had just had three hugely profitable years in a row and were regarded as the best healthcare team at the firm. None of them particularly liked Martoma. All three were startled to see the Wyeth shares appear in SAC's account, and they started to ask around.

"Why is the firm making a billion-dollar bet on Wyeth?" Karp asked Cohen.

"It's Wayne's position," Cohen told him. That was supposed to be the end of it.

The name aroused awe on SAC's trading floor. Wayne Holman was a former SAC portfolio manager, a graduate of Yale and the NYU School of Medicine who had worked as a pharmaceutical analyst at Merrill Lynch before coming to work at SAC. Cohen had tried to hire him multiple times before the compensation finally won him over; once at SAC, he quickly started to make more money than almost anyone else. Martoma referred to Holman as a "healthcare god."

When Holman left SAC to start his own hedge fund, called Ridgeback Capital Management, in 2006, Cohen contributed $800 million, on much more flexible terms than he typically gave to the new ventures of former traders. Cohen was so unhappy about the prospect of investing in health-care stocks without Holman's input that he asked Holman to continue giving him advice. Holman signed a consulting agreement codifying his willingness to talk to Cohen about Wyeth even though he no longer worked for SAC. In exchange, SAC agreed to pay Holman an "advisor's fee" of 20 to 30 percent of SAC's returns on the investment. Cohen didn't usually offer deals like that, but Holman was worth it.

Holman believed that the more rational way to make a bet on bapi was by investing in Wyeth, which was bigger and had more products than Elan, meaning that if bapi didn't work out, it was less likely to suffer. Elan, on the other hand, had its future tied up in the Alzheimer's trial. It had only one other viable drug in development, Tysabri, which was designed to treat multiple sclerosis. But Tysabri had proven problematic, causing brain infections in some patients. Holman predicted that if bapi didn't work out, Elan shares would get crushed. It was, given all that, a nakedly risky investment. Even though Holman was his healthcare god, Cohen seemed to ignore him when it came to Elan and told everyone that Martoma was the one he trusted. Martoma was "tagged" for the position in Cohen's account, which meant that he was considered responsible for the Elan investment and would share in the profits it generated. He was tagged for Wyeth, too.

Munno and Slate couldn't understand why Cohen was risking so much on two volatile drug companies. SAC made aggressive investments all the time, but Cohen prided himself on his risk management skills. Carefully assessing whether the money you might make on a trade offset the potential losses was crucial to a hedge fund's survival. Making a bet that was so big that a single drug trial result could wipe out all of the fund's profits for the year was not prudent. Munno and Slate approached Martoma several times, asking if he'd be open to discussing his views on the stocks and the bapi trial.

"Let's share notes," Munno would say.

"It's okay," Martoma would reply, infuriating Munno, who felt that SAC shouldn't be invested in Elan at all.

At first, Munno and Slate tried to figure out where Martoma's confidence might be coming from, by trying to retrace his likely steps in the research process. They were certain, given their expertise in the field— Munno had a PhD in neuroscience—that they could replicate whatever work he'd done that led him to his conclusions. But over time they became convinced he was just wrong. The only other explanation was that there was something shady going on. They took their concerns to Karp.

"Can *you* figure out what this guy is doing?" they asked.

Karp started to get genuinely worried. Munno and Slate were the brightest healthcare analysts at the firm, in his opinion. If they thought that the position was a potentially catastrophic risk, he wanted to protect the company. *His* bonus was at stake, too, after all. When he approached Cohen to talk about Martoma, though, he got nowhere.

"Just let him be," Cohen said. "Don't talk to him—he's not your employee, just stop going down that hole."

"Do you think they *know* something, or do they have a very strong *feeling*?" Munno asked, referring to Martoma and Holman.

"Tough one," Cohen said. "I think Mat is closest to it."

A few days later, Slate asked Cohen the same thing again. "Seems like Mat has a lot of good relationships in this area," Cohen said vaguely, waving him off. He accused Munno and Slate of "pissing on the parade" with their negativity. He was starting to get annoyed.

With all the hyperaggressive hedge fund traders in the market, investing successfully in stocks had become harder than winning at poker. Not only did you have to know what cards the other players had, you had to know what they *thought* of their cards. Sometimes, companies announced positive news but their stocks went down, because traders were already expecting it. Guessing what everyone else was anticipating became as important as understanding a company's products. Knowing this, Munno started trying to map out just how good bapi's results would have to be in order to register as positive for all the investors betting on the drug trial.

Over and over, Munno, Slate, and Karp nagged Cohen: Does Martoma *think* he knows what the results will be, or does he *know*? Cohen refused to answer.

SAC was one of the most powerful hedge funds in the world, and its most talented employees had been reduced to acting like teenagers, bickering and scheming behind one another's backs.

Though Martoma kept up a hard front, he felt increasingly vulnerable. He was starting to feel like Munno was trying to sabotage his career by going behind his back and sowing doubts about him with Cohen. He tried to double-check some of the information he was getting from Gilman with another doctor working on the trial, whom he found through a different expert network firm, Wall Street Access. Then in April, Martoma begged Gilman, his prized contact, to talk with Munno and Slate and encourage them to calm down a little.

The debate continued inside SAC's office, but Cohen didn't change his position. Finally he told Munno and Slate to back off for good. He didn't want to hear any more from them on the subject of Elan.

As part of his role as an advisor to the more junior traders, Jason Karp developed a system for categorizing information that he taught to all of his analysts, a way to understand what was safe and what might be illegal.

There was "white edge," which was obvious, readily available information that anyone could find in a research report or a public document, information that wasn't worth much, frankly, but wasn't going to get anyone in trouble.

Then there was "gray edge," which was trickier. Any analyst doing his job well would come across this sort of information all the time. For example, an investor-relations person at a company might say something like, "Yeah, things are trending a little lower than we thought. . . ." Was that material nonpublic information? The only way to be sure was to talk to SAC's legal counsel, Peter Nussbaum, who'd been with Cohen since 2000. Nussbaum was not an imposing figure, but he had a drawing of a shark lurching out of the water on the wall outside his office, which some employees interpreted as a bit of art direction intended to make himself seem intimidating.

If Nussbaum decided that a particular bit of information could get SAC in trouble, the stock in question was put on the restricted list and they couldn't trade it. Of course, for that very reason, traders only went to him if they absolutely had to. Nussbaum was the firm's equivalent of Internal Affairs.

Karp's third category of information was "black edge," information that was obviously illegal. If traders came into possession of this sort of information, the stock should be restricted immediately—at least in theory. In the course of doing their work, analysts inevitably came across this type of information—a company's specific earnings numbers before they were released, say, or knowledge that the company was about to get a big investment—although the vast majority of what the traders trafficked in was gray. Karp found the color-coded euphemisms to be helpful for the guys working for him; it enabled them to talk more openly about what they were doing. "If you do one thing wrong, you're in jail and your life is ruined," Karp told them. "There is no trade that's ever worth it."

In reality, of course, they were all playing a game, trying to get the most valuable information they could without getting into trouble. Edge was the water, and they were swimming in it. And Cohen prided himself on hiring the most determined swimmers.

In Karp's view, Martoma was disregarding simple rules for assessing the quality and legality of his information. The thought crossed Karp's mind that Martoma might also be bluffing. He'd seen it before, portfolio managers faking conviction to prompt Cohen to build a big position, essentially a gamble that would earn them a huge bonus if it happened to turn out well. Or maybe there was something illegal going on.

Munno suspected something similar when he typed out another aggravated email to his colleagues, complaining about the fact that Cohen was listening to Martoma instead of them. "We're idiots for getting involved in this to begin with," he wrote to Slate. "Stupid on so many levels." There was no way for them to win, Munno said, when Martoma was telling people that he had "black edge."

CHAPTER 7

STUFF THAT LEGENDS
ARE MADE OF

As SAC's traders struggled not to lose money through the spring, as the financial crisis deepened, the government's insider trading investigation was finally beginning to gather momentum. In early 2008, Bear Stearns was sold to JPMorgan Chase in an emergency rescue negotiated by the government. From that point on, investors found themselves in an environment they had never seen before. Nothing they tried seemed to work. Even when traders were able to gather valuable information, it turned out to be useless for trading purposes. Companies would report earnings that were better than expected, and their stocks would plunge anyway. The market was headed in one direction, and that was down.

Just as the market worsened, an application to wiretap Raj Rajaratnam's cellphone was submitted in secret to a federal court, accompanied by an affidavit signed by B. J. Kang. Permission for the government to listen in on private phone conversations is not something courts give lightly. The application is first reviewed by the Justice Department in Washington, D.C., before being submitted to the court with jurisdiction over the area where the crime is alleged to be taking place. For the request to be granted, the FBI must show evidence that a crime is in progress over the specific phone line they are interested in tapping and that other investigative methods—such as reviewing documents and finding cooperators—have been exhausted or are not likely to work. They must show that a wiretap, known as a "Title III," is the only way for the government to put a stop to the criminal activity.

On March 7, 2008, after twelve months of digging by the SEC and the FBI, prosecutors at the Southern District of New York persuaded Judge Gerard Lynch to authorize a thirty-day tap on Rajaratnam. For almost the first time, the FBI was eavesdropping on Wall Street professionals doing their jobs.

Cohen, meanwhile, was growing increasingly pessimistic about the economy, signaling to his employees that he saw a market crash coming. "Unless oil trades down dramatically, I don't see how the market holds these levels," he wrote in one firm-wide email. "I would use rallies to sell."

Strangely, this pessimism did not extend to SAC's huge, unhedged positions in Elan and Wyeth, positions so large that they violated the firm's risk management protocols. Rather, Cohen's confidence in Martoma's views on bapi was buttressed when Martoma arranged a private dinner at Cohen's Greenwich mansion on June 4, 2008, with Elan's CEO, a former Merrill Lynch investment banker named Kelly Martin. Most investors would never have the opportunity to have a private conversation with the chief executive of a multibillion-dollar company, let alone a dinner, but Cohen was different from other investors. He probably could have bought the company if he wanted to, and most chief executives would likely agree to give him some personal time if he asked for it.

Martoma hoped that meeting Martin might give his boss additional confidence about their investment, especially in the face of David Munno and Ben Slate's ongoing campaign to convince Cohen to sell. Elan had a history of worrisome accounting problems, and Cohen agreed that some face-to-face interaction would help him feel more comfortable about owning so much stock. He had always felt good about his intuition about people and wanted to get to know Martin a little, to get a sense of him as a person.

Martoma and Cohen strategized ahead of time about the best way to elicit hints about how the drug trial was going. Martoma drew up a list of carefully crafted questions he planned to ask. The plan was to pay close attention to Martin's body language in addition to what came out of his mouth, looking for nonverbal cues as to what was going on. "More recently, there has been increased emphasis on AAB-001 in your communications," read the first point Martoma planned to raise. "How important is the success of AAB in this phase II trial towards establishing your lead/dominance in this space?"

During the meal, Cohen watched Martin as he spoke. Martin struck him as subdued, almost downcast, not focused and energetic, the way you would expect someone leading a company that was about to solve one of the world's great medical crises to behave. Cohen's gut told him that things weren't going to work out with bapi.

After Martin left, Cohen turned to Martoma. "That doesn't sound like a guy who just solved Alzheimer's," he said.

Two weeks later, there was positive news: On June 17, 2008, Elan and Wyeth announced "encouraging top-line results" from Phase II of the trial. It was only a preliminary indication of how things were going, but it was hopeful. Both companies publicly reaffirmed their decision to launch a Phase III study. Martoma was elated. He sent Cohen an email about it before the market opened.

"Yee-haw," Cohen wrote back. "Well done."

Munno, the most vocal Elan dissenter in the office, was frustrated. He still believed that Elan was a bigger risk than it was worth. When he expressed as much to Cohen, again, Cohen gloated.

"Here we go again, round 2," Cohen said. "And round 1 to Martoma."

When the market opened, both companies' stock prices popped up a few dollars. Cohen and Martoma bought hundreds of thousands more shares of each. By the end of that month, CR Intrinsic owned $233 million worth of Elan and $80 million of Wyeth. Cohen also had a large position in his own portfolio, with another $400 million invested in the two stocks—altogether, more than $700 million.

Jason Karp, Munno and Slate's boss, was still annoyed about how much time Munno and Slate were wasting on their rivalry with Martoma, and he admonished them. "So now he looks smart and you guys look stupid," he said. "And now *I* look stupid because you spent so much time trying to make an example out of him. Just let it go."

Martoma, meanwhile, kept buying more. As the position ballooned, Cohen's personal assistant, who listened to nearly every conversation her boss had all day long via the "Steve-cam," applied to senior management at SAC for permission to open a personal trading account. There were only two stocks she wanted to buy: Elan and Wyeth.

The two drug companies were scheduled to announce the final results of the bapi trial at the annual International Conference on Alzheimer's Disease, on July 28, 2008, in Chicago. It was one of the most hotly anticipated medical research announcements in recent memory. By the standards of the science world, the conference was a glitzy affair, held over five days at the Hyatt McCormick Place Hotel. Hundreds of Wall Street analysts were signed up to attend, along with scientists and researchers from around the world.

Three weeks before the conference, Elan notified Gilman that he had been selected to present the final data from the bapi study. It was a huge honor, the sort of opportunity that Gilman would normally have jumped at, but his health was failing. He had just been diagnosed with lymphoma and was undergoing chemotherapy treatment. "The hair on my head is just about all gone," he wrote despairingly to Elan's medical director. "With my current appearance, I could fill in the role of an evil scientist in an Indiana Jones movie. I am looking for a diamond stud for my shirt so that I can look like Daddy Warbucks."

Executives at the drug companies assured him that he was the person they wanted to do it, bald or not. Was he well enough? Gilman said yes. Though his role was supposed to be secret, he immediately told Martoma. As the keynote presenter at the conference, Gilman would be one of the first people to have access to the full, unblinded bapi test results. Elan and Wyeth worked to ensure that there wouldn't be any leaks.

While Gilman was getting ready to present the drug trial results to the rest of the world, the stock market continued to crash. On July 15, the SEC issued an emergency ban on short selling of financial stocks in an attempt to calm the market, a desperate measure that only served to scare investors even more. Watching SAC's portfolios lose money every day was an unusual experience for Cohen, and one he did not enjoy. He had lost all confidence that the situation could be brought under control through government intervention or anything else. He sent a company-wide email, warning of further financial violence. "I want to be clear that any rally that comes will be a 1–2 month affair followed by additional weakness," he wrote. "Let me reiterate that the indices could see new lows over the next couple of weeks."

On July 15, Gilman flew by chartered plane to Elan's medical facility in San Francisco, where he huddled with the teams who had overseen the Phase II trial. They were joined by a group of statisticians whose job it was to assist the doctors in interpreting the data. It was a defining moment in the quest to find a cure for Alzheimer's disease. This was when the data would be "unblinded"—all of the parts that had been kept secret would be revealed for the first time in their entirety. Before they began, Dr. Allison Hulme, who led the bapi study for Elan, reminded Gilman again that everything he was about to see had to remain secret.

Looking through the data, Gilman felt a sense of excitement. Upon first glance, it seemed that the drug had indeed exerted significant benefits on the group of patients that did not have a gene that made them predisposed to Alzheimer's. Even the group that did have the genetic weakness showed a positive trend. He couldn't help but feel inspired by the potential implications.

But as he scrutinized the data more closely, a problem jumped out at him. There was a lack of dose response, meaning that the symptoms of the disease did not respond to increasing doses of the drug. Gilman liked to explain this phenomenon by using the example of someone with a headache reaching into their medicine cabinet. Usually, he would say, "if you have a headache and you take one aspirin, you get a little bit of relief. If you take two aspirin, you get a little better relief. Take three aspirin, you get even more relief." He saw no evidence of that, however, in the bapi results. There was no way that the treatment was working if its effects didn't get stronger with larger doses.

He tried to focus on the more positive aspects, which suggested that the Phase III trial, which had already started, was worth continuing. Bapi also appeared to be safe for patients to take, which was important. There were a few minor side effects and one major one, vasogenic edema, the brain swelling. It was potentially serious, but the study seemed to show that doctors could manage it by lowering the dose of the medication until the symptoms went away; once they subsided, they could ramp the dose back up again.

Editing the enormous amount of data down to a twelve-minute PowerPoint presentation that would best capture the results was a task that Gilman tackled earnestly, along with the rest of the Elan team. Gilman flew back east the next day. Dr. Hulme, of Elan, emailed him a draft of the presentation the following day so they could work on polishing it. "ICAD presentation confidential. Do not distribute," read the subject line. The presentation was enclosed as a password-protected attachment. "I'll send the password by separate email," Hulme wrote.

Another email arrived an hour later.

"Dear Sid," it read. "The password is 'nuggets.'"

At home that evening, Gilman looked through the presentation again, trying to draw conclusions from the tables and charts. These were the moments of scientific inquiry that he lived for, the excitement of discovery and revelation. He couldn't wait to share the news with someone.

Then his telephone rang. It was Martoma. The first thing he asked about were the trial findings.

"I'm very excited about these results," Gilman told him. "I do have some concerns about the decline in the placebo group, and the lack of a dose effect." He also explained that bapi had shown stronger effects in patients who did not carry the gene that made them predisposed to Alzheimer's than in those who were carriers of the Alzheimer's gene, which wasn't ideal. Still, the results showed that the way the drug functioned, with a protein designed to attack the plaque buildup in the brain, could work.

They spent an hour and a half going over the slides in detail. Martoma displayed little emotion as he asked dozens of questions. Gilman prattled on: "This would certainly warrant a Phase III trial. . . . I am very, very optimistic."

Then Martoma made a noise, signaling a change in subject.

"Sid," Martoma said, "my uncle passed away a couple of months ago and I was too busy to go to the funeral. I feel really bad." He let his voice trail off. His uncle had lived in Ann Arbor, Martoma said, and he was planning a visit to his family. "I'm going to be there on Saturday. Will you be around? I'd like to drop by."

Gilman thought about it for a moment. "Yes, sure, you can drop in," he said. He would be in his office, working, as he had been nearly every Saturday that he could remember.

Two days later, Gilman drove to the campus and parked his car in the lot adjacent to the North Ingalls Building. Just after 10 A.M., he swiped his badge to get into the deserted complex through the garage and made his way to his office, where he quickly became absorbed in his work. Around 2 P.M., his phone rang. Martoma was outside.

"Have you already had some lunch?" Gilman said as he led Martoma down the hall to his office. "We could go out and get something."

"No thanks," Martoma said.

"Shall we just sit and chat, then?" Gilman asked.

Then, Gilman later recounted, Martoma got straight to the point: "I'd like to see the ICAD slides."

Gilman hesitated. Then he went to his computer and pulled up the latest version of the presentation, stepping aside so that Martoma could scroll through it. Gilman narrated while Martoma squinted at the charts and images. Gilman paused over the slide showing the dose response to the medication.

"What is your view of the results?" Martoma asked.

Gilman, who was still feeling hopeful about the data, and perhaps a bit defensive, reiterated his concerns about the lack of dose response and the decline of symptoms in the placebo group. But he didn't think either of these negated the obvious benefits of bapineuzumab. "These are relative concerns, not huge concerns. They're the first results showing a treatment that is effective, that appears to be effective, at least in the Phase II study," he said, becoming lively, as he always did when he was talking about neuroscience. "I think these are certainly results worthy of Phase III, another larger trial. I'm very excited."

In spite of Gilman's enthusiasm, Martoma could see as he flipped through the slides that the results were a huge disappointment from an investor perspective. Bapi had proven to be effective for only a small subgroup of patients; based on the methodology of the trial, even that was uncertain. More testing would be necessary to know for sure.

Expectations for bapi had become massively inflated. The results wouldn't be released to the public for another nine days, but Martoma could see clearly how this would be interpreted by the market: Elan and Wyeth shares would crash once this news got out.

When they finished looking through the slides, Martoma asked to use Gilman's phone. He placed a call to the cabdriver who had collected him at the Detroit airport that morning, who was waiting nearby. He and Gilman walked out together and said goodbye. Martoma climbed into the waiting car and headed back to the airport, where he boarded a 4 P.M. Delta Airlines flight back to JFK.

Gilman returned to his office and continued working for the rest of the afternoon. That night he and his wife went out to dinner with their friends Maxine and Ronnie, and the doctor tried his best to forget about what had just happened.

"Is there a good time to catch up with you this morning?" Martoma typed in the subject line of an email. "It's important."

Weekend mornings were times when most people lounged around

with coffee and the newspaper, but early on Sunday, July 20, 2008, the morning after his return from Michigan, Martoma was as alert as he'd ever been. He needed to talk to Steve Cohen right away.

Cohen replied by emailing his home phone number.

At 9:45 A.M., Martoma called Cohen. They talked for twenty minutes. After they hung up the phone, Martoma emailed Cohen again, listing all of their holdings in Elan and Wyeth stock, which by now totaled more than $1 billion in value. Then Cohen typed out a message to his top trader, Phillipp Villhauer. He wanted to start selling off their Elan shares as soon as possible. And he wanted it done quietly.

Cohen then wrote out an email to Wayne Holman, his healthcare guru. "I am driving back early today," he wrote. He explained that he was returning sooner than expected because bad weather was going to prevent him from taking the helicopter later on, as he normally would. "We need to talk on eln, wye," he wrote, using shorthand for Elan and Wyeth.

The next morning, Villhauer arrived at the office early to prepare to execute Cohen's orders. Cohen had instructed him to find some accounts that weren't visible to the rest of the firm, so that no one could see the Elan and Wyeth sales taking place. It was an unusual way to sell off a position, not something Villhauer had been asked to do before in his twelve years at SAC. But it wasn't easy for Cohen to make a big trade without people noticing and without affecting the stock price.

Like Cohen's other traders, Villhauer had also learned through experience not to stick his nose into things that didn't directly concern him. The stock sales at issue on this day were particularly likely to attract attention. Elan and Wyeth were among the firm's largest holdings, so both SAC portfolio managers and brokers at outside firms would notice. SAC had over four hundred brokerage accounts open, and any one of them was likely to start talking.

He checked with the operations guys, who told him that two accounts were reserved for "low visibility" sales and that he should execute the trades there. Villhauer then told Doug Schiff, the backup execution trader, that he was stepping out of the office and that Schiff should take over. He reminded Schiff to maintain close communication with Cohen.

The Elan shares were in three accounts: Cohen's, Martoma's, and a general CR Intrinsic account. Villhauer stayed in contact with Schiff as he made the trades over the course of the day.

After the market closed, Villhauer sent Martoma an update: They'd sold roughly 1.5 million shares for an average price of $35.

"Obviously no one knows except me you and Steve," Villhauer wrote.

The next morning, Cohen asked him to sell 1.5 million more.

"400k at 34.97 all dark pools," Villhauer wrote to Cohen by instant message at 8:50 A.M., referring to private stock exchanges where trades were executed anonymously. The market hadn't even opened yet.

Then at 9:11 A.M.: "550k at 34.93," indicating that he'd sold 150,000 more.

Then: "660k 34.91."

"Keep selling," Cohen wrote back.

Over the next nine days, Cohen's trader sold 10.5 million shares of Elan. Another trader did the same thing with SAC's Wyeth position. No one in the market could see that SAC was selling.

Even after liquidating his position, Cohen wasn't finished. Once the selling was done, Cohen shorted 4.5 million shares of Elan, worth $960 million. In just over a week, he had turned his bet on the stock completely around.

The same day that Villhauer started selling off the firm's Elan, a man named Harvey Pitt arrived at SAC's offices in Stamford. It was early evening, and the stock market had just closed. After stepping down as chairman of the SEC in 2003, Pitt had founded a consulting firm called Kalorama Partners, selling his services to the private sector as an expert in compliance and regulatory issues. SAC had hired him to give a presentation to its staff on insider trading, a subject Pitt knew well. During his career in private practice as a corporate lawyer at Fried, Frank, Harris, Shriver & Jacobson, he played a central role in the Michael Milken case, when he served as Ivan Boesky's personal defense lawyer and negotiated a plea bargain for the notorious arbitrageur.

Pitt wasn't terribly familiar with Cohen and his company. All he knew was that SAC was a very successful, very large hedge fund, and if history was any guide, insider trading training was likely overdue.

Pitt had noticed in particular that younger traders on Wall Street who hadn't lived through the scandals of the 1980s and 1990s needed constant reminding about what was legal and what wasn't. Otherwise, the past was destined to repeat itself. He planned to deliver a talk he'd given many times before, reviewing the current state of securities law and the definition of material nonpublic information, as well as teaching some commonsense strategies for staying out of trouble. Senior SAC managers made it clear that everyone at the firm was expected to attend, no exceptions. One of SAC's compliance officers personally rousted traders from their desks, practically dragging them to the cafeteria.

Pitt was led into the packed room, where cameras had been set up to broadcast his presentation to SAC's satellite offices. He spoke in a low, rumbling growl that projected authority. As he started, he looked around the room, and noticed instantly that Cohen wasn't there. Pitt began by reminding the traders and portfolio managers in the room that insider trading was illegal in every state in the United States as well as every other country where SAC did business. "Insider trading is a hot topic for regulators," he said, explaining that over one hundred insider trading cases had been brought against hedge funds in the previous year alone.

The press, he pointed out, was also eager to publish stories about traders accused of breaking the law—there was no more perfect villain. "Don't write or send any email or other electronic communication, or leave any voicemail message for anyone, if you wouldn't want to see it in the media or have it read by regulators," he warned. Cohen's absence through all of it struck him as strange. Usually, the head of a company made a point of sitting in the front row at Pitt's talks. "I've done these all over, and everybody usually attends," Pitt later recalled. "*Particularly* the CEOs, because they want to make a statement."

But Pitt didn't let Cohen's absence hold him back. "Stop and think before trading," he told his audience. "If the trade seems too good to be true, it probably is."

As the former SEC chairman launched into a meditation about the dangers of using outside expert network consultants because they might inadvertently disclose confidential information, a small drama was playing out elsewhere in SAC's offices. A corporate announcement appeared on the news wires just before 5 P.M.: Brocade Communications Systems, a data networking company based in Silicon Valley, revealed that it was buying Foundry Networks, which produced switches and routers for Internet service providers. SAC's CR Intrinsic unit owned 120,000 shares of Foundry stock—an investment that had been recommended by the analyst Ron Dennis, who was a member of Jon Horvath and Jesse Tortora's "fight club" of information-sharing. Dennis had learned about the Foundry takeover three days earlier from a friend at a hedge fund in California, who had heard about it from Foundry's chief information officer.

"When is information 'nonpublic'?" read one of the slides that Pitt had just displayed to SAC's staff. "If it is not widely disseminated or if received with the expectation it will remain confidential." A merger that hadn't been announced yet was clearly inside information, based on Pitt's or anyone else's definition. After getting the tip, Dennis had told his portfolio manager at SAC about the impending deal, and he had bought a lot of stock. When Foundry went up 32 percent after the takeover was announced, SAC made $550,000.*

After Pitt's lecture was over, he was told that the greatest trader on Wall Street wanted to meet the former SEC chairman, and he was escorted to Cohen's office. The two shook hands.

"Thanks for coming," Cohen said. Then he turned back to his trading station, and Pitt was shown his way out.

Joel Ross strolled through the lobby of the Hyatt McCormick Place Hotel in downtown Chicago on the afternoon of July 28. A large, bland tower overlooking Lake Michigan that was a popular venue for large industry

---

* Dennis settled civil insider-trading charges with the SEC in 2014 and agreed to be barred from the securities industry and pay a two-hundred-thousand-dollar fine, without admitting or denying the allegations.

gatherings, the hotel was at that moment overflowing with scientists. It was the first day of the International Conference on Alzheimer's Disease, and Gilman's presentation of the bapi results was scheduled for the following afternoon. Ross was a gerontologist with a thriving medical practice in New Jersey, and he had treated twenty-five patients enrolled in the study. He had a flair for the theatrical, with a thick mustache and a taste for eye-catching ties.

All of the physicians who had participated in the bapi study were invited to a private dinner that night in a small conference room in the hotel, where they would be treated to an early presentation of the Phase II results. Ross took his seat and signed a confidentiality reminder that was distributed to everyone in the room. Allison Hulme, from Elan, appeared at the podium and explained how bapi worked and what the study had hoped to achieve. She reiterated the design of the trial and the demographics and characteristics of the patients who participated. Then came one of the slides Ross had been waiting for: "Post Hoc Efficacy Analysis."

He felt depressed as he stared at the numbers on the screen. There was no dose response. Ross leaned over to another doctor, a well-known Alzheimer's researcher from Harvard Medical School. "Pardon me," he said. "I'm not statistically oriented. What's the bottom line here—does this mean the drug is a failure, it doesn't work?"

The other doctor nodded somberly. "The drug did not work," she said. "The drug failed."

Ross rushed out to the hotel lobby. He had arranged ahead of time to meet with Mathew Martoma, who was also attending the conference. Martoma had contacted him during the drug trial, and the two had been holding consultations through an expert network Ross worked with.

Martoma was waiting for him in front of a glass wall that overlooked the hotel's atrium. "How was it?" he asked.

"The results were negative," Ross said. "The drug failed to show efficacy." Ross thought about the billions of dollars that had been funneled into bapi research, the dozens of hopeful patients and their families who participated in the trial—all that effort, for nothing. He also felt personally discouraged. He was sure that some of his patients had benefited from the drug, and he hoped they'd be able to continue taking it. He told Martoma that in spite of the negative results, he was still hopeful that bapi might work, because he had observed some improvements in his own patients who were taking it.

"I don't know how you can say that when the statistical evidence shows otherwise," Martoma said. He cited the exact p-values, a number that indicated whether a result was statistically significant or not, and a handful of other specific figures that had just been included in the presentation to the investigators. The results still hadn't been publicly released.

Ross was flabbergasted. How could Martoma possibly know about those details? It was as if Martoma had seen the presentation he had just seen. But he knew that was impossible.

"And what about the dose effect?" Martoma said. "How can you be so high on it when you look at the dose effect?"

"I don't care about the dose effect," Ross said, sounding irritated. "I just know my patients." He found himself wondering how he could have gotten mixed up with someone who was so indifferent to the human suffering behind Alzheimer's disease. Didn't Martoma care about all those elderly people, relegated to miserable deaths in hospital wards? They needed bapi to work. Ross said goodbye and walked back to his hotel room.

The hotel ballroom was filled the following afternoon for the formal presentation. All 1,700 seats were taken, with additional people standing in the aisles and along the back wall. It either was—or was not—going to be the setting of one of the great breakthroughs in medicine.

Gilman was not feeling well. He'd had a series of chemotherapy treatments that week, and he was depleted. He approached the stage and adjusted his eyeglasses, grasping the podium with both hands. The room grew quiet. Then Gilman started talking about the first of his twenty-two slides. "Encouraging Clinical Data from Passive Immunotherapy in Alzheimer's Disease," read the title of his presentation. He described the objectives and the design of the Phase II study. Then he moved into the safety characteristics of the drug.

As he cycled through six slides containing the efficacy analysis of the drug, showing a series of blue and green bar charts indicating that there wasn't much of a relationship between patients' cognitive improvement and strength of dose, the auditorium began crackling like a switchboard. Wall Street analysts were furiously typing on their BlackBerrys, sending messages back to their funds to sell Elan and Wyeth even though the stock market had already closed.

"I can remember gasping," said one analyst in the audience, who texted out his own Code Red.

As soon as the presentation ended, Katie Lyndon, an SAC analyst who worked for Martoma, got up from her seat and rushed back to her hotel room. She hadn't seen Martoma all day. Typically, when they both attended industry events like this, they kept separate schedules, to maximize the number of presentations they could watch, and then compared notes later. She was anxious to see what was going on with their portfolio and logged into Panorama, SAC's internal system that tracked its positions. She was sure that Elan and Wyeth were going to get killed as soon as the market opened the next day. The only question was how much they would go down.

As she stared at Panorama, she stopped breathing for a moment. Money was moving around the system in and out of the different portfolios faster than she'd ever seen before. She couldn't tell what was going on.

Shortly after midnight, Martoma sent her an email. "What was your impression of data?" he wrote. "Any buzz at dinner?"

"I thought the data was okay, not as great as I was hoping, but probably also not meriting the euphoria with which it was greeted by the shorts," she replied. She was dying to know what was going on with their position. "I saw what u did with WYE yesterday," she continued, "and I'd be interested to hear your thoughts about that going into the data."

That same evening, back at SAC's offices, Tim Jandovitz was sitting at his desk when the press release announcing the bapi results crawled across his Bloomberg monitor.

"That does not look good," he thought as he clicked on the headline.

The market was closed, but the stocks had already dropped significantly in aftermarket trading. Jandovitz looked at Panorama, too, hoping that someone had reduced SAC's position or at least put some hedges in place. But he didn't see any Elan or Wyeth sales recorded. He was certain they'd lost at least $100 million. A disaster.

At the same time, as the news was filtering out of the ICAD meeting, Ben Slate and David Munno started furiously emailing Jason Karp. "The drug failed," they wrote.

Karp felt ill.

Slate and Munno knew better than to gloat. After all, as far as they knew, SAC had just lost a devastating amount of money, possibly enough to throw the future of the firm into doubt. Still, Munno couldn't help but feel vindicated. Martoma had been wrong all along.

Even though he had gotten into the habit of working out of the New York office a couple of days a week, Jandovitz made a point of reporting to SAC's main office in Stamford the next morning. He was fairly certain that Martoma would be fired. There was a decent chance he would be fired, too. He couldn't remember witnessing such a catastrophic loss; it was multiples greater than anything he'd ever been involved in. He briefly wondered what else he could do with his life, whether another firm would ever hire someone associated with a loss of this scale.

When he got to his desk, he checked Panorama again. It reflected no positions in Elan and Wyeth at all, but the market hadn't opened yet. Something wasn't making sense. He finally reached Martoma on his cellphone. "What happened to our Elan?" Jandovitz asked.

"We no longer own the stock," Martoma told him curtly.

Jandovitz felt a sense of relief. Maybe he still had a job after all.

Just before the stocks opened for trading, Jandovitz got an instant message from a friend, a salesman at JPMorgan whom he'd known since they were five years old.

"TELL ME MARTOMA GOT OUT OF ELAN," his friend wrote.

"W/out getting into detail," Jandovitz wrote back, "Wednesday and this week has been GREAT for us."

"I LOVE IT . . . I LOVE IT . . . I LOVE IT . . . GREAT STUFF, MY MAN, GREAT STUFF," his friend replied.

"Stuff that legends are made of," Jandovitz answered. He imagined that the decision to sell all of the firm's Elan—and then short it before the disastrous trial announcement—would someday end up on a list of the most celebrated trades in Wall Street history. "We'll catch up over a beer, and I'll tell you a tad bit more."

Jandovitz was still bewildered as to how they'd avoided the Elan-Wyeth disaster. He recalled all the times Martoma had promoted the stocks, claiming a conviction rating of 9 in the idea. Something had happened to cause Martoma and Cohen to suddenly change their minds, and it had happened in secret.

Elan shares had closed at just under $33 before the ICAD presentation. The scientists who had looked at the bapi results were divided about what they meant. Some felt that the drug still had potential, while others interpreted the data negatively. The results, Alzheimer's researchers agreed, were confusing. Wall Street, however, was clear about how it felt: Elan opened at $21.74 that morning and fell below $10 within two days. Wyeth fared a little better. The massive losses investors suffered in the two stocks became the talk of Wall Street, as traders tried to figure out who might have been put out of business and who made millions taking the other sides of those trades. Anyone who had purchased shares in recent weeks and held on to them without the benefit of knowing the secret trial results lost money.

Martoma arrived for lunch with Gilman at the Peninsula Hotel's Shanghai Terrace in Chicago the day the market was reacting to the news about bapi. It was considered to have the best Peking duck in the city, served by waitresses wearing cheongsams. "Did you hear about what happened to Elan's stock?" Martoma asked Gilman once they'd sat down.

Gilman was annoyed at the question. "No," he said. "That's not what I do."

"Well, it dropped like a rock," Martoma told him. More than 30 percent, in fact.

Gilman was surprised. He thought bapineuzumab still had promise and that it might come out of Phase III testing with some commercial potential. "Did I do something wrong in my presentation?"

"The market doesn't like a drug that only helps half the population," Martoma said.

A few days later, when Martoma was back in Stamford, he called Jandovitz into his office. Jandovitz was still fuming about not being included in the decision about the Elan trade.

Martoma apologized for what had happened. "Steve told me not to tell you about our decision to sell," Martoma said.

"Why?" Jandovitz said. He was offended. He was the healthcare trader, after all, the one who had built the position up over months. Why was he suddenly excluded?

"Steve told me to keep it between me and Villhauer," Martoma said. After feeling confident all those months, Martoma had changed his mind about the drug trial, he added, and thank god for that. "I reviewed my notes over the last couple of weeks and just didn't feel confident anymore."

Gilman slowly recovered from his lymphoma treatment over the course of the summer. He was still weak, but his hair was starting to grow back.

He waited for weeks to hear from Martoma, but there was no word. He was surprised by it. He couldn't believe his friend wouldn't at least check in on him, given his cancer and everything else—in the past, Martoma always showed such concern for Gilman and his health. Finally, in September, Gilman broke down and typed out an email. "Hi Mat, I haven't heard from you in a while and hope that all is well with you," he wrote, trying to sound cheerful. "I hope that you have not been too seriously set back by the great turmoil in the markets, plus the disappointing drop in Elan stock." As he watched the stock market plunging day after day and saw headlines about bank rescues and financial panic, Gilman had been worried about his friend and his young family. "Anyway," he added, "no need to call, I have nothing new. I just wonder how you are faring. Best Regards, Sid."

Martoma scheduled an appointment through GLG to meet with Gilman a few months later at a medical conference in Seattle, but Martoma canceled the meeting. They never saw each other again.

There was more drama to come that summer. While Elan stock was still going down as a result of the drug trial results, the SAC technology analyst Jon Horvath got a piece of information that he was sure would make him and his boss, Mike Steinberg, a lot of money. Jesse Tortora, Horvath's friend and the ringleader of their stock-tip-sharing circle, had learned that Dell's earnings were going to be a disappointment. Tortora had a connection, a former colleague named Sandeep Goyal, who had a friend who worked at Dell. The hedge fund Tortora worked for, Diamondback Capital, was paying Goyal for his Dell tips by wiring $75,000 a year to Goyal's wife because the firm Goyal worked for wouldn't let him do outside consulting. Apparently Dell's gross margins were looking like they would be lower than what people were expecting, in contrast to the relatively strong performance of the stock.[*]

Typically, Tortora sent this kind of information first to Todd Newman, his boss at Diamondback; he was like a cat, whose job it was to bring the dead mouse to the people paying his own bonus first. Then Tortora would forward it to Horvath, Sam Adondakis, their friend at Level Global, and the others in the email group. "Dell checks," Tortora wrote them on August 5, three weeks before earnings were going to be publicly announced. "gm looking 17.5% vs street 18.3%. Doesn't sound good, but still very prelim and could change." This was where figuring out what others in the market were expecting became critical to betting the right way. Horvath figured that the 17.5 percent gross margin number, which gave a sense of the strength of the company's sales numbers compared with its costs, was

---

[*] Goyal's wife was never accused of any wrongdoing.

likely to send the stock down. Steinberg started shorting Dell in anticipation of the company's earnings announcement at the end of the month.

Horvath was desperate to prove his value to Steinberg and Cohen. He was still doing legitimate research into his computer companies, building spreadsheets and cultivating the investor relations staff and pressing them for information. But he was also feeding Steinberg the updates he was getting from Tortora. Typically, in the last month of each quarter, before Dell announced its earnings, Tortora would send Horvath a flurry of details about what was coming. He never specified where he was getting his information from, but it was clear that it was coming from someone fairly senior inside the company.

On August 18, 2008, Horvath left for a long-planned trip to Cabo San Lucas, where he had rented a condo near the beach. While there, he tried his best to stay in touch about the Dell position. Tortora called him with another update that confirmed what he'd been saying for the last couple of months: The earnings were going to be more than disappointing, they were horrendous. "Please be extra sensitive with these numbers," Tortora told him.

Horvath immediately called Steinberg and passed along what Tortora had conveyed to him. After he hung up, he grew worried that he hadn't been clear enough about keeping it quiet, so he followed up with an email. "Pls keep the Dell stuff especially on the down low," he wrote. "Just mentioning because JT asked me specifically to be extra sensitive with the info."

By August 25, three days before the earnings release date, Steinberg had a short position on Dell of over $3 million. That day, Horvath received an email from Cohen's "steveideas" account. "Cohen Sector Position Alert," read the subject line. "Please reply with any comments or updates you have on the Cohen Account positions below." The accompanying chart showed that Cohen's personal SAC trading account was long Dell. Horvath experienced a clenching sensation in his stomach. He and Steinberg were betting Dell would go down, and Cohen was betting it would go up.

"Steve didn't like losing money," Horvath said later—a mild understatement. "You were kind of in the bad books if you lost him money."

Horvath forwarded the email to Steinberg with the note, "steve is long DELL. . . ."

Steinberg, who was at his weekend house in the Hamptons, was feeling uneasy. What if Horvath was wrong? By this point, they were short almost $10 million worth of stock, which was a big position for him. Short positions were especially risky. If things didn't go the way they were expecting, it was going to hurt. "Interesting . . . I have not mentioned anything to him yet," Steinberg replied. "I would like to express our view to him, but we need to properly weigh the r.r. [risk/reward] of doing so. How high is your conviction here, scale of 1–10, 10 being maximal conviction?"

They spent the next twenty-four hours debating how, and what, to tell Cohen. They emailed back and forth with another SAC portfolio manager named Gabe Plotkin, who had a $60 million long investment in Dell, to try to figure out how good his information was.

It was clear that within the star system at SAC, Plotkin was on the rise. He had developed a formula for studying credit card data and shopping mall traffic that he claimed helped him make winning trades in consumer stocks. Whatever he was doing, it seemed to be working. He was making huge profits. Like Cohen, he could have millions at risk in the market and still go home and have the best night's sleep of his life. And Cohen had been listening to him more and more. Plotkin was the one who had convinced him to buy Dell in the first place.

The following day, August 26, Steinberg emailed Plotkin and Horvath, asking them to share their thoughts on Dell, as they appeared to have opposing views. "Gabe," Steinberg wrote at 12:37 P.M., "we think GMs are at risk this qtr." He went on to add, in stock market dialect, that he thought Dell investors were expecting the numbers to be better than they actually were. "Any thoughts on this—or related points?"

"I do think that is the biggest risk," Plotkin replied. He had a more optimistic opinion than Horvath evidently did, however. He listed the factors that he thought would influence the company's gross margin number. "Where are you modeling gm%? What are your insights . . . ?"

Plotkin then called Cohen. They spoke for several minutes.

Horvath had been reluctant to put a conviction number on Dell's earnings. But at 1:09 P.M., he wrote out another email message from Mexico. He needed to indicate just how solid he felt his information was.

"I have a 2nd hand read from someone at the company—this is 3rd quarter I have gotten this read from them and it has been very good in the last two quarters," Horvath wrote. He added that his source was predicting that gross margins and earnings would miss the estimates most Dell analysts were using. Then he pressed the send button.

Plotkin took a few minutes to absorb what Horvath was saying. "Well—if your checks are right, that is certainly a negative," Plotkin replied. "I will say however that it seems like recently (more in consumer) everytime someone hits me with a check, it ends up being off. . . . So we will have to see."

Steinberg asked Plotkin to be careful with the information Horvath had just shared.

"I will," Plotkin answered.

Plotkin viewed Horvath's "check" with some skepticism. Still, he forwarded the "2nd hand read" email to Anthony Vaccarino, an SAC trader who had been instructed to keep Cohen informed about Dell. Plotkin then sold 300,000 shares from his portfolio, leaving him with a 2.1-million-share long position—still a large amount of exposure.

Vaccarino's official job was "research trader." He was responsible for monitoring what all of the portfolio managers who traded retail and consumer stocks were doing and making sure Cohen knew about it. Privately, Cohen called Vaccarino his "conduit." Cohen knew that his portfolio managers sometimes misled him, talking about how much they loved a stock and then selling it in their own portfolios, possibly so that his own, usually larger, volume of trading wouldn't interfere with theirs. He had five research traders, and he instructed them to follow the trading activity inside SAC like hawks. Cohen wanted to know immediately if someone made a trade of even one share against whatever position he was holding. "Watch what they do, not what they say," Cohen told Vaccarino on more than one occasion.

Vaccarino immediately forwarded the "2nd hand read" email to

Cohen, who was working out of his house in East Hampton. Then he placed a call to Cohen's cellphone.

Minutes after that phone call, Cohen started selling Dell. Over the next two hours, he sold his entire long position of 500,000 shares.

Just over forty-eight hours later, the moment that they had all been debating and dancing around for months arrived: Dell reported its earnings at 4 P.M., right after the market closed. The numbers were almost as bad as Tortora had been predicting, down 17 percent. The next day, the stock dropped from $25.21 to $21.73, a fall of 13.8 percent, its largest sell-off in eight years. By selling his shares, Cohen had avoided $1.5 million in losses.

"Great call and good work from top to bottom," Steinberg wrote to Horvath after he'd had a chance to look more closely at the numbers.

Horvath allowed himself to enjoy his success for a few minutes. He had done something right for a change. He wrote a message to Tortora: "Nice man!!! You nailed it!!!"

Horvath didn't know it at the time, but he wasn't the only genius at SAC when it came to Dell's second-quarter earnings announcement. Tortora and Ron Dennis, the other SAC analyst who was part of Tortora's information-sharing group, had also spoken on the afternoon of August 28, and Tortora had shared the same information about Dell's income and gross margins. Within an hour of their conversation, Dennis's portfolio manager at CR Intrinsic started shorting Dell, too. After Dell's earnings came out, Tortora sent Dennis an instant message: "your welcome," it said.

"You da man!!" Dennis answered. "I owe you." His boss covered his short and made $800,000 in profit on the trade.

As was often the case when good information led to a big prize, though, the thrill of success was overshadowed almost immediately by anxiety about how they would do it again. Each time the inside information worked, it raised the expectations for the next quarter, and the next quarter, and the quarter after that. The pressure to find more edge was that much greater. It was like a drug.

Later that evening, Cohen sent Steinberg an email. "Nice job on dell," he wrote.

"Thanks," Steinberg responded. "This ole dog can still hunt."

PART
THREE

CHAPTER 8

THE INFORMANT

On a chilly night in January 2009, a broad-shouldered, unshaven man in his early thirties was walking home from the Equinox gym in Tribeca, his shoulders curled inward against the cold. It was around 8:30 P.M., and Jonathan Hollander had just finished a ninety-minute workout, lifting weights and circuit training. He was damp and hungry, looking forward to getting takeout, going home, and doing a little work. As he hurried down Murray Street, he heard a voice behind him. "Mr. Hollander!"

It wasn't a friendly tone. He turned around and saw a man in a dark overcoat, open enough to show a gun on his belt. There was a slightly larger guy right behind him, dressed the same way.

"Where are you going?" said the second man. "We need to talk to you."

The first man held a badge in front of Hollander's face, too close for him to actually read it. "I'm David Makol, with the FBI," he said. "We want to talk to you about insider trading. Where can we go to talk?"

Hollander was confused. His blood sugar was low, and he was starving. As his heart rate accelerated, the scene started to take on a surreal, almost dreamlike effect. He told the FBI agents that he needed to eat, so they walked in awkward silence for two blocks and entered the brightly lit Whole Foods on the corner. Makol and his partner stood to the side, watching Hollander as he filled a carton at the salad bar. "Can I get you anything?" asked Hollander, heading to the register, where he got in line behind a woman in designer yoga wear. The agents declined.

They walked up the stairs to the seating area and sat down at a table in the corner. Makol talked while Hollander ate, his mind spinning.

"We know you committed insider trading while you were employed at SAC Capital," Makol began. "We know you're guilty. But you can help yourself."

Hollander tried to stay calm. He knew what to do in situations like this. At SAC he'd participated in something called Tactical Behavior Assessment training, a strategy for learning how to read people's body language for signs of deception. Cohen had brought in a group of former CIA operatives to train his staff in the technique, thinking that it might help the firm's traders and analysts tell when company executives weren't being forthcoming about things like their earnings or accounting methods. The most critical thing was to appear relaxed. Squirming, Hollander recalled, picking lint off your clothes, or fiddling with your eyeglasses all could signal that you were lying. He tried to avoid saying words like *honestly* or *frankly*, which were common signifiers of dishonesty.

At SAC, Hollander had been a junior-level analyst with CR Intrinsic, the firm's elite research unit. He was someone who had very little contact with the top-level people. To make a trade, Hollander had to go through his boss, Jason Karp. Though seen as having less-than-infallible judgment, Hollander was widely liked around the office. He was a quirky guy. Outside of work, he volunteered as a baseball coach to underprivileged kids in Harlem, and he had an ownership stake in a trendy Mexican restaurant in downtown Manhattan. He was constantly injuring himself playing sports, tearing tendons and dislocating shoulders. One time, Hollander had gotten into a bar fight after someone allegedly insulted his girlfriend; he punched the guy in the face and broke his own hand in the process. That kind of thing didn't go over well with senior management at SAC, so Karp and his other colleagues told everyone he had been hurt in a softball accident.

Makol seemed to be well aware that Hollander had left CR Intrinsic a few weeks earlier. Dozens of people had been let go after SAC dropped 28 percent in 2008, the fund's only negative year in the sixteen years it had been in business. After canceling the expensive flower deliveries, the full-time massage therapists and the free Snapple, Cohen embarked on the most drastic layoffs the firm had ever seen. CR Intrinsic was shut down. Hollander was fired—which made him, potentially, an ideal cooperator.

In fact, Makol seemed to know a lot about what Hollander had worked on while he was at SAC. The FBI knew that Hollander had traded stock in Albertsons, a supermarket chain—a friend of Hollander's who was involved in a takeover of the company had leaked it to him ahead of time, Makol said. "We arrested Ramesh," Makol went on, referring to the friend, who worked at the Blackstone Group in London and who was at that moment being confronted by FBI agents at JFK airport. "Your two other friends are going to jail. You're going to jail, too, if you don't help yourself."*

There was no use fighting, Makol said. Rich Wall Street guys didn't stand a chance in front of a New York jury.

Hollander was indignant. The agents seemed to him to have no idea what they were talking about. Yes, he acknowledged, he had traded Albertsons shares, but the company had been a rumored takeover target forever, and he traded in and out of it for six months. He had a whole binder of financial analysis he'd done before SAC made the investment, concluding that the company's real estate holdings were worth more than the price where the stock was trading. This was an area he knew intimately. After earning his MBA from Stanford in 2003, he had worked with his dad finding "triple net lease" opportunities in Maryland. They would buy the real estate under a chain restaurant or store, like an Outback Steakhouse or a Walgreens, and then lease the property back to the chain. In exchange for taking on the burden of taxes and property costs, the tenant paid rents that were generally lower than the norm but still left a nice margin for a landlord with access to cheap financing. The strategy

---

* At SEC's request the charges against Ramesh were dismissed with leave to refile. They appear not to have been refiled.

worked best when the investor understood the neighborhood and the market extremely well.

This experience was why SAC hired him, Hollander tried to explain. They wanted his expertise in real estate financing. The Albertsons trades were a textbook case of him applying it. There was nothing illegal about it.

The agents appeared unconvinced. Makol mentioned more names of Hollander's friends at different firms who were supposedly going to end up in jail. Then he pulled a piece of paper out of his pocket and unfolded it dramatically. It was a face chart, the sort of thing Hollander had seen in cop movies, usually tacked on walls with yarns of various colors pinned all over it: the map of a criminal conspiracy. Raj Rajaratnam, the Galleon co-founder, was on it, along with at least twenty other portfolio managers and traders, some of whom Hollander had worked with, some not.

At the center was a face he recognized. It was Steve Cohen.

"There's a lot you don't know about Steve," Makol said, pointing at Cohen's face. He was involved in all sorts of shadowy things Hollander might not be aware of, boiler room sort of stuff. Makol talked about him as if he were a gangster. "You'll need protection from him, but don't worry, we're here to take care of you."

Hollander had no idea if any of it was true, or how much they were exaggerating, but he felt anxious.

"We already have three people inside SAC who are wired up, working for us," Makol said. "You're over here," he went on, pointing to a far corner of the page, the face chart equivalent of Siberia. "You're not even on here yet. We don't want you to end up on here. But you've got to help us help you." They wanted him to become an informant.

Hollander said that he needed to think about it.

The agents let him leave, and Hollander trudged home to his apartment, still in his ratty gym shorts and T-shirt. His roommate had just moved out, so he was alone. He pulled out all his Albertsons files and started leafing through them. There was a twenty-five-slide PowerPoint presentation he'd given to his colleagues at CR Intrinsic in 2005, a year before any of the stuff the FBI was talking about. The presentation included detailed financial analyses and a model showing how much the company could make selling off various assets. He had done a tremendous amount of work developing his Albertsons idea.

He called a woman he'd gone out with a couple of times, who was an attorney at the law firm Schulte Roth & Zabel. Hollander asked her about finding a lawyer to help him.

Within half an hour, around 10:30 P.M., his home phone rang. It was Peter Nussbaum, SAC's legal counsel, on the line.

"We hear you got picked up by the FBI," Nussbaum said.

Hollander was stunned. How did Nussbaum find out?

"This happens all the time," Nussbaum said. "We doubt you did anything wrong. Don't worry. We'll defend you, cover your attorney's fees, anything you need. Everything's going to be okay."

Special Agent B. J. Kang strode across the concourse of a federal building on lower Broadway and turned left onto Duane Street, fighting his way through a wind tunnel as he headed toward Foley Square. It was a chilly March morning, and his suit jacket flapped open in the gusts—he liked his blazers on the boxy side, to conceal the pistol he always carried on his hip. Kang held a packet of compact discs in his hand as he hurried to meet with his colleagues at the U.S. Attorney's Office.

Kang had been consumed by the Raj Rajaratnam investigation for more than a year. It had expanded far beyond Raj to include dozens of other traders and hedge fund managers all over Wall Street. Over the preceding months, the investigation had fallen into a satisfying rhythm. The FBI would flip a cooperator, use him to gather new evidence against another trader, and then apply for a wiretap on the new trader. With each new wiretap, the FBI amassed more recordings that Kang and other agents could then use to flip more witnesses. The list of names kept getting longer, and Kang had thought of little else for as long as he could remember, moving the puzzle pieces around in his mind, trying to plan out his next move.

It was clear to the FBI investigators and the prosecutors working on the case by this time that Rajaratnam was going to be convicted. The question was, how many others could they take down with him? The wiretaps had been up for over a year, and they were going to have to make some decisions about how to move forward. They had a tremendous amount of evidence implicating Rajaratnam and his friends, perhaps more than they needed. But every day, new recordings filled with new names were piling up, other traders at other funds who were engaged in insider trading, spawning new investigations of their own. Each one took up precious resources and time. How long should they let it go on before deciding that they had enough fish and should pull the net up into the boat? By waiting to arrest people, they ran the risk that Raj or others would find out that they were about to be caught and destroy evidence or even leave the country. The FBI, the prosecutors at the Manhattan U.S. Attorney's Office, and their counterparts at the SEC debated the arguments for letting the investigation continue without making any arrests, to see how many more traders could be drawn in. They understood that as soon as Raj was arrested, all of Wall Street would be alerted to the fact that the FBI was listening to their phone calls.

More important, the government knew that arresting Raj would give its ultimate target, Steven Cohen, and his hundreds of traders and portfolio managers a warning that they might be next.

Their biggest challenge was that, at that moment, the two lead FBI agents on the case, Kang and Dave Makol, were locked in a bitter turf war. Like Kang, Makol was an excellent, motivated agent. Each time a promising new lead surfaced on the wire or through a cooperator, they both raced to see who could investigate it first. Because the insider trading rings they were pursuing were so complex, affecting dozens of interconnected hedge funds, law firms, and corporate executives, they often intersected with one another, with a witness that one agent was pursuing suddenly turning up in the middle of another agent's case. Makol would spend weeks working sixteen-hour days gathering evidence—only to find that Kang was already working on it.

Though they were competitive with one another, both agents were very good at what they did. Prosecutors who worked with them in the U.S. Attorney's Office in Manhattan joked that if they could only fuse them together, they'd have an unstoppable superagent and securities crime would be eradicated from the earth.

Kang tried to put the rivalry out of his mind as he arrived at 1 St. Andrew's Plaza and rode the elevator up to meet the head of the securities unit. Kang was there to brainstorm and talk about how they should move forward with the investigation, with Makol and two of the prosecutors working on the case, Andrew Michaelson and Reed Brodsky. In spite of their differences, the two FBI agents were in agreement on one thing: that there was enough evidence developing to go beyond Rajaratnam and his immediate circle and mount a much broader attack on the hedge fund industry. They were eager to go forward. Michaelson and Brodsky looked at each other. It was an intriguing idea. The arguments in favor were obvious: an end to corruption across a powerful industry that had been operating largely in the dark; a thrilling series of prosecutions that would generate headlines; a rebuke to the critics who insisted that law enforcement shied away from Wall Street cases. Ray Lohier, their boss, asked what the risks were to moving ahead aggressively.

Well, the FBI agents said, the more people they pursued and the more witnesses they flipped, the greater the possibility that someone would start to talk. The whole investigation was secret right now; only a handful of people, mainly the agents and prosecutors in the room, knew about it. They needed more cooperators if they wanted to go after the biggest targets, which would naturally increase the risk of a leak. Lohier and the prosecutors agreed that, as a first step, the FBI should take some of the new wiretap evidence they'd gathered and use it to approach a few new traders—Ali Far, a hedge fund manager in California who once worked for Rajaratnam, and his partner, C. B. Lee, who had previously worked at SAC; Karl Motey, who ran his own investment research firm and was also in California; and a fund manager in Boston named Steve Fortuna—and try to flip them and see where it led. All were in agreement that it was a risky step. The whole investigation could come apart if a potential witness told them to go to hell and then warned his friends that the FBI was tapping their phones.

The two FBI squads chose April 1 as the day. Kang would approach Far first, and Makol would talk to Motey. Another agent would try to flip Fortuna. There were contingency plans in place in case things didn't go as they hoped. They hoped to have their new cooperators ready and new wires running in time for the second-quarter earnings season, when insider trading was sure to spike. Kang immediately started planning out his trip, booking airline flights and a hotel room.

There had been moments like this in the investigation before, when it seemed as if some new event might alter the course of what followed, but this one seemed more significant somehow. As April 1 arrived, Brodsky, Michaelson, and others at the U.S. Attorney's Office waited anxiously to hear how the approaches had gone. Would a year of intense, backbreaking work blow up in a single day? They were about to find out how strong their case really was.

Two weeks later, on April 16, 2009, B. J. Kang's new cooperating witnesses arrived at the U.S. Attorney's Office in downtown Manhattan. Although Ali Far and C. B. Lee were best friends and had been running a hedge fund together, neither knew that the other was in the building. Kang had approached them both separately in California, and they had independently agreed, at least in theory, to flip. As far as the FBI knew, they hadn't talked to each other since Kang had first spoken to them at their front doors.

An agent met Ali Far in the lobby and escorted him to a conference room on the sixth floor; after making sure the elevator was clear, Andrew Michaelson met Far's partner, C. B. Lee, and brought him to the fifth floor. Michaelson and another prosecutor, Josh Klein, raced back and forth between the two rooms, trying to act as if nothing unusual was going on. The goal was to play them off against one another and try to pressure them to cooperate fully, all without alienating them. It was a delicate situation.

"Lying to a federal agent is a separate crime," Klein reminded Lee. If he said something that wasn't true during the interview, they could charge him with perjury.

Initially, Lee and Far were reluctant to admit they had done anything illegal, which was the first step of cooperating. The prosecutors made an argument that both men had heard before, from Kang: that cooperating was the only way to avoid being prosecuted. The strategy was to play a bit of a tape-recorded conversation that contained just enough evidence to show them that the government had the proof—without revealing too much about how they had gotten it. Lee and Far, meanwhile, were being instructed by their lawyers not to say much or admit to anything until they knew whether or not the government was bluffing.

"I didn't do anything," Lee said. "I went to Taiwan to meet with companies, but I didn't get revenue numbers."

"Really?" Kang said. "No revenue numbers?"

Kang opened his laptop and pressed play on a digital sound file in which Lee was heard getting earnings numbers for Nvidia, a semiconductor manufacturer. The government had evidence that Lee had been wiring $2,000 payments every quarter to a small army of consultants in Asia, who were gathering inside information about semiconductor companies and giving it to Lee.

"Okay," Kang said. "Let's cut the shit."

Lee and Far were agonizing over what to do. People accused of serious crimes are often in personal turmoil. They have trouble sleeping, sometimes resort to drugs, and have to juggle all sorts of related crises, money problems, angry significant others, anxiety disorders. Lee had a remoteness about him. He seemed more analytical and less emotional than his partner. Far, on the other hand, seemed like he might have a mental breakdown at any moment. Both of them were worried about saving not only themselves but also what was left of their business.

At one point, Lee's lawyer pulled Michaelson aside. "I want to help my guy, I want to help you, but help me figure this out," he said. "What do you have on my client? Share a little something with me so that I know that cooperation makes sense." Then Kang played more recordings.

"This is your one chance," Klein said to Lee. "If you don't cooperate, we will prosecute you, we will convict you, and you will go to jail."

Ever so slowly, Lee and Far began to give in.

One of the first things Lee and Far had to do was close their fund down without drawing undue suspicion from their friends on Wall Street. Once they were working as FBI informants, they couldn't continue trading for their investors. The fund had been doing relatively well, up 10 percent the previous year, so suddenly shutting down without an explanation was bound to raise questions. They needed a cover story. With help from their FBI handlers, they agreed to publicly offer the fact that they had been fighting about how to divide the fund's profits as the reason for going out of business. As soon as word reached New York that Lee was unemployed, he was inundated with job offers from other hedge funds.

Lee and Far were now, officially, B. J. Kang's personal helpers, effectively required to be available at any hour for any task, from answering questions to calling former colleagues and recording them to showing up to a meeting wearing a wire. They would even have to betray their best friends if they were asked to.

While Rajaratnam ran a major hedge fund, it increasingly looked to the government like SAC Capital was the sun that everyone else was orbiting. FBI agents had heard from numerous sources that Cohen was the one fund manager Rajaratnam felt most competitive with. Raj took pride in hiring traders who had worked at SAC—even ones whom Cohen had fired. Stevie Cohen was a legend, people on Wall Street said over and over, the best in the business. Still, Cohen's company had remained obscure to the FBI. They were determined to find out more. C. B. Lee had been a semiconductor analyst at SAC from 1999 until 2004. The possibility that he could tell them about how Cohen's fund worked was intriguing.

Lee told Kang how things operated at SAC. He had worked at other investment firms before, but once he got to Cohen's fund, he explained, his employers pushed him to be much more aggressive. The only way to satisfy them, Lee felt, was to get inside information. Lee had been at SAC when technology companies were moving most of their manufacturing business out of the United States to Asia. He was fluent in Chinese and knew people in Taiwan and mainland China. Most of the Taiwanese firms didn't care about America's regulatory rules or whether they might be violating them by sharing confidential information with Lee. He was smart and knew what to do with this information once he got it. Over time he developed an intuitive feel for the semiconductor manufacturing cycle, which he was able to exploit to come up with profitable trading ideas.

Lee also described the internal landscape of SAC and its unusual structure. It was organized like a bicycle wheel, with the spokes consisting of about a hundred portfolio managers with their own teams of analysts and traders. Cohen was the hub, sitting at the center of everything. Information made it all move. Each team had an industry it specialized in, comprising thirty or more stocks—technology, healthcare, consumer companies like Target and GE—and they were pitted against the other teams to come up with the trading ideas that would make the most money.

The teams rarely shared ideas with one another, just with Cohen, who took their best ideas and traded on them himself. The arrangement was different from the way most other hedge funds operated, where people tended to work on the same portfolio rather than against one another. Cohen could see what everyone around him was doing, while all the others stayed isolated from one another.

If Cohen caught someone making a trade before giving the idea to him, he became infuriated. And if someone working for him lost money for a stupid reason, sometimes even once, his anger was hard to describe in human terms. If a trader did well there, he was paid like a professional athlete, Lee said. But if he didn't, he was dumped as quickly as a bad investment. It was not a happy place to work.

Part of his job, as Lee understood it, was to get inside information for Cohen to trade on. "I was expected to call companies and get the numbers," he told Kang. Lee also said he thought SAC was "dirty."

That was just what Kang wanted to hear.

Lee also explained how SAC was organized to insulate Cohen from the behavior of the lower-level traders and analysts. All of the ideas for trades were filtered through layers of portfolio managers and assigned codes for how strong they were before they reached him—a "high conviction" idea might be given to the boss without explaining why the analyst was so sure about it. Cohen wanted guaranteed moneymaking ideas; the system was designed so that Cohen did not need to know what his traders had to do to get them.

Because he had left SAC more than five years earlier, the information Lee provided on specific trades was too old to prosecute. But the insight he offered into Cohen's world was revelatory.

At first, Kang wasn't sure what to make of what Lee was telling him. Here was an enormously profitable hedge fund that seemed to be on the right side of every investment it made, almost as if it could predict the future. The fund made huge profits, year after year, evidently without the ups and downs that other funds went through. The analysts and traders working there were under intense pressure to deliver and were paid huge bonuses when they did.

"Okay, so what?" Kang thought. Squeezing your employees wasn't illegal. If it was, half of Wall Street would have to shut down.

But then Kang started to compare what Lee was telling him with what he was hearing from his other sources on Wall Street. Traders he talked to at other funds kept saying things like, "You think *my* fund is dirty? You should check out what SAC is doing." There was an expectation at SAC that traders would try to get inside information, Kang was told, or even try to manipulate stock prices by spreading false information.

"This has got to be more than just smoke," Kang thought.

For the people in the middle of it, the insider trading investigation had taken on huge implications. Making decisions about what next steps to take meant confronting difficult questions and possible trade-offs. Was all of this effort, the months of wiretaps and flips and working late, and all the evidence, in the end just about charging Raj Rajaratnam and a couple of his friends? Or was this case going to be something bigger, an indictment of the greed and corruption and win-at-any-cost culture that permeated Wall Street?

There were two obvious new avenues they could pursue to expand the investigation even further, and both involved becoming much more ambitious.

One was the opportunity to break into the labyrinthine world of the expert network firms, which investors paid to connect them with employees at public companies for consultations. The use of these expert networks was widespread in the hedge fund industry—once a few funds started using them, everyone else had to do so as well to try to keep up with their competitors. It had become obvious to investigators that many of the expert networks provided a cover for the exchange of inside information, and that traders were making money using this information at the expense of other investors.

The second avenue was attempting to gather enough evidence to go after Cohen. Shutting SAC down would set a powerful example for the rest of the industry.

The next steps in building the expert network case were straightforward enough: They needed more wiretaps. The FBI believed that Primary Global Research, or PGR, was one of the worst offenders, based on a handful of phone calls that Kang and other agents had heard on the tapes. C. B. Lee had been able to demonstrate what expert network calls were like by posing as a hedge fund investor and contacting PGR consultants.

To Kang, the whole concept of the expert network business model sounded corrupt. He could see that certain expert consultants got hired again and again because word had spread through the hedge fund industry about how "good" they were—meaning that the information they provided was, in Kang's view, probably illegal. Why would savvy hedge fund guys pay thousands of dollars to get information from these consultants that was publicly available elsewhere? Some funds that used them suspected that PGR saved its "best" consultants for its highest-paying clients. And who would those be? One of PGR's biggest customers, running up a tab of $520,000 in 2009, was SAC.

Two FBI agents, Dave Makol and James Hinkle, started gathering evidence for an application to wiretap PGR's phone line. They were sure there was much more going on.

At that point, the tension that had been building between Kang and

Makol exploded into the open. The two agents were leading separate FBI squads—C-1 for Kang, C-35 for Makol—investigating insider trading, and they had been circling each other's territory for the previous year like wolves. Every time one of them thought about approaching a new cooperator, Kang or Makol had to check with the other squad to make sure that it wouldn't disrupt whatever they were doing. Each agent was reluctant to divulge his activities, which meant that progress on the investigation was slowing down. And each side was constantly trying to get credit for the progress that was happening.

Kang got upset when Makol took the lead in the expert network case, arguing that he had been tipped off to PGR first, when it had surfaced on the C. B. Lee and Ali Far wiretaps. The chief of the securities unit, Lohier, had a special gift for diplomacy, and spent much of his time trying to make peace between the two sides. But eventually, even his boundless patience was tested. The Kang-Makol war became a joke in the office. After the fight over PGR, Lohier got so exasperated that he ordered the two of them to report to his office.

"You two need to talk," he said. He told Kang and Makol in no uncertain terms that they were not to come out until they had made up, and then left them alone. The two agents made a grudging commitment to try to get along.

In the spirit of cooperation, the prosecutors and FBI agents working on the insider trading investigation gathered again to brainstorm their options for pursuing their other target, Steve Cohen. To build a case against him, they basically had two choices: find a cooperator who was close to him who could wear a wire and collect evidence that he was trading on illegal information, or try to get permission to wiretap Cohen's phone.

If they wanted to wiretap, they would need one of their existing cooperators to elicit a dirty call with Cohen for the application. If they wanted to flip someone new who was close to Cohen, they needed evidence they could use to try to compel that person to cooperate. The choice of which confidant to approach for a flip wasn't easy. It needed to be a person who was intimate enough with Cohen that he was likely to have access to incriminating information about his trading, but not so close that he would tell Cohen what the FBI was up to.

On the question of whether to wiretap or try to flip someone, Makol and Kang were, not surprisingly, on opposite sides. Kang argued that they had a well-positioned cooperator in C. B. Lee, someone who used to work for Cohen and who could easily get him on the phone and collect evidence for a wiretap application.

Makol, meanwhile, had identified a potential cooperator, an SAC portfolio manager who was managing a $500 million portfolio for SAC, who seemed to be someone Cohen trusted. Makol was confident the portfolio manager would flip. He just needed more time to prepare.

The prosecutors weren't sure they could wait that much longer. To Makol's consternation, Lohier and the rest of the group decided to pursue a wiretap on Cohen's phone instead of going after the portfolio manager. Kang started coaching C. B. Lee to prepare to make a call to Cohen and try to get the evidence they needed. Kang came up with a plan whereby C.B. would phone Cohen and ask if he could have his old job back. He could talk about what "edge" he had and try to entice his old boss by listing all his valuable connections. If the plan worked, they'd have their wiretap *and* a mole inside SAC Capital.

The FBI had learned about Cohen's Sunday Ideas Meetings, during which his portfolio managers called him to talk about their trading ideas for the week, and the agents decided to target those calls first. They weren't sure where Cohen usually was when those calls took place, however. They had to choose one phone line for the wiretap application, and there were four choices: his Stamford office line, his home phone in Greenwich, his house in East Hampton, or his cellphone. They decided to pursue the line in Greenwich. Kang and Michaelson prepared a Title III application, requesting permission to wiretap Cohen's home phone for thirty days beginning in July. This would coincide with the third-quarter earnings season.

There was one important and rather obvious factor that the FBI and the U.S. Attorney's Office failed to consider, however: During the summer months, when the humidity in New York City often reached rainforest levels, everyone of any significance in the financial industry fled to the Hamptons. Traditionally, Wall Street executives' wives moved out there with their children and domestic staff, while the men commuted back and forth to the city. In July and August, seaplanes and helicopters ferrying billionaires buzzed around the skies of Long Island like drones, and Cohen was often in one of them. He was barely in Greenwich at all during the first month of the government's wire. Still, there were a few conversations that took place over the phone line that prosecutors used to get permission to extend the wiretap for an additional thirty days.

Kang called Michaelson every day with updates on what the wiretaps were yielding, but Cohen was proving to be a far more discreet information broker than Raj Rajaratnam. Typically, Cohen's portfolio managers would call and say vague things like "I talked to my guy" before sharing earnings numbers and other data. Crucial pieces that would be needed to prove a case against him in court were simply not present. The "guy" under discussion could be just about anybody: a company insider or an outside consultant or even another fund manager. SAC's portfolio managers sometimes relayed information in code.

One call in particular got the investigators excited: Cohen was heard receiving what sounded like suspicious numbers from an analyst who made references to "channel checks," which are looks at different points along a company's supply chain that indicate how much business it's doing. Still, it wasn't specific enough.

After listening to Cohen's calls, the prosecutors had the impression that he was someone who could have many conversations with people in which inside information was being communicated in a way that would make it exceedingly hard to prove that anything inappropriate was happening. They hypothesized that his exchanges often seemed to be based on a prior understanding about what was being discussed and where the information was coming from. Where Raj was arrogant and loose, rarely passing up a chance to tell everyone how connected he was, Cohen was careful and calculating. They would need something more than what was in these calls to charge Cohen.

The second wiretap on Cohen's phone ran out, and this time the judge was not willing to extend it.

Late in the afternoon on August 16, 2009, a phone rang inside the New York offices of the Securities and Exchange Commission. An enforcement attorney named Sanjay Wadhwa turned away from the mountains of paper on his desk and looked out the window, which faced directly into the corporate gym of Goldman Sachs, where investment bankers in compression shorts lifted weights and ran on treadmills. Wall Street's most profitable investment bank had just built its world headquarters next door, a couple of blocks north of the World Trade Center site. Wadhwa had an unobstructed view of the bank's roof garden, a series of grassy plots on the tenth floor that had probably cost five times more to landscape than most government attorneys made in a year.

Wadhwa tried not to dwell on it.

There are two things that dominate the thoughts of a typical SEC employee: how much more money he or she could be making at a big law firm, and how little credit he or she received for forgoing that opportunity to fight the excesses of Wall Street. It was less than a year into the worst financial crisis in eighty years. The previous fall, Lehman Brothers had gone bankrupt, banks were collapsing, and millions of people were watching the value of their retirement savings go down with the plunging stock market. House prices had plummeted, revealing the corrupt machinery inside investment banks that had packaged low-quality subprime mortgages and sold them to investors all over the world. Bernie Madoff's $20 billion Ponzi scheme had been discovered, along with the fact that the SEC missed obvious warning signs for many years. Morale had never been lower.

For decades after its founding in 1934, the SEC was a feared and respected force on Wall Street, its lawyers priding themselves on their discretion and political independence. Over the previous few years, however, the culture at the SEC had changed; incompetence had become ingrained. The SEC enforcement staff was openly discouraged from pursuing ambitious cases, and getting permission to send out subpoenas required four levels of managerial approval, often taking weeks. This was partly a reflection of the SEC's chairman, Christopher Cox, a Republican congressman from California who had been appointed by George W. Bush in 2005. Cox was a reluctant regulator who made no secret of his staunchly free market, pro-business views. He felt that regulatory agencies had no business trying to tell big banks and major investors on Wall Street what to do and that the financial industry could monitor itself for bad behavior.

Wadhwa was frustrated by the atmosphere at the SEC but was in no way defeated. Despite everything, he loved his job. He had spent the previous two years quietly helping to build the Rajaratnam case, by far the biggest breakthrough of his career. The case had started as a routine regulatory complaint at the SEC in 2006 and had grown into one of the most significant projects the agency had ever taken on. Investigating it had been one of the most exhilarating experiences of his life.

Born in India, Wadhwa had moved to the United States at age nineteen, but he was still deeply influenced by his native country's left-leaning politics. His father had been a high-level executive at a company in Calcutta that produced paper packaging for British consumer products conglomerates, and his mother a schoolteacher, and they were relatively well-off in a country besieged by wrenching poverty. Wadhwa's parents decided to move with their three children to Florida in the 1980s to escape the atmosphere of declining political and economic opportunity in India. Because of the country's restrictions on expatriation of personal assets, the family lost everything when they moved. Wadhwa's father had to take a job at a Rite Aid, and Wadhwa joined him there to help sustain the family. After graduating from a Texas law school that most people had never heard of and getting a master's degree from NYU, he passed a few unhappy years as an associate at Skadden, Arps, Slate, Meagher & Flom, a powerhouse law firm closely allied with Wall Street. In 2003

Wadhwa applied for a job at the SEC. As soon as he joined, he started focusing on insider trading cases.

He had spent the summer of 2009 working closely with the FBI on the Rajaratnam investigation and the other hedge fund cases that grew out of it; he and the FBI agents involved in the insider trading cases sometimes spoke multiple times a day.

The number on Wadhwa's caller ID screen was blocked, which meant one thing. Wadhwa grabbed for the phone.

It was Kang on the line. "Look, I can't get into details right now," he said, "but I have reason to believe something big happened at SAC last summer. A huge trade, huge profits. It generated a lot of talk at the firm."

Wadhwa had heard of SAC, of course, as well as its secretive founder. Cohen's name had come up multiple times in the Raj case. He knew that SAC held a powerful allure on Wall Street. Cohen had built a massive personal fortune in a way that was not supposed to be sustainable, by placing high-volume bets on upticks and downticks in the market. He was not the sort of investor who took large stakes in companies and held them for years, who immersed himself in how businesses worked and understood the levers of the economy. Cohen was the anti–Warren Buffett.

On the phone with Wadhwa, Kang didn't elaborate on what the "something big" was. Even though they had been working together for months, Kang had access to information that could not be shared, by law, with those involved in civil enforcement, including anyone at the SEC. Specifically, anything to do with wiretaps.

"Do you know what sector?" Wadhwa asked.

"Pharmaceuticals."

Paper had overtaken Wadhwa's office. There were bankers boxes of files, stacks of complaints, deposition testimony, and subpoena applications, some creeping like a stain across the lumpy couch, where he theoretically could take naps but never did. Copies of *The Wall Street Journal* yellowed on the windowsill. It wasn't the most cluttered office in the SEC, but it stood in contrast to Wadhwa himself, who was fastidiously clean-shaven and always wore a suit and tie.

The mechanism for reporting and tracking suspicious activity in the stock market was tragically antiquated. Financial regulators were like sad, old librarians overseeing a paper card catalog long after the rest of the world had gone digital. Except that these librarians happened to be responsible for ensuring the stability of a market in which trillions of dollars change hands each day. When strange activity was detected—a sudden increase in trading in options of a company the day before a takeover was announced, for example—by a bank employee or an investor, that person was encouraged to report it to the Financial Industry Regulatory Authority. FINRA would then spit out a referral—essentially a letter pointing out that a suspicious trade had occurred, without providing much in the way of details or context. These referrals were then passed along to the SEC, which was supposed to investigate them.

The problem was, minimal effort was made to put all the pieces of evidence together. FINRA's referrals, which were the vital seeds of securities fraud cases, were forwarded to the SEC's office in Washington, D.C., where they were entered into a self-contained database. And there they would sit.

After the call from Kang, Wadhwa called the chief of the Office of Market Surveillance.

"Did we receive a referral from FINRA last summer concerning a really big trade done by a fund called SAC Capital?" Wadhwa said. "It would have been around some sort of events announcement." He knew that most trades that yielded huge profits occurred before news that drove a stock dramatically up or down.

"It's funny you should mention that," the unit chief said, chuckling. "Yeah, I have a referral sitting here. . . . I was leafing through it the other day because it got bounced back." He meant that it had been returned to him without any SEC lawyer agreeing to investigate it.

"Really?" Wadhwa asked. "What is it?"

"Oh, you know, it's a referral," the unit chief said, without going into detail. "The total amount is massive."

Wadhwa asked how long it had been sitting there.

"Almost a year," he said.

The answer made Wadhwa cringe. The chief explained that he'd been "shopping it around" the enforcement division, trying to find someone to look into it. He had presented it to various associate directors in the D.C. office, but nobody had expressed interest in it.

To make an insider trading case, the SEC would have to prove that there had been an illegal tip and that the trader in question had been in communication with someone who had access to information from inside a company. Before even getting to the point where he or she could subpoena mind-numbing reams of data, however, the staff attorney would have to go before the full commission to ask for formal permission to send subpoenas and solicit documents. The Republican commissioners, at a minimum, could be counted on to ask a lot of questions.

From the sound of it, the referral didn't have the makings of a quick "stats point" case of the sort that was institutionally encouraged.

"Why don't you send it to me?" Wadhwa said.

The next day Wadhwa received an email from the Office of Market Surveillance with the referral attached. "Oh my god," he thought as he looked it over. "This must have been what B.J. was talking about."

"On July 29 2008 at 5 pm, scientists from Elan and Wyeth gave a presentation at the International Conference on Alzheimer's Disease in Chicago on Phase 2 trial data on their Alzheimer drug that is under development," read the letter, dated September 5, 2008. "This event was widely attended by the media, research analysts and institutional investors." The letter went on to observe that the hedge fund SAC Capital had made notable advantageous trades across fifteen accounts in the two days prior to the news. It estimated the firm's profits and avoided losses at $182 million. "The extraordinary size and net potential benefit of these timely trades," the letter read, "required that this Referral be made." Apparently a trader at a brokerage firm called RBC Capital Markets had noticed the trades and made the complaint.

Seeing that, Wadhwa couldn't help but wonder what else was going on at SAC. He tried to think about who was available to take on a new case like this—one that had the potential, he thought, to be even bigger than Raj.

There was a new branch chief in the New York office, Amelia Cottrell, and she had a new attorney named Charles Riely in her group who didn't yet have a full load of cases.

Wadhwa typed up an email to Riely. "Hi Charles, can you come by for a second?"

Riely had just returned from his summer vacation when he got Wadhwa's message. Young, eager, and almost impossibly straightlaced, Riely was a year into his time at the SEC and had yet to file his first case. He was frustrated.

He scurried across the hallway that separated his office from Wadhwa's and joined him at the conference table, next to Cottrell. "I want to show you guys something," Wadhwa said. He laid the Elan referral on the table in front of them. They all stared at it.

In the context of what the SEC had been looking at recently, the amount of money involved was breathtaking. In the Rajaratnam case, which had consumed Wadhwa's every waking minute for almost three years, they had only found $55 million in alleged illegal profits in eleven different trades that they felt they could prove, which in itself was one of the largest insider trading cases ever. SAC's "lucky" drug stock trades blew that out of the water. The chances of an experienced fund manager making such a large bet on anything less than a sure thing were slim.

The name SAC Capital has come up before, Wadhwa said. The first question the SEC attorneys had was whether the information in the referral could possibly be correct. It was rare, in their experience, for a fund to make such a large bet on one or two stocks. Managing risk was an important element of success for traders. You simply didn't last long in the business engaging in investments that could blow up the whole company if they didn't work out. Perhaps there was some error, or maybe the trade had involved several people.

The SEC didn't have much to go on, but the referral had the potential to finally bring the SEC inside SAC, an organization that had one of the worst reputations on Wall Street. Riely felt himself growing excited. Maybe this case was the break he was waiting for.

All through the summer and fall of 2009, as he was piecing together bits about SAC and Cohen, B. J. Kang was monitoring Raj Rajaratnam's telephone calls with a special electronic recorder called a pen register, on guard for any signs that he might be planning to leave the country. Each time Raj dialed out or a call came in, Kang checked the phone number. He had a fairly good understanding of Raj's communication patterns and which people he was likely to be speaking to.

Early in the morning on October 15, Kang was jolted awake by the sound of a text message on his smartphone. There was activity on Rajaratnam's line. At first, he wasn't going to bother checking it, because it was the middle of the night, but then he decided to look into it anyway. Kang could see that Raj was calling his daughter. It was 3 A.M., a weird time to be calling anyone. Almost unconsciously, Kang started getting dressed; he was certain that his day was about to take a dramatic turn. He contacted the Office of Customs and Border Protection, which monitored border traffic, and was told that Raj had just purchased a plane ticket to go to London the following day, October 16. That set off a five-alarm response. Kang called his supervisor to let him know that it was an emergency, and together they tried to wake up the rest of the FBI's New York office.

Kang rushed out of his house and hopped into his agency-issued Crown Victoria and practically lifted off of the New Jersey Turnpike as he sped into the office. His colleagues agreed that they could not let Rajaratnam get on the plane to London. The FBI decided to arrest him and a handful of his associates right away rather than risk letting them leave the country, which would mean they would have to go through a time-consuming extradition process that might last years. The FBI rushed to assemble teams to carry out the arrests.

At 6 A.M. the following morning, the FBI cordoned off a portion of East Fifty-third Street, and a team of agents descended on Rajaratnam's Sutton Place duplex. A few minutes later, Kang came out with Rajaratnam in handcuffs.

CHAPTER 9

THE DEATH OF KINGS

A thick, concrete low-rise, 1 St. Andrew's Plaza sits behind the federal courthouses in lower Manhattan out of view of the street—which is, perhaps, for the best. Inside, the security guards look indifferent, the carpet is so thin that it's almost translucent, and it's advisable not to look too closely at the bathroom floor. But that the office's physical surroundings exist in apparent opposition to the power wielded by those who work there is partly the point. The prosecutors in the Southern District are too important, and likely too arrogant, to care. They are doing exalted work for a fraction of the salary they could be making in private practice. The scruffy offices are a source of pride.

On this particular afternoon, Preet Bharara was sitting at his desk, looking out at the East River. Raj Rajaratnam had just been arrested, only eight weeks after Bharara's August swearing-in ceremony. As the new U.S. Attorney for the Southern District, Bharara finally had the position he had dreamed about since he was a child. The Southern District is arguably the most prestigious and influential branch of the Justice Department, responsible for prosecuting federal cases in Manhattan, the Bronx, and other parts of New York State, including Westchester County. Because of its location, it brings most of the biggest cases in the country dealing with terrorism, narcotics, organized crime, and the most significant financial crimes cases. Bharara was still trying to familiarize himself with the dozens of cases being prosecuted by the office's two hundred assistant U.S. attorneys when he was thrust into a whirlwind of attention. There was the prosecution of a Somali pirate accused of hijacking an American cargo ship, and the case of a former detainee from Guantánamo Bay prison. But financial cases were what the public seemed to care the most about at that moment. The Raj case had become a media sensation.

People across the country were struggling to deal with the fallout from the financial crisis, and public sentiment had turned strongly against Wall Street. Families were being evicted from their homes while traders at AIG and other companies that had been bailed out by the government were once again pocketing eight-figure bonuses. Although they weren't directly connected to the financial crisis, the insider trading cases were at the top of Bharara's list of priorities. Up until the moment of Rajaratnam's arrest, the insider trading investigation had been moving quietly forward, driven by a handful of government employees whose names were unknown. With Bharara's appointment, the investigation finally had a public face, a mediagenic front man with political ambition who wanted to make Wall Street crime the centerpiece of his career. And he had the resources to make it happen. Rudy Giuliani, a previous Manhattan U.S. Attorney to whom Bharara was sometimes compared, had earned a national reputation with his pursuit of Michael Milken and Ivan Boesky in the late 1980s. This historical precedent was not lost on the new U.S. Attorney.

Preetinder Bharara was a toddler when his parents brought him to the United States from India and settled in Monmouth County, New Jersey. Like so many other immigrants before them—and like Wadhwa at the SEC—his parents were trying to escape poverty and political uncertainty at home. Bharara watched as his father worked to become licensed to practice medicine in the United States and opened a pediatric clinic in Asbury Park. His parents put all their resources into their children's future. Bharara and his brother, Vinit, were enrolled in an elite prep school and Bharara's parents expected them to be exemplary students from an early age. "If you got a 98," Bharara said of his father, "he wanted to know why you didn't get a 100." The plan was for both brothers to become doctors. Vinit described their father as a stern disciplinarian. "School, studying, grades," he said. "It was ultra-competitive."

Preet graduated as high school valedictorian and went to Harvard, class of 1990, where he majored in government and political theory. Some of his classmates were impressed by how well he did considering how little he seemed to study. He spent most weekends with his girlfriend, a student at Wellesley, and engaged in alcohol-fueled political debates with his friends. He went on to Columbia Law School, where he took a course in trial practice taught by Michael Mukasey, the district court judge who later became attorney general under President George W. Bush. The class inspired Bharara to become a prosecutor. He worked as an assistant U.S. attorney in the Southern District from 2000 until 2005, when he became chief legal counsel to Senator Charles Schumer. There he helped lead an inquiry into Bush's firing of eight United States Attorneys around the country, a politically motivated purge that Bharara worked to expose—the scandal ultimately led to the resignation in 2007 of Bush's attorney general, Alberto Gonzales. Bharara was working as Schumer's chief counsel when President Barack Obama appointed him to lead the Southern District. The headline in *The New York Times* on the day Bharara was sworn in by the Senate read: "Schumer Aide Is Confirmed as United States Attorney." He didn't intend to be referred to as anybody's "aide" for long.

As soon as Bharara took over, lawyers inside and outside the U.S. Attorney's Office noticed a change in atmosphere. He had an acidic sense of humor that often veered into sarcasm and generated constant press attention. Under Bharara's most recent predecessors, the office's outdated media operation did little to bring attention to what the office was doing—and for years, that was how the prosecutors in the office wanted it. The work they did and the cases they prosecuted were supposed to speak for themselves.

Bharara took a different approach. He brought in a professional media relations staff and tasked them with publicizing his accomplishments. He held press conferences and gave speeches. Suddenly, questions about how things would play out in the media started to creep into internal discussions about particular cases and how to handle them. In everything he did, Bharara made it clear that he saw himself moving on to bigger things.

Hours after Rajaratnam was arrested, Bharara held a news conference. Television crews lined the back wall of a foyer on the first floor of 1 St. Andrew's Plaza, and rows of folding chairs were filled with reporters scribbling on notepads. Bharara had rarely seen so many cameras. Standing at a podium emblazoned with the Department of Justice seal, Bharara announced that he was there to discuss an insider trading case that was "unprecedented" in nature, involving hedge funds managing billions of dollars and a handful of corporate insiders who leaked company secrets to them.

"Today, we take decisive action against fraud on Wall Street," Bharara said, his green eyes glinting, before outlining charges against Rajaratnam and five other people. "The defendants operated in a world of, 'You scratch my back, I'll scratch your back.'" He waited a second. "Greed, sometimes, is not good."

Positioned at his trading station inside the New York offices of SAC Capital's Manhattan office, Michael Steinberg couldn't believe what he was reading. Raj ran a multi-billion-dollar hedge fund, and he was widely respected as an investor and a philanthropist. Raj's brother Rengan had even worked at SAC in 2003, until Cohen fired him. It was hard to believe that the FBI could just show up at Raj's doorstep without warning and take him away in handcuffs.

He spotted Horvath walking by his office and gestured for him to come inside.

"What's up?" Horvath said, oblivious to the news that was rocking trading desks across the city.

"Raj was arrested this morning," Steinberg said.

Horvath tried to remain calm. Inside, though, his stomach was churning.

As soon as he was able to make a graceful exit, Horvath ran back to his desk and started scanning news reports about the arrest. He had to talk to Jesse Tortora right away. If there was a massive dragnet going on, their "fight club" emails had surely caught some regulators' attention. SAC's offices crackled with gossip about how the FBI had suddenly become aggressive about insider trading. The SEC had evidently started doing its job as well. So far, at least, few details about the extent of the investigation had been revealed. People could only speculate about who might be cooperating. A few days after the arrest, Horvath, Tortora, and Sam Adondakis met for an emergency lunch in Midtown Manhattan. They resolved to stop using email to communicate. They would have conference calls instead.

Day by day, Steinberg seemed to Horvath to grow increasingly paranoid. "Don't talk to other investors that you don't really trust," he told Horvath. "There are telephone conversations being recorded, and people are running around wearing wires."

The street outside his office was noisy with Midtown traffic, as usual, but Michael Bowe fumbled to answer his cellphone anyway.

"Yeah?" he said, a touch apprehensively.

It had been a difficult few months for the forty-three-year-old Kasowitz Benson lawyer. Biovail's lawsuit against SAC had been dismissed, which had been humiliating. The case had consumed most of Bowe's time and energy for two years. But the far greater shame came from the fact that Biovail itself had fallen under scrutiny over its own accounting. The SEC had charged the company with fraud the previous year, accusing it of hiding losses from its investors. Biovail agreed to pay $10 million to settle the case. Bowe was catching a lot of flak for taking the case in the first place. Some of what the hedge funds had said about the company was right: It *was* a fraud. Bowe feared that it would be hanging around his neck for the rest of his career.

It was Patricia Cohen on the phone, Steven Cohen's ex-wife. Bowe hadn't spoken with her in months. He wondered what had happened to her.

She sounded excited. "Something big is going to happen," she told him. "There's going to be a RICO case filed against Steve."

Since they first spoke three years earlier, Patricia had been busy with her own investigation into her former husband's activities, one that oddly paralleled what the FBI was doing. She was on a mission to make Cohen pay.

Patricia's kids were grown, and the project infused her with a sense of purpose. In 2006, she filed a Freedom of Information Act request with the SEC to obtain the files in the RCA-GE insider trading investigation from the mid-1980s. She got a copy of Cohen's deposition in which he had taken the Fifth with the SEC, refusing to answer any questions. She had had no idea that the SEC's investigation had gone as far as it had. She also called several of Cohen's former colleagues from Gruntal to get a better sense of how much money he had been making when they were married—and what he had done with it.

In the course of reading the SEC files about Cohen, she came across a mention of an old case file that the court had to retrieve out of storage, from 1987. It was another revelation.

Unbeknownst to Patricia, Cohen had sued Brett Lurie, his former friend and real estate lawyer, over a real estate deal they had made in the 1980s. During their divorce, he claimed that the real estate investment with Lurie was worth nothing, which sharply reduced the amount of money he gave Patricia. Apparently there was a long and bitter litigation between Cohen and Lurie before they settled the case. At the end of it, Lurie was bankrupt, a wrecked man.

Patricia was astonished by what she was reading. It looked to her as if Steve had definitely hidden assets from her. She was shocked by the way he seemed to have treated Lurie, his former friend. She also found a list of other accounts and mortgage loans that she never knew existed.

A few weeks after her call to Bowe, Patricia filed a lawsuit charging Cohen, SAC Capital Advisors, and Cohen's brother Donald with violat-

ing the Racketeer Influenced and Corrupt Organizations Act by conspir-
ing to defraud her over a period of years. She included everything she
had found in her complaint: her interviews with Cohen's former Gruntal
colleagues, the Lurie deal that had gone so bad, the documents she had
acquired from the SEC. She alleged that her husband had confessed to
trading in RCA based on inside information that he'd gotten from Bruce
Newberg, a Wharton buddy who had worked as a trader for Michael
Milken at Drexel Burnham Lambert until he was charged with securities
fraud. Newberg, she alleged, had gotten the information from Dennis
Levine, another Drexel executive who was later convicted. RICO was a
federal law that had been passed in 1970 specifically to target organized
crime. Patricia was using it to claim marital fraud. As part of her suit she
demanded $300 million in damages. It was a bombshell. Cohen strenu-
ously denied the allegations.

Bowe shook his head as he read through it. He still couldn't believe
that rather than paying his ex-wife some money Cohen had chosen to
fight her over it.

Dozens of people—drug company executives, board members, lawyers,
bankers, investor relations staff, and doctors—were involved one way or
another in the bapi drug trial. These were the so-called insiders, people at
Elan and other companies who had access to closely guarded nonpublic
information, such as details about how the trial was going. Charles Riely
intended to track them down. He didn't care how long it took. In order
for this case to go anywhere, he needed to figure out who could have
tipped off someone at SAC about the trial results.

In late 2009, Riely began issuing subpoenas for each of the insiders'
phone records. Then he looked carefully through them, trying to figure
out who had contacts inside the investment community. With the help of
Neil Hendelman, an SEC investigator who specialized in analyzing phone
data, they built a spreadsheet that quickly grew to dozens of pages.

Riely's childhood had prepared him for this sort of labor. He was
the son of a nurse and a fighter pilot who flew a C-130 in Vietnam, and

his upbringing in North Dakota was something out of a made-for-television movie. His father had died in a training mission when Riely was six; his mother raised four boys on her own, filling them with a deep commitment to Catholicism, hard work, and personal discipline. Riely ran track at Yale before attending law school at the University of Michigan and working as an associate at the law firm Akin Gump Strauss Hauer & Feld. His older brother had gone to medical school at Johns Hopkins and his younger brother was a pilot, as their father had been, and Riely felt that he had a lot to live up to. Since joining the SEC in 2008 he had developed a reputation as a hard worker and an unwavering follower of rules. He did everything, even minor tasks, strictly as he was supposed to.

As Riely squinted at the list of names on his computer screen, two people stood out. Both were doctors. One was Sidney Gilman, the presenter of the information at the medical conference that had prompted the Elan and Wyeth stocks to plunge in July 2008. The other was Joel Ross, one of the clinical investigators who had participated in the trial. From looking at Ross's phone records, Riely and Hendelman were able to see numerous conversations with someone at an SAC number. Still, the records didn't indicate which portfolio manager or trader at SAC Ross had been talking to. Riely started cross-referencing the mystery SAC number with other numbers of SAC employees the SEC had in its database. He googled incessantly and ran the numbers through directories. It required hours and hours of tedious work.

Who was the trader? The question nagged at him. There had to be a way to find out.

As the SEC was gathering more details of the Elan and Wyeth trades, Mathew Martoma was struggling to repeat his spectacular success at SAC. His bet on bapineuzumab had been one of those once-in-a-lifetime accomplishments, one naturally followed by a severe case of performance anxiety. Martoma had received a $9.38 million bonus that year. Finding that level of success again wasn't going to be easy.

Cohen was eager to see whether his bapi trade could be replicated. Martoma had the potential to be one of the most valuable portfolio managers at the firm, ascending to the ranks of those whom Cohen relied on for ideas year after year. Martoma felt the weight of his colleagues' expectations as he worked to come up with an investment idea as profitable as bapi.

In 2010 he seized on InterMune, a biotechnology startup in California that didn't have a single product on the market. What it did have was a drug in development, called Esbriet, that was designed to fight pulmonary fibrosis, a disease that afflicted roughly a hundred thousand people in the United States. An investment in InterMune was almost entirely a bet on whether Esbriet would obtain FDA approval. There were clinical trials under way and a great deal of hype, with analysts predicting that the drug could reach $1 billion in annual sales if it worked.

Martoma aggressively recommended InterMune to Cohen. By the end of April, SAC and Cohen had accumulated almost 4.5 million shares. When, on May 4, the FDA announced that it would not be approving Esbriet, the effects were immediate and devastating. After closing at $45 the night before, the stock plunged to $9 the morning after the news came out as hedge funds sold their shares in a panic. Cohen owned more than 8 percent of the company. It was the kind of calamity that could end a trader's career.

After adding up the losses, Cohen met with his top deputies to discuss what to do with Martoma. He had hit his "down-and-out," the amount of loss his portfolio could sustain before it triggered an automatic termination. But Martoma had goodwill in reserve because of the incredible profits he brought to the firm in 2008, an otherwise disastrous year for SAC. David Atlas, SAC's chief risk officer, argued that they should fire him immediately; Tom Conheeney and Sol Kumin, who had recruited Martoma, thought that they should let him stay and try again. They eventually persuaded Atlas to their view. Cohen agreed to give Martoma another chance. But he was clear that this would be it.

Ecstatic to hear the news, Martoma wrote an effusive email to Cohen. "I want to THANK YOU again for your decision last week," it began. "I realize the outcome could have been different. Clearly, there is a long road ahead for me to restore your faith in my process, performance and risk management. I will do everything in my power to bounce back quickly." He went on to explain that he had "debriefed" the CEO of Inter-Mune, who had explained that the FDA's decision was tipped in the "negative direction" at the last minute, the result of some sort of unusual intervention by a senior official.

"SAC is a special place to me," Martoma continued. "Having attended graduate and undergraduate programs at Harvard, Stanford and Duke; founded/sold my own healthcare company; and worked as a Director at the largest federally funded science initiative in the last 3 decades, I have a variety of experiences to compare against my time at SAC. Through it all, it's clear to me that I am in my element here at SAC. . . . I want people outside the firm to realize how inspiring this place is." He went on: "This week's events were extremely disappointing to me, but I believe they are just a speed bump on my path here. I still have a lot to offer, and am thankful that you are giving me a chance to prove it. Respectfully yours, Mat."

His painful attempts at flattery would get Martoma only so far. He soon learned how SAC was structured to punish portfolio managers who lost money. The firm reduced the amount of capital he could invest, which made it more difficult to make up for his losses; it created a sort of self-fulfilling vortex that was almost impossible to get out of. Martoma quickly hit his loss limits again.

Finally, in May 2010, Atlas again recommended that Martoma be let go. This time, Conheeney agreed. Martoma was "expendable," Conheeney argued, and SAC had plenty of other portfolio managers who did what he did, only more consistently and without the big losses. Conheeney also pointed out that, aside from the bapi trade, Martoma hadn't suggested any other profitable ideas during his almost four years at the firm. In an email to Cohen, Conheeney wrote: "He's really been a one trick pony with Elan."

Just after 10 P.M. on Friday night, November 19, 2010, *The Wall Street Journal* posted an article on its website that would appear in the newspaper the next morning. "U.S. in Vast Insider Trading Probe," the headline read. It was like the setup to a legal thriller.

"Federal authorities, capping a three-year investigation, are preparing insider-trading charges that could ensnare consultants, investment bankers, hedge-fund and mutual-fund traders, and analysts across the nation, according to people familiar with the matter," it began. "The investigations, if they bear fruit, have the potential to expose a culture of pervasive insider trading in U.S. financial markets, including new ways non-public information is passed to traders through experts tied to specific industries or companies, federal authorities say."

The article had a shocking number of details about what the FBI and the SEC were doing—things that up until then had been completely secret. It identified the expert network firm PGR as one of the main targets of the investigation. It mentioned a handful of drug companies the government was looking at. It also reported that Richard Grodin, C. B. Lee's former boss at SAC, had received a subpoena.

For the government, it was a devastating leak that would alter the course of the investigation. Wall Street was now on notice that the Justice Department was waging a campaign that was much bigger than anyone had suspected. The Raj Rajaratnam case was only the beginning.

A former SAC portfolio manager named Donald Longueuil reacted to the story with particular alarm. He had been fired from SAC for poor performance the previous April. He was looking for another high-paying hedge fund job, and his wedding was only three weeks away. Now he had this to deal with.

Longueuil was intensely competitive, a mindset he brought to his work. Tall and lean, with a shaved head, he spent most of his free time training for cycling races. He was also a winter sports enthusiast and had tried to make the 2002 U.S. Olympic speed-skating team after graduating from Northeastern University. In 2008 he joined SAC as a technology portfolio manager. During his time there, he became friends with another SAC portfolio manager in Boston named Noah Freeman, a Harvard graduate whom he'd met competing with the Bay State Speedskating Club. Both men were in their early thirties and driven by an obsession with winning their various athletic endeavors. Freeman was so intense about it that one triathlon group, known as "Team Psycho," kicked him off for being unsportsmanlike.

At home in Midtown Manhattan with his fiancée, Longueuil read the article again. It was as if the piece were about him and his hedge fund friends. He looked at his fiancée, wondering if his life was about to blow apart. He still couldn't quite believe that she was marrying him. In addition to being blond and just about perfect-looking, she had a biology degree from Princeton and an MBA from Wharton, where she'd been a competitive rower, and she now had a great job at the Boston Consulting Group. Freeman was going to be his best man.

During his eight years on Wall Street, Longueuil had built an extensive network of information sources, including at Apple and Texas Instruments. He seduced them with expensive dinners and golf outings, as well as the occasional night at a strip club. And they, in turn, supplied him with inside information that he had traded on while he was at SAC.

Because the material he got from his sources was so voluminous, he'd become a diligent note-taker, saving details from every conversation so that he could track the quality of the information over time. He and Freeman shared the information and traded on it together, along with another friend of theirs, Samir Barai, the manager of a small hedge fund. Still, even with that extra boost, things had been difficult at SAC. Longueuil used to complain that even with all the cheating going on, you still couldn't make that much money because the market had gotten so competitive. Hence the firing by Cohen.

Longueuil glared at his bedroom table, where he kept his USB flash drive. He and Freeman had nicknamed it "the log." It contained his notes from his sources. It almost seemed to be mocking him, saying: "You're toast."

Longueuil grabbed the USB drive and the two other external hard drives he used to store notes from his information exchanges with Freeman and Barai. All along he'd been exceedingly careful, never saving any of the illegal information on his SAC computer, and never writing any-thing incriminating in his work email. All of his questionable dealings had been conducted via one of his numbered Gmail accounts on his lap-top, with all his notes saved on the external drives. He tried to do most of his instant-message chats through Skype, which he was sure couldn't be wiretapped.

He tore around his apartment looking for a pair of pliers, which he used to rip the USB and hard drives apart, stripping them into little bits. Then he divided the pieces into four ziplock bags. He stuffed the bags into the pockets of his North Face jacket and turned to his fiancée.

"We're going for a walk," he said.

At 1:52 A.M., in the early hours of the morning of Saturday, November 20, video surveillance captured them hurrying through the lobby of their condominium building, past the doorman and down an elegant slate walkway lined with bamboo plants. They turned past the Chinese restau-rant next door and took a tour through the neighborhood. Longueuil looked for garbage trucks making the rounds. When he spotted one he ran it down and tossed one of the bags of hard-drive parts into the back. Over the next thirty minutes he dispersed the bags into four different trucks. As he threw each one, he wondered what would happen if the Feds found them. Maybe it would have made more sense to dump them in the East River? He was pretty sure they were so damaged it would be impossible to read any of the data, even if by some miracle the FBI got its hands on them.*

They didn't get home until 2:30 A.M. Everything was gone. He felt much better.

That same night, Samir Barai, Longueuil's friend and the founder of Barai Capital, had read the same *Wall Street Journal* article and had a similar panic attack. At thirty-nine, Barai had succeeded on Wall Street through sheer exertion. He had a severe hearing impediment, and when he was

---

* Longueuil's fiancée was never charged with any wrongdoing.

young, nobody thought he would ever amount to much. He got through NYU and then Harvard Business School by sitting in the front row and reading his professors' lips.

He had been trading extensively on inside information at his small hedge fund, something that anyone who worked for him quickly discovered as he demanded that they get inside information, too. Barai and Longueuil had developed a close, if nasty, friendship, making wisecracks about Freeman behind his back, laughing at the thought of him having sex with their various sources, even jokingly referring to him as "the Jew." (Barai's nickname, meanwhile, was "the Hindu," while Longueuil was "the Catholic.")

The news of the government investigation of PGR couldn't have come at a worse time. Barai was already distracted by his ongoing, increasingly ugly divorce, and he was a heavy PGR user as well as a close friend of the company's chief financial officer. Barai pulled information from a wide range of strange characters. One, a consultant named Doug Munro— nickname "10k"—ran a company called World Wide Market Research. Munro maintained an email account under the name JUICYLUCY_ XXX@yahoo.com; in it, Munro would compose emails containing inside information about Cisco and other companies but leave them in the "drafts" folder, where they supposedly would not create an email trail. Barai paid him around $8,000 a month, and Freeman paid him, too; in return, both had the password to the email account. Whenever there was something new, Munro sent Barai an email: "Lucy is wet." Then the men would log in and read whatever was there.

Barai, Freeman, and Longueuil had pet names for most of their sources. "Cha-Ching" was their guy at Intel; "Saigon" was their consultant who gave them information about National Semiconductor. Their best source was Winifred Jiau. Her nicknames were "Winnie the Pooh" and "the Poohster," and she was a little nutty. She had a statistics degree from Stanford, had worked at Taiwan Semiconductor, and had friends all over Silicon Valley, although "friends" in her case had a loose definition. The Poohster was available by special arrangement through the expert network PGR, which paid her a $10,000-a-month retainer to speak with a select group of its clients through its private network. Jiau badgered PGR constantly about money, acting desperate and paranoid, as if she would never see another paycheck. She referred to her tippers inside companies as "cooks" and often threatened Barai and Freeman that they'd go on strike. "Cooks don't talk to me without sugar!" she screamed. After one particularly useful session, she requested a $500 gift certificate to the Cheesecake Factory in addition to the cash Barai and Freeman sent her each month. Another time, Freeman, acting on Jiau's request, asked his secretary to have twelve live lobsters delivered to the capricious source. The lobsters ended up dying at the FedEx office near Jiau's residence in California because she couldn't be bothered to go pick them up.

The reason Jiau was able to get away with this was that she was good. Her information was by far the most valuable they got from anyone. She had numbers for revenue, gross margin, and earnings for Marvell and Nvidia, two volatile semiconductor companies Barai, Freeman, and Longueuil loved to trade, that were accurate down to the decimal point. The Poohster offered them something they couldn't live without.

Because of Barai's hearing problems, he made his research analyst, a thirty-eight-year-old named Jason Pflaum, secretly listen in and record almost all of his calls. Pflaum had only a minimal understanding of who Jiau was, but he would eavesdrop and send instant messages to his boss explaining what she was saying so that Barai could keep up with his end of the conversation. Pflaum also took extensive notes so Barai could go back and review the information later, since he usually missed many of the details the first time.

"Who are your sources?" Barai had asked Jiau at one point, incredulous.

"You should not ask who my sources are," Jiau replied.

Reading the *Wall Street Journal* article, Barai's mind filled with what-if scenarios and questions about just how he was going to get himself out of legal jeopardy. He sent an instant message to Pflaum. "Did you see the

PGR article?" wrote Barai, quoting the story. "Key parts of the probes are at a late stage. . . . Federal grand jury has heard evidence." He had read the article ten times, he said.

"So another reuters article," he wrote a few minutes later after a follow-up news story was posted. "This scope is said to focus on the use of so-called expert network firms. . . . concern for years that some experts may be passing on confi info about public cos to traders. . . . PGR was only one named!!!!"

Then, a minute later: "Fuuuuuck."

His next act was to order Pflaum to delete all of their BlackBerry messages.

The following morning, Pflaum sent Barai a message. "Yo. Deleted them. Didn't sleep so well last night. What else do you think we need to do?"

"I dunno," Barai wrote. "I think we ok tho. I think u just go into office, shred as much as you can. Put all ur data files onto an encrypted drive." He told Pflaum to erase all of his emails with PGR executives. Rather than waiting for Pflaum to go in and destroy all the evidence, Barai rushed to their office on Third Avenue and Forty-sixth Street and started shredding everything he could get his hands on. Then he went back home.

As he raced around in a panic, Barai started to see a way through the disaster. Maybe they wouldn't be able to nail him with anything. He had talked to people, sure, but that wasn't illegal. He would hire a lawyer, the best money could buy, and he would fight. They had to prove that he had acted on the information, and that was sure to be difficult. He told himself that he'd invested using the "mosaic theory"—an approach to analyzing stocks that involved collecting disparate bits of public information about a company's operations and putting them all together to create a "mosaic" about the business. It was a long-standing defense argument traders used to explain what prosecutors often thought of as insider trading. Everyone did it, Barai told himself. There was nothing wrong with it.

Just to be safe, he instructed Pflaum to leave his laptop with his doorman on Sunday night so that Barai could pick it up and do a "Department of Defense delete," an erase of the hard drive that couldn't be undone. Barai collected the computer and brought it to his fiancée's apartment, where he copied all the notes onto a thumb drive he had just bought and then tried to wipe the laptop clean. He spent all night downloading software from the Internet that promised to help him erase everything permanently, but he was never able to get it to work.

On Saturday morning, just as the print version of the newspaper was being picked up from the doormats of buildings across the Upper East Side, Pflaum met with B. J. Kang on the street near his apartment. Pflaum had been cooperating with the FBI for a month. He showed Kang his BlackBerry messages with Barai from the night before. Kang took pictures of the entire exchange, including the orders to shred his documents and delete his email.

As Kang read one of Barai's messages—"Fuuuuuck"—from the night before, he had the same exact feeling. Guys all over Wall Street were probably destroying their hard drives. The FBI had to do something.

CHAPTER 10

OCCAM'S RAZOR

Early Monday morning, November 22, 2010, two days after *The Wall Street Journal* set off a weekend of frantic evidence destruction, a fleet of unmarked cars pulled up outside 1 Landmark Square, an office tower in the center of Stamford, Connecticut. A dozen federal agents were inside the vehicles.

Special Agent Dave Makol was a block away. He pulled out his cellphone and dialed a number.

Inside the office tower, a phone rang.

"Hello?" a man answered.

Makol identified himself as an FBI agent. "We know you've been involved in insider trading," he said. "There's going to be a lot of stuff going down later, and it's going to affect you and your family. Your life is never going to be the same."

Their investigation was focused on expert networks, Makol continued, and they wanted the man to cooperate. When the man asked for more information, Makol said he couldn't be more specific. "We're at the McDonald's next door," he said. "If you want to come down and talk to us, that'd be great."

The man wasn't sure what to do. He was scared to say anything. He told Makol that he needed to think about it.

Makol said they didn't have much time to wait.

The man was Todd Newman, a forty-five-year-old portfolio manager at a hedge fund called Diamondback Capital. He hung up the phone and ran one floor down to the Diamondback general counsel's office. He relayed the whole exchange to the company's legal counsel and its COO, John Hagarty.

"Is there something you did?" Hagarty asked, staring into Newman's eyes. Hagarty had only been on the job for three months. For a moment, he wondered whether Newman was wearing a wire or something, the situation was so bizarre. The look on Newman's face was one of terror.

No, Newman said, he hadn't done anything. "I'll just go over there and talk to them. I don't have anything to hide."

"I don't know if you want to do that," Hagarty said.

"I think I need a lawyer," Newman said.

The legal counsel threw out a few names of lawyers he knew, and Newman decided to walk over to the office of one of them, just up the street. Incredibly, even though the block was crawling with FBI agents, he walked unnoticed out the front door of the building.

As Newman made his way down the street, the elevators opened on the fourteenth floor, just outside Diamondback's reception area, and a team of FBI agents fanned out wearing bulletproof vests. This was the moment when it seemed as if a man with a bullhorn might jump out and yell "Cut!" and things would go back to normal. The agents looked like they were ready to charge into a terrorist safe house rather than an office filled with Wharton graduates tapping away on keyboards.

"FBI!" they shouted, flashing their badges.

Startled receptionists and traders sat up in their chairs, unsure what to do. Agents filed between the rows of desks, commanding people to back away from their computers. Hagarty watched in shock as the agents carted out files and hard drives. His father had been a New York City police officer for twenty-seven years, and his brother was an FBI agent who had helped bring down John Gotti. He had worked in finance for more than fifteen years; he had never imagined that he would be employed by a company that was the target of a federal raid. He asked the agents for a copy of the search warrant.

Rumors had been making their way through the hedge fund industry that the government was going after SAC Capital, Hagarty knew, and Diamondback and SAC were closely connected. Diamondback's founders, Larry Sapanski and Richard Schimel, had been two of Steve Cohen's most successful traders before they went out on their own in 2005. When they told Cohen they were leaving SAC to start their own fund, Cohen threatened to destroy them. As far as Cohen was concerned, they had been nothing when they came to work for him; how dare they go into business against him? To make matters worse, Schimel had married Cohen's sister Wendy—which made bar mitzvahs and weddings pretty awkward. Several of Diamondback's other key employees had come from SAC as well. If you wanted a proxy for Cohen's firm, Diamondback was about as close as you could get.

Storming into a hedge fund wasn't how the FBI had intended for this part of the investigation to play out. These were drastic measures, but Makol didn't see any other choice.

While Diamondback's hard drives were being carried out the door, David Ganek was driving into the offices of Level Global, the hedge fund he founded after leaving SAC, across the street from Carnegie Hall. When he got there, he found five of his employees milling around on the street. Not just the smokers but nonsmokers as well. They looked stressed.

"What's going on?" Ganek asked.

"We've been raided," one said. "The FBI is upstairs."

"What?" Ganek said. His mind flashed briefly to a film he'd seen recently, about the siege of the U.S. embassy in Tehran, where embassy workers furiously shredded documents as a mob of Iranians battered the door down. When he thought of the word *raid,* that was the sort of thing that came to mind.

He called his general counsel, who advised him not to go inside. The office was swarming with federal agents, the counsel said, and they had a search warrant signed by a judge over the weekend.

Ganek had read the *Wall Street Journal* article over the weekend. He was a regular presence on the Manhattan social scene, a trustee of the Guggenheim Museum who lived in a $19 million penthouse on Park Avenue. That Saturday night he had gone to the bar mitzvah of the child of a prominent Wall Street figure, and the investigation had been all that anyone there could talk about. Thirty-six hours later, a dozen agents were inside his office, collecting cellphones, laptops, and notepads and making images of the firm's servers to be analyzed later.

It was like a nightmare. Just a few months earlier, at the end of March, he had worked out a deal to sell a 15 percent stake in his $4 billion fund to Goldman Sachs. Level Global was his life's work.

Watching his employees waiting on the sidewalk, Ganek exhaled deeply. Then he turned around and left.

In early December, a couple of weeks after the raids on Diamondback and Level Global, Donald Longueuil was still feeling insecure. After smashing his hard drives he was hopeful that he had destroyed any evidence that would implicate him in any illegal trading. Still, he told his friend Noah Freeman, they should communicate from now on only by Skype.

Freeman, since his firing from SAC the previous January, had attempted to turn his life around. He had a wife and a baby daughter and was trying to be a hands-on father, a present father. He had started teaching economics at the Winsor School in Boston, a private all-girls academy. He missed the money from his old life, but he felt better about himself.

One afternoon, as he was crossing the school's leafy campus, Freeman noticed a man waiting for him by his car. "I'd like to talk to you," B. J. Kang said.

Kang invited Freeman into his car so they could speak privately. Freeman climbed in. Then Kang prepared to release his grenade. As Freeman sat there awkwardly, his spine as stiff as a board, Kang played a snippet of a recording of a phone call. It sounded like Freeman talking to his expert network consultant Wini Jiau on the phone. Kang let the recording do his work for him. Then he suggested that Freeman should help himself by working with the FBI. Freeman had been a copious user of PGR experts when he managed $300 million for SAC. He knew he was in trouble.

"It's better to be the first one to cooperate," Kang told him.

A few days later, on December 16, Freeman arrived at 1 St. Andrew's Plaza with two attorneys. They sat down with Kang and a pair of prosecutors, Avi Weitzman and David Leibowitz. Freeman had agreed to talk to them, but the prosecutors weren't sure what to expect. Kang first asked about Freeman's background, writing down the name of Freeman's wife and the various analysts he'd worked with at his different jobs. Then Freeman started describing his sources, at companies like Cisco Systems, Fairchild Semiconductor, and Broadcom, and the information he got from each and how he took pains to store it safely. He had barely hesitated before implicating Longueuil, his best friend, in all of it.

Freeman recounted how he and Longueuil, whom Freeman had nicknamed "Long Dong," collaborated to get nonpublic information and shared it with each other when they were at SAC. Longueuil had been trading on inside information in his personal account as well as at work, Freeman said. His cooperation agreement with the FBI required that he report information he had about any crimes that had been committed by himself or anyone else, even if they had nothing to do with securities fraud. Freeman told Kang that he had occasionally smoked marijuana and gave the name of the person he had bought it from. Freeman also told them he had cheated in his triathlons by blood doping with EPO.

Weitzman had worked for three years prosecuting organized crime cases. The most dramatic one had been a murder case involving the Albanian mob in which two brothers killed their best friend after mistakenly concluding that he was working as an informant and then tossed the gun into the bay under the Verrazano Bridge. Even though the people involved in those kinds of cases were often committing heinous crimes, murdering and extorting and stealing from vulnerable people, Weitzman observed that they operated by a code that said you did not betray your friends and family. The bonds of loyalty were strong.

In the Wall Street cases, by contrast, people turned on one another with very little prompting. There was no code at all, nothing beyond a shared lust for making money. Freeman hewed to type. He barely hesitated before flipping on Longueuil, who had been the best man at his wedding.

Kang began asking Freeman about the environment at SAC. At SAC, Freeman said, there were four ways of communicating with Cohen: in person, by phone, by email, and through portfolio writeups every Friday. Freeman recalled instances when he'd shared inside information with other SAC portfolio managers. He remembered a time when Cohen, whose desk Freeman could see from his own, became animated during a phone call. He hung up the phone and announced that he wanted to go long on financials—that is, to buy bank stocks. Given that it was in the middle of the financial crisis, Freeman thought it seemed like a brazen, possibly self-sabotaging move. The following Saturday, Fannie Mae and Freddie Mac were nationalized, and Freeman couldn't help but wonder whether Cohen had known it was going to happen. As with many of the other stories Kang heard, it was intriguing, but it wasn't enough to make a case.

Kang leaned across the table and stared at him.

"What did Steve want you to do?" he asked.

"You were expected to provide your best trading ideas to Steve," Freeman said without hesitation. "I understood that this involved giving him inside information." Freeman was adamant that he was not alone in this understanding.

After Freeman left, the prosecutors ran into their boss's office to update him. There was definitely insider trading taking place inside SAC, they said, and they finally had a witness to testify about it. With Freeman's testimony, they felt that they had enough concrete evidence to open a case on SAC directly. The securities chief of the Manhattan U.S. Attorney's Office wrote "In Re: SAC Capital" down on a folder.

SAC was finally, officially, the subject of its own investigation.

Weitzman asked Kang to send him every set of interview notes he had that mentioned Cohen or SAC Capital. The notes were accounts of conversations with witnesses written by FBI agents, who weren't known for their elegant prose. A few hours later, two four-inch binders full of notes were dropped on Weitzman's desk. He started reading through them.

He was immediately struck by how many interview subjects had said that Cohen was trading on inside information or that people who worked at SAC were doing so with Cohen's knowledge. At the same time, few had any hard evidence to back up their claims. There was clearly a culture of insider trading at the firm but also strong mechanisms in place to protect Cohen from what was going on. People fed tips into Cohen's portfolio by using a numbered "conviction rating" to convey how sure they were about the value of the tip. This meant Cohen was insulated.

Noah Freeman tried not to shake as Kang fitted him with a hidden recording device a few days later. If Freeman hadn't condemned his friend already, he was about to do so now. He made his way over to Longueuil's apartment on East Fifty-ninth Street and checked in with the doorman before stepping into the elevator and ascending to the tenth floor. Longueuil had become increasingly insecure about any communication other than face–to–face, and he had stored up a few things he wanted to talk about.

Feeling sweaty and sick to his stomach, Freeman proceeded to try to implicate his friend, sounding as self-conscious as a sixth-grade boy asking a girl to dance. He brought up the *Wall Street Journal* article from the previous month and all the drama it had caused.

"What do you think, worst case, they could get us in trouble for?" he asked Longueuil, and the conversation instantly turned to the most egregious of the things they had done: obtaining inside information about Marvell from the PGR consultant Wini Jiau.

"I got it from Wini. I gave it to you. So we both . . . I guess in theory, there's that," Freeman said, his voice trailing off. "Did you trade on the Wini P&L? We both did, didn't we?"

"Yeah," Longueuil replied.

"The Wini thing, that was detailed. That was fucking detailed," Freeman continued. "I gave that to you."

"That was '08," Longueuil said, playing right along. "The first half of '08."

"So I traded on that," Freeman said. "You, you said you traded on that. Sam sure as hell traded on that."

Later in the conversation, Freeman asked his friend whether he was worried about Jiau cooperating with the government.

"I guess," Longueuil said. "But do they have proof that she gave it to us? I mean, I can tell you whatever you fucking want to hear, or don't want to. I can lie, whatever. So, yeah, we talked to Wini. It's 'he said, she said.'"

"So if she says, 'I gave them the fucking EPS number' and then we say . . ."

"Where's the proof?" Longueuil responded. "I don't remember it like that."

Freeman asked him about "the log." Where was it? It would be devastating if the FBI got its hands on it.

Yeah, Longueuil acknowledged, the log would be damning. It had the list of all of their sources at the different companies. But Longueuil had taken care of that problem. "The night the *Wall Street Journal* article came out, I pressed the eject button and everything's fucking gone," he said.

"Is the log gone?" Freeman asked.

"Destroyed," Longueuil said. "Everything's gone."

"How did you do it?" he asked.

"I chopped it up," Longueuil said. "Chopped up everything."

"I don't see how you get rid of that shit."

"Oh, it's easy," Longueuil said. "You take two pairs of pliers and you rip it open." He said he also had two external hard drives that had wafer numbers on them, which he pulled apart and put into different baggies. "At 2 A.M. I leave the apartment and go on like a twenty-block walk around the city and threw the shit in the back of like random garbage trucks."

"I can see the Feds trying to find it," Freeman said.

"Well, they can find it, but it's all fuckin' ripped apart," Longueuil replied. "Everything's gone."

At night, after taking the train home to Jersey City and helping his wife
put their four kids to bed, the SEC lawyer Charles Riely stayed up late,
combing through sheets of data, looking for connections. It was early
2011, more than a year after his new case had launched, and he still didn't
know who the Elan trader at SAC was. It was driving him crazy.

It wasn't until May 2011, the same month that Raj Rajaratnam was
convicted on fourteen counts of conspiracy and securities fraud, that
Riely had his breakthrough. He had sent out a subpoena for Sid Gilman's
phone records several months before, but they were taking forever to
come back. When he finally got them, he was able to identify a phone
number on the list: It belonged to a portfolio manager at SAC named
Mathew Martoma. The SEC had his name in a database. Suddenly, everything fit together. The doctor and the trader had spoken dozens of times.
Riely had his trader.

He went to tell his boss, Sanjay Wadhwa, that they finally had a suspect. Then Wadhwa placed a call to the head of the securities unit at the
U.S. Attorney's Office.

Frankly, Wadhwa was feeling frustrated. The SEC's Elan investigation
had been going on for more than a year. During that time, mostly through
analysis of the limited phone records they were able to get, they had
pieced together elements of a massive financial fraud. Now, thanks to
Riely's work, they had two suspects, Martoma and Gilman. And the case
also appeared to envelop Cohen himself, the whale they had all been
chasing for the previous few years. Despite all that, though, the U.S. Attorney's Office still had not assigned a prosecutor to the case, giving the
SEC the distinct sense that they did not think it was important. He had
already urged them twice to put a prosecutor on the Elan case, and nothing had happened.

The three interrelated groups involved in federal securities investigations—the SEC lawyers, FBI agents, and federal prosecutors—formed

a sort of unsteady but codependent triumvirate. Although they often worked together closely and the FBI was technically a subsidiary of the Justice Department, each felt some resentment toward the others, and members of each group wondered whether they were putting in most of the effort and receiving insufficient credit for the cases being filed. The FBI prided itself on being the tough guys who did the dangerous work of flipping witnesses and wiretapping people. FBI agents hated it when people suggested that the SEC ever arrested people, a misunderstanding they had to correct with maddening frequency. The SEC believed, not without reason, that it was the brains behind most securities cases—the only ones who truly understood the complex securities laws. Many SEC attorneys felt underappreciated and sometimes disrespected. The prosecutors, who were drawn heavily from the graduating classes of elite Ivy League law schools, tended to believe that cases weren't important until they got involved and did all the preparation required to bring them to trial. Preet Bharara's pattern of announcing new charges at press conferences threw gasoline on the smoldering resentment. He usually thanked his "partners" at the FBI and the SEC, but the optics made clear that he was the one bringing the Wall Street criminals to justice.

"Where are you guys?" Wadhwa asked the chief of the securities unit in Bharara's office and his deputy when he got them on the phone. "There's a really good case here, but we need you to get involved."

Wadhwa, and the SEC generally, were under more than the usual amount of pressure.

Senator Charles Grassley, an influential Republican senator from Iowa, had started complaining—loudly and publicly—that the SEC was not doing its job policing the stock market. The previous month, Grassley's office had received a tip from someone suggesting that the Senate Judiciary Committee look into a rogue hedge fund called SAC Capital.

Grassley had been a vocal critic of the Obama administration's response to the financial crisis, arguing in interviews and press conferences that the president's financial reform proposals weren't strong enough. The SAC case looked like a ripe opportunity to criticize regulators again for missing the next Madoff in their midst. Ironically, Grassley had attended a fundraiser at SAC's offices in 2008, but he still had little idea what the fund did. In April 2011, a month into the Raj Rajaratnam trial, one of Grassley's staff members asked FINRA, which monitored stock market activity, to send over every referral it had involving suspicious trading by SAC. Cohen and his firm looked like the perfect bludgeons to use to disparage the SEC. If anything significant came back and the regulatory agency hadn't done anything about it, Grassley would have cause for a loud and public campaign.

A few days later, a folder containing a stack of referrals concerning trading in twenty different stocks arrived at Grassley's congressional office. The young aide who opened it wasn't an expert on hedge funds, but it sure looked bad.

There was a referral from May 9, 2007, reporting suspicious trades by the SAC unit CR Intrinsic in something called Connetics Corporation. Another referral from October 26, 2007, flagged SAC trades in Fidelity Bankshares. Another referral, from December 14, 2007, read: "The investigation identified timely purchase of INGR shares by two hedge funds located in Greenwich, CT that had contact with INGR during the period of June 26, 2006 through August 31, 2006." The funds were part of SAC, and the purchases happened right before a buyout of INGR was announced. The list went on and on: problematic trades in United Therapeutics, Sirtris Pharmaceuticals, Third Wave Technologies, Cougar Biotechnology, Synutra International. Some of the trades had happened as recently as 2010. Included in the pile was the September 5, 2008, referral about Elan and Wyeth and the massive stock sales SAC had made a week before the drug trial announcement.

Grassley demanded to know whether the SEC had done anything about the referrals. He released a letter to the media outlining his concerns about the SEC's ability to enforce the securities regulations. Look at SAC, he said. Signs of suspicious activity were rampant, and the SEC hadn't taken any action—it was another useless government agency.

Cohen watched the senator's actions with growing discomfort. Any time someone suggested something improper was going on at SAC, he became defensive. He ordered his executives to do something about the criticism from Washington. A few days after the senator's letter became public, on May 10, 2011, SAC dispatched a group of executives from Connecticut to Grassley's offices to try to calm the situation.

Cohen's advisors seemed confident that they could "charm" the Senate staffers into dropping their concerns about SAC. Tom Conheeney, SAC's president, Peter Nussbaum, its general counsel, and an SAC executive in Washington named Michael Sullivan descended on Grassley's office. Sullivan was a former advisor to another powerful Republican senator, a Washington operator through and through, and Cohen had hired him specifically to address this kind of problem. Sullivan argued to the senator's investigators that the firm took its compliance seriously and that they should lighten up.

"Steve is very civic-minded," Sullivan told Grassley's staffers. "He's thinking about taking a stake in the New York Mets."

The staff members stared at him, unable to comprehend what they were hearing. "Oooh, I'm a Mets fan—he *must* be a good guy," thought one member of Grassley's staff sarcastically.

The meeting ended awkwardly and, from Cohen's perspective, fruitlessly. On May 24, Grassley released another letter to the media, this time accusing the SEC of failing to investigate SAC and demanding a meeting with the chair of the SEC. "I have had a longstanding interest in whether the Securities and Exchange Commission is properly policing and regulating our financial markets," Grassley wrote. He explained that he had recently obtained twenty referrals of suspicious trades at SAC from FINRA and demanded a written explanation as to how the SEC had resolved each one.

By the time Wadhwa got a call from the SEC's enforcement chief about it, the Grassley campaign was threatening to escalate into a full-blown scandal.

"We have got to get ahead of this," Wadhwa's boss told him. "Can you look into it?"

After hearing from the SEC about the Gilman-Martoma connection to the Elan case, the head of the securities unit at the U.S. Attorney's Office agreed that it was time to look again at what the SEC had found. Two criminal prosecutors, Avi Weitzman, who was working on the Noah Freeman and Donald Longueuil cases, and Arlo Devlin-Brown, who was in the middle of a high-profile case involving illegal Internet gambling sites, walked over to the SEC's offices. B. J. Kang came, too.

Charles Riely still wasn't positive about what had happened with Elan, but he had a theory. He tried to describe the criminal conspiracy as clearly as he could. "We think it's most likely that Gilman, or another doctor, tipped Martoma," he said. It was famously difficult to build an insider trading case on circumstantial evidence alone, but every new document that came in supported the narrative that was emerging. Riely felt in his bones that this was going to be a huge case.

To everyone in the room, the link seemed obvious: There was a major drug announcement that caused a stock to plunge; that announcement was made by a doctor who had access to the information well in advance; that doctor had been paid a fortune to consult with a trader at SAC, who was paid a fortune by Cohen, who made millions of dollars trading the stock the week before the news came out. It was like Occam's razor, or the law of parsimony: Among competing hypotheses, the simplest one was usually correct. Any other explanation defied common sense.

"Guys," Wadhwa said to the prosecutors. "This is a really important case. If you don't start doing something, we'll have to go forward alone." He couldn't have cared less about Martoma personally, he added. The big catch here was Cohen.

"You're right," said the head of the securities unit. "We need to move on this."

Kang had to leave the meeting early, but he had heard enough to be convinced about Elan. He had developed a skeptical view of what was happening on Wall Street, to put it mildly. He'd heard over and over from his cooperators and sources that cheating was rampant. When the incentives were so huge and you had so many funds competing to the death—

all of them with the same Wharton-trained wizards on staff, the same state-of-the-art technology systems, the same expert network consultants, the same greed and determination—how else could you rise above everyone else and beat the market year after year? In the Galleon case, they had charged Raj Rajaratnam and a few others over eleven trades and alleged a $64 million illegal profit. With Elan and Wyeth, the profit was four times as large.

The FBI finally had a live lead, Gilman, who was ready for an approach.

When Kang got back to his office, he plugged Martoma's Social Security number into the FBI's database. It turned out that Mathew Martoma had a particular status called "known to the Bureau." He had apparently been interviewed by an FBI agent in 2000 as a potential witness in connection with a separate fraud investigation.

Something else showed up, too: Martoma was not his real name. In the early part of his life, he was known as Ajai Thomas. That was the name that appeared on the old FBI notes from the previous case. It struck Kang as strange.

Even more intriguing, there was a reference in the old interview notes to Martoma having to leave Harvard Law School abruptly. Kang immediately shared it with the prosecutors, Devlin-Brown and Weitzman. They had both gone to Harvard Law School, too. They were apparently there at the same time as Martoma. The prosecutors made a note to look into it.

Kang's first priority was Dr. Gilman, who seemed like he had a lot to gain by cooperating. Kang chose the week before Labor Day for the approach. Gilman looked like an easy target, a distinguished older gentleman who would never want to contemplate losing his job and spending what was left of his life in jail.

Around 5 P.M. on August 31, 2011, Kang and a partner drove to Gilman's house, which was located on a residential cul-de-sac in Ann Arbor not too far from the University of Michigan. They parked just down the street and knocked on the door. Gilman's wife answered. After the agents identified themselves, she explained that her husband was at the hospital, doing his rounds. "He should be back later this evening," she said. She looked extremely nervous. The agents waited for about an hour and then left.

The next morning, the FBI agents came back and waited until Gilman left the house. They followed him on his drive to the hospital, pulling up alongside him as he parked his car. Kang hopped out and tapped on the window.

"Dr. Gilman, can we speak with you?" he said.

"Yes, of course," Gilman replied. Kang suggested that they go inside and find a quiet place to talk.

"We're here to talk to you about insider trading," Kang said once they sat down. "Did you disclose confidential information to Mathew Martoma?"

Gilman was not the first person to become panic-stricken when confronted by armed federal agents and to start behaving irrationally. Although it had been three years since his last contact with Martoma and he had forgotten many of the details, Gilman knew that he had broken the law. He had spent the time since his last contact with Martoma, in fact, trying to forget the whole Elan thing had happened. He also knew that lying to the agents was likely to make matters worse. This was, of course, what the FBI *wanted* to happen: Once someone lied, the FBI had a hook in them for a perjury case.

Gilman pushed reason aside and lied anyway.

"I don't know what you're talking about," he told Kang.

"We have you on tape giving Martoma inside information," Kang said, looking hard at Gilman. He let a few seconds pass, until the silence became uncomfortable. Kang was saying something that wasn't true. There was no wiretap. But Kang's philosophy was "Whatever it takes."

Gilman kept shaking his head.

"We know you told Martoma about the bapineuzumab trial," Kang said. "We have everything on tape." There was no point in fighting, he insisted. You have too much to lose—your reputation, your professorship, your research grants.

Gilman kept denying it and denying it until, finally, he said: "If you really believe that I shared confidential information and you have tapes of my calls, then it's likely I did it, but I didn't mean to." He paused. "I don't remember what I told him, exactly. It was three years ago."

Kang continued with his usual line of persuasion, telling Gilman it would be a shame to throw his career away by refusing to help them and help himself. Especially when he was an insignificant player in the entire scheme.

Then Kang stared directly at him. "Dr. Gilman, you are only a grain of sand," he said. "So is Martoma. The person we're really after is Steven Cohen."

Flying Pond is a magnificent tree-lined lake just north of Augusta, Maine, and Charles Riely retreated there for a vacation during the last week of August. As the SEC attorney prepared to go out for a long run through the woods, bending down to tie his shoes, he imagined, for the twentieth time that day, that he could hear the faint trill of his cellphone. Even though the biggest case of his career was about to move into a new, crucial phase, Riely didn't dare suggest not going on the trip to his wife. He was distracted, though, and spent most of the week trying to find a cell signal so that he could check his voicemail for an update on the approach of Gilman. He was dying to know whether Gilman flipped. Finally, Riely got the call.

"It went pretty well," Kang told him, trying to put the most positive spin possible on the situation. They both knew from experience that people rarely start sharing everything they know at the first meeting, so Gilman's refusal to answer questions wasn't necessarily a rejection. There had been a bit of hope. Gilman had said he "might have" done it, Kang repeated. Getting someone to flip was like training for a long-distance run. You had to build up to it.

Now that Gilman had been approached, the investigation was no longer a secret, and the SEC was free to start sending subpoenas for his personal and professional data. His calendars, his files from the University of Michigan, everything on his laptop. They were able to go back to Elan with more specific details about what they were looking for, including anything relating to Gilman's role in the bapi trial. They could see from the phone records that Martoma and Gilman had often talked for over an hour at a time.

"I don't think I've ever had a conversation that lasted that long in my life," Kang said to Riely at one point. "Can you imagine sitting on the phone for an hour and twenty minutes?"

After the approach by Kang, Gilman had agreed, at least in principle, to cooperate. But it was far from clear that he was actually prepared to go ahead with it. Not remembering anything didn't count as helping the government to the best of his ability.

After dragging the discussion out for months, citing his client's hectic conference schedule, Gilman's lawyer finally agreed that he would come in to speak with the SEC and the prosecutors to see how he could help them. Even then, the lawyer made it clear, he wasn't going to make things easy for the government. His client held the key to an enormous case, and everyone knew it. He had plenty of leverage to cut a good deal.

Gilman had hired Marc Mukasey to represent him. Mukasey was a former prosecutor in the Southern District securities unit, and an SEC lawyer before that, who was now a partner at Bracewell and Giuliani. He was also the son of Michael Mukasey, who was a former federal judge who had served as attorney general under President George W. Bush, a fact that his son reminded people of at every opportunity. Mukasey quickly distinguished himself as someone who was going to be difficult. He employed the full arsenal of defensive tactics. He occasionally yelled. He cited Gilman's age as an excuse. "My client wants to do the right thing, but he's an old man who is sick and very busy," Mukasey said when the prosecutors pushed to schedule a meeting. "I'll check and get back to you."

As the SEC was still trying to pin down a meeting time with Gilman, Riely made a startling discovery while looking through a batch of phone records: Martoma had apparently placed a twenty-minute call to Cohen's home phone on the morning of Sunday, July 20, 2008, at 9:45 A.M. It was an odd time for a work conversation. The following morning, Monday, trading records showed that SAC started liquidating its Elan and Wyeth shares, a nearly $1 billion investment. Martoma had to have told Cohen why they should reverse course and sell all their stock.

"Holy crap," Riely thought as he walked through the implications of this new discovery. Now it seemed like they might have a case against Steve Cohen, too.

After he was branded a "one-trick pony" and fired from his job at SAC, Mathew Martoma had moved with his wife and kids to Florida. Ostensibly, it was to be closer to their parents. But Florida also had generous tax shelter laws, allowing residents to shield their primary residences and other assets from bankruptcy and other kinds of judgments.

The Martomas bought a five-bedroom, $1.9 million house at the Royal Palm Yacht and Country Club in Boca Raton. It was an ornate, Spanish-style mansion featuring an elevator, marble surfaces, and miles of heavy drapery. Out back was a swimming pool in the shape of a clover. Neither Martoma nor his wife was working, so they dedicated themselves to competitive parenting: Managing young Joshua, Ava, and David's golf lessons, spelling bees, Mandarin tutoring, and private school education was a full-time occupation. They liked the idea of becoming philanthropists and placed $1 million into the Mathew and Rosemary Martoma Foundation, which gave them a generous tax deduction.

On the evening of November 8, 2011, Martoma and his wife came home to find B. J. Kang and his partner, Matthew Callahan, waiting in front of their house.

"I'm Special Agent Kang, from the FBI," Kang said. He introduced Callahan. Then he said: "Your former business partner, Stephen Chan, is about to get out of jail." Recognition flickered across Martoma's face. "I'd like to talk to you about it."

Kang had thought carefully about his first line. He wanted Martoma to know that he had done his research. By this point, he knew everything about Martoma and his life, things his wife probably wasn't even aware of. The opening line was about communicating the seriousness of the situation, that they weren't just there to see what they could find out and then go home.

Rosemary's eyes were wide as the moon. She remembered that their children were in the house, probably wondering what was going on. She said she would be right back and went inside to check on them.

As soon as she was gone, Kang turned back to Martoma.

"Listen," he said. "We aren't here because we want to talk about Chan. We are here to talk about insider trading while you were at SAC." He paused and watched the color drain from Martoma's face. "We want to talk about Elan and July 2008."

Right there in his own driveway, Martoma fainted.

CHAPTER 11

UNDEFEATABLE

Like many people who immigrate to America from faraway places, Mathew Martoma's parents dreamed of what their children might eventually achieve there. They had especially high expectations for their firstborn son, whom they named Ajai Mathew Mariamdani Thomas. Martoma's mother, Lizzie Thomas, was a twenty-six-year-old medical resident in Michigan when he was born, in 1974. Both she and Martoma's father, Bobby Martoma, were Christians from Kerala, located in India's tropical south. Bobby emigrated in 1964 at age nineteen to study mechanical engineering in the United States; after graduating from Howard University, he took a job as an engineer with the Ford Motor Company in Michigan. When Martoma was a toddler, the family moved to Florida.

Bobby fantasized that a child of his might one day attend Harvard. The family was active in their church in Coral Springs, and Bobby prayed for Harvard every day. His son's grades in school were a subject of intense interest. Martoma was enrolled in gifted classes at the Christian elementary school he attended and went on to graduate as the co-valedictorian of his class at Merritt Island High School, in Rockledge, Florida. Still, Mathew's performance wasn't enough to get him into Harvard, and his father was furious at his son. His anger drove him to a stunning act of paternal cruelty. A few weeks after Mathew's eighteenth birthday, he presented his son with a plaque that said: "Son Who Shattered His Father's Dream."

Martoma ended up going to Duke, where he majored in biology and spent his free time engaged in résumé-bolstering extracurricular activities. He volunteered with Alzheimer's patients and lived in a community-service-oriented dormitory. He went by his given name, Ajai Mathew Thomas, although people called him "Mat."

At every step of his academic career, Martoma proved skilled at cultivating mentors, particularly male ones, who served as surrogate father figures. One of his professors, Bruce Payne, who taught a course on ethics and policy-making, recalled Martoma as eager and hardworking, someone who stood out because he dressed more formally than the other students, as if he might at any moment be called up for a job interview. "What was interesting about Mat was that he was actually more interested in the field of ethics than most of my students," Payne recalled. "Mat got a handle on the class pretty quickly, and understood how to do the kind of analysis that I was looking for and hoping for." Early in the semester, Martoma campaigned to be made head teaching assistant for the class, and Payne agreed.

Martoma spent the year after graduation at the National Institutes of Health, in Bethesda, Maryland, working on the National Genome Project. "He was ambitious, he wanted to make something of his life," said Ronald Green, a Dartmouth professor who supervised Martoma during his year at NIH. "To some extent, I felt like Mathew was an adopted son."

While he was at NIH, Martoma applied to law school. When a thick envelope arrived from Harvard Law School bearing the news that he had been accepted, Martoma's father was ecstatic. In the fall of 1997, Bobby drove Mathew from Florida to Massachusetts in a U-Haul to get him moved in. In many ways, Martoma was a typical Harvard Law student—which is to say, someone who did very little in the way of relaxation, and spent his time almost exclusively on activities that would enhance his curriculum vitae. He tried to make the most of his time there, co-founding a campus group called the Society of Law and Ethics and serving as an editor of an on-campus law journal.

During his second year, though, Martoma began struggling with his coursework. This was due in part to his heavy load of extracurricular activities, something his father had warned him about. His grades started to go down. In the late fall, his classmates began applying for prestigious summer clerkships, a common rite for the most ambitious students, but Martoma's grades weren't quite what he'd hoped. The students with straight As, he knew, would take all the coveted slots.

He was determined to get a clerkship anyway, which led him to a fateful decision. Martoma's academic performance wasn't good enough—so he would *make* it good enough. He spent an afternoon in December meticulously altering the grades on his transcript in his Civil Procedure, Contracts, and Criminal Law classes, changing them to As from the B, B+, and B he'd actually received. Then he sent applications off to twenty-three judges.

That January he was invited to interview with three judges on the Washington, D.C., Circuit Court of Appeals. Second only to the Supreme Court in stature, it plays a crucial role in shaping legislation and rulings on the reach of the federal government. The judges had already received his transcript and had been impressed. In person, they were struck by Martoma's handsome appearance, his deference, and, of course, his dazzling academic record. Two of the three rated him as an "excellent" candidate. One of the judges called Martoma on the night of February 2, 1999, to offer him a clerkship. It was late, and a bleary-sounding Martoma answered the phone. He seemed so disoriented that the judge suggested that Martoma call him back the following day. When Martoma failed to return the call, the judge's clerk tried to reach him and left a message asking that Martoma call the judge back. The clerk tried again, on February 4, and left another message.

Unbeknownst to the judge, during the few days between the interviews and phone calls, the foundation that upheld Martoma's world had started to crumble.

A clerk working for one of the judges had noticed something suspicious about Martoma's transcript and had placed a call to the school. On the afternoon of February 2, Martoma was summoned to see Registrar Stephen Kane.

As he walked to Kane's office at the edge of campus, Martoma wasn't sure why he had been called in for the meeting. But he had an awful feeling.

The year before, Kane had expelled a Harvard Law student who had submitted faked transcripts in order to gain admission, and he was prepared to do the same with Martoma. Kane didn't waste time with casual conversation and asked Martoma directly if he had doctored his transcript. Martoma went into shock. His future, his father's pride, the years of sacrifice and hard work—he felt it all slipping away. He made desperate attempts to explain, insisting that his application was just a joke and that he didn't really intend to pursue a clerkship.

"I already sent withdrawal letters to the judges," he said, implausibly. Kane gave him a look that said, *You have got to be kidding me.*

Martoma left determined to undo the damage. There had to be a way out of this. He came up with a plan, but it wasn't a good one.

That night, Martoma sat down at his computer and tried to construct an electronic paper trail that would bolster the defense he had offered to Kane, that his clerkship applications weren't serious and had already been retracted.

"Please don't mail out any recommendations on my behalf as I am no longer looking for a clerkship," he wrote to the secretary of one of his professors who was sending out recommendation letters on his behalf. Martoma sent letters to all of the judges he'd applied to, attempting to retroactively withdraw his clerkship applications. The letters were all dated January 31, though they were postmarked February 3, the day after Kane confronted him over his transcript.

Kane and the dean of students were sure that Martoma was lying, but expulsion was a serious matter at Harvard—the nuclear option, as it were. So they gave Martoma the benefit of the doubt and took their time with the investigation.

For three months, Kane conducted a full autopsy of what had occurred. He made phone calls and examined documents. The law school's administrative board launched a formal investigation and collected email records. In April and May, the board held four days of hearings, during which Martoma, his parents, and his younger brother all testified.

The Martomas all told the same fantastical story: Martoma had created the fake transcript expressly for the purpose of showing it to his parents, who expected him to achieve near-perfect grades. However, he told the board, a few days later he realized that what he had done was wrong, and he gave his parents his real, unaltered transcript. In the confusion surrounding these events, he left the doctored transcript lying on his desk in his parents' house and then hopped on a flight to California for an "impromptu" job interview. While he was away, he asked his brother to help finish his clerkship applications for him. His brother had allegedly taken the doctored transcript and included it with the applications, against Martoma's intentions, and put everything into envelopes Martoma had already prepared. His mother then mailed them off without looking at them.

Most members of the board had a hard time believing the story. The whole thing struck them as preposterous. Each element was riddled with implausibilities: Changing the grades to impress his parents, spontaneously deciding to come clean with them, leaving the doctored transcript lying around, entrusting his younger brother with the task of assembling the applications. It was one huge "dog ate my homework" excuse.

Martoma also held firm to his defense regarding the timing of the emails and letters he'd sent withdrawing his clerkship applications. He was adamant that he had composed the email to the professor's secretary, withdrawing his application, the day *before* Kane had confronted him, on February 1, but that it inexplicably hadn't been transmitted until the following night, *after* Kane confronted him. He presented emails with the earlier date on them, even though the recipients' emails indicated that they'd been received the following day. A computer forensics expert who had been scheduled to appear on Martoma's behalf backed out, saying that "he did not feel that he was in a position to authenticate Mathew's version of the events."

Throughout the process, the board members found Martoma to be evasive and unforthcoming. He was acting guilty.

Some board members were conflicted, because of the great promise Martoma had shown as a student. His academic record was outstanding, and he was heavily involved in law school community activities. But the administrative board concluded that Martoma had presented a cascading series of lies in an attempt to cover his original deception, and on May 12, 1999, they voted to expel him. In its final report, using Martoma's original last name, the board noted: "Mr. Thomas was apparently under extreme parental pressure to excel academically."

Expulsion did not put an end to Martoma's Harvard experience. He moved off campus and began plotting ways to get himself reinstated. By his analysis, it all came down to the timing of the emails. If he could convince the law school board that he had withdrawn his clerkship applications before being caught, he would be readmitted and get his life back on course. A light clicked on in his mind: He would create a company to authenticate the disputed dates on the emails.

The scheme seemed brilliant. It would both exonerate him at Harvard and plant the seeds of a new startup company that would ultimately make him rich, too. He would be vindicated on two fronts. He told his parents about his plan, and they agreed to help him. His father took out a second mortgage on their house and lent him a million dollars to launch the company. Martoma was hardly a computer expert, so he had to find someone with technical skills to help him. He quickly settled on the perfect candidate, a talented young programmer named Stephen Chan.

Chan had a great-looking résumé. A couple of years older than Martoma, he had graduated from MIT in 1993 and then gone to work for IBM. He and Martoma immediately got along. Both had excelled in school. Both had immigrant parents with high expectations. And both had a propensity to bend rules, a habit that had recently landed them in serious trouble.

On June 30, 1999, Martoma and Chan's new company, Computer Data

Forensics, issued a four-page report filled with techno-gobbledygook that validated the timeline Martoma had presented to the Harvard board regarding the contested dates on the clerkship emails. "Our conclusion is that the computer data forensics evidence corroborates Mr. Thomas' assertion that he created the withdrawal letters on January 31, 1999 and sent the subject e-mail . . . at 10:20 PM the night of Monday, February 1, 1999," the report read.

It was signed by three "Case Analysts," notarized and stamped, and mailed off to the Harvard Law School Administrative Board in Cambridge. There was, of course, no mention of the fact that the forensic analysis had been done by Martoma's own company. Martoma also took a polygraph test, which he allegedly passed. He sent those results to Harvard as well, and waited to hear back.

He eagerly anticipated his vindication, but it never came. The law school declined to reinstate him.

Martoma quickly reoriented his ambition and resolved to try to make a success of his and Chan's new company. He moved into the apartment complex where Chan lived. They worked out together, took martial arts training five or six days a week, and enrolled in ballroom lessons at the local Arthur Murray Dance Studio, with the aim of impressing women. In September, Martoma asked Chan to sign on as a full partner with the company and promised to pay him $25,000. Four full-time employees were hired in New York—a project manager, an engineer, a quality control specialist, and an administrator. The employees all believed Martoma was a lawyer named "Jay Hale."

The staff began making preparations for a booth at an upcoming trade show in Las Vegas, but as October came and went, Chan started to wonder about his partner's background. Martoma had kept details about himself vague and had a habit of deflecting questions. Chan started to get suspicious and wondered whether Martoma was hiding something. He poked around on his own and eventually confronted Martoma about the circumstances of his departure from Harvard and the fact that he had been misrepresenting himself on various company applications and leases with a fake name. Martoma broke down and apologized. He promised never to deceive Chan again. He acknowledged that he had doctored his Harvard transcripts and had lied to cover it up.

While Chan and Martoma bickered, their employees hung around the office surfing the Internet and going out to lunch. "We were like rent-a-friends," Chuck Clarke, the firm's "Case Analyst and Project Manager," later said. He and the other employees figured that "Hale" and Chan were rich kids who didn't have anything better to do. The company burned through most of the million dollars Martoma's father had provided in a matter of months, at which point Bobby flew to New York to meet with Chan and Martoma and talk about the business. They asked him for more money to keep the venture going, but Martoma's father could see that it wasn't working. He felt his temper rising. He told his son that he was a "complete liability."

In mid-December, when he should have been halfway through his second year of law school, Martoma boarded a flight and flew back to his parents' house in Florida. His employees were locked out of the office; their paychecks bounced. The aggrieved employees collaborated on a letter to Martoma's parents. "His disappearance is unprofessional and bizarre," they wrote. "The fact that his family is hiding him is incomprehensible and disgraceful. We are owed expense reimbursements. We are owed stock. We are owed bonuses. We are owed commissions." They threatened legal action if they didn't receive a satisfactory response. "You have caused us to have an unpleasant Christmas holiday," they concluded. "If this is the way you treat people, we intend to reciprocate one hundred fold worse."

While their employees were revolting, the relationship between Martoma and Chan continued to deteriorate, and on January 3, 2000, Martoma filed for a restraining order against Chan. Their heated arguments, he said, had become violent. Chan also, allegedly, called Martoma a "faggot" and "not a man." Martoma portrayed himself as a battered spouse and said that his parents had intervened to "remove Plaintiff from his relationship with Defendant" after observing the bruises all over his body. Chan refuted these accusations, but the restraining order was granted.

It turned out that Chan had more serious problems than his breakup with Martoma to deal with. A few months before they met, Chan and six partners had been charged with fraud, for allegedly setting up a sham data storage company that stole millions of dollars from various banks. By the time Chan pleaded guilty to one count of conspiracy and one count of mail fraud in the case, Martoma was about to embark on a new life. He had come up with a plan to reinvent himself as a financier.

In 2000, Stanford University's MBA program was vying with Harvard's for the top business-school ranking in the country and was a favorite recruiting ground for Wall Street banks, consulting firms, and the burgeoning technology giants of Silicon Valley. Martoma had decided to go into finance, and getting an MBA was a crucial first step. Harvard was out of the question, for obvious reasons, so he set his sights on Stanford. The program had a 7 percent admission rate.

Martoma began the process of contacting his old mentors and college professors, asking for letters of recommendation. He wrote to his ethics professor from Duke, Bruce Payne, and asked if he would write a letter on his behalf. Payne had always been fond of Martoma and felt that he was one of the brightest students he'd ever had. He was happy to help.

Payne had already written recommendations for Martoma on two occasions. The first instance was when Martoma applied for a position as a genetics research fellow at the National Institutes of Health, in 1995, the year he graduated from Duke. In that letter, Payne wrote admiringly of Martoma's scholarship and his passion for ethics, and said: "Mathew would be an asset in any program that suited his talents and interests." A few months after that, in September, Martoma had asked for another letter, this time for his application to Harvard Law School. Payne pulled the first letter up and changed a few of the details. He had always thought that Martoma would make a superb law student, and he said so.

Since then, Payne hadn't heard much from Martoma. He assumed that he had finished law school and was working at a prestigious firm somewhere. So when the new request came, in the fall of 2000, for a business school letter, Payne was confused. He asked Martoma to let him know what he'd been doing since he had applied to law school five years earlier, so that he might freshen up the letter. Payne briefly wondered why Martoma would be asking him, rather than some of his law school professors from Harvard, but he brushed the question aside.

Martoma did what came naturally to him: He concocted a story. He said that he had left NIH to start his own business in New York providing biotech companies with corporate infrastructure and 3D computer modeling software. The dotcom boom was under way, and students were dropping out of school to launch startups every day, so it didn't seem all that unusual. Things had been going great, Martoma told Payne, but then he had had to put his business on hold to move back to Florida to help one of his relatives deal with a health crisis. He did not mention Harvard Law School.

Payne took him at his word and updated the letter, writing about how selfless Martoma was to put his own professional goals aside to return home to support his family and what a serious, earnest student he had been.

The following fall, Martoma arrived at Stanford's campus south of San Francisco, ready to begin business school. Just days before, he had legally changed his name from Ajai Mathew Mariamdani Thomas to Mathew Martoma. His transformation was complete. Harvard, Chan: It was all behind him. By the time he arrived at Steve Cohen's office at SAC five years later, he had learned that there was no problem he couldn't overcome if he put his mind to it.

Standing outside Martoma's Boca Raton house in November 2011, B. J. Kang bent down to make sure that Martoma was okay. He thought about the times in the past when a suspect he approached had fainted. It had happened before. The one notion that kept coming to mind was that an innocent person was unlikely to pass out after hearing the words *insider trading*.

Just then Rosemary came rushing out of the house, dark hair flying. When she saw her husband on the ground, she screamed.

"Would you like us to call an ambulance?" Kang asked.

"No!" Rosemary sobbed. "I'm a doctor." She crouched down.

A few minutes later a woozy Martoma pulled himself up off the ground, and Kang continued with what he had to say. "We know about the trade in 2008," he said.

Martoma and Rosemary looked at each other. They understood immediately what Kang was referring to: Elan, the stock that had changed their lives.

"Your whole life is going to be turned upside down," Kang went on. He said that he knew Martoma had been involved in insider trading, and then launched into his well-practiced pitch about doing what was right at the darkest time of his life by cooperating. Besides, Kang said, they weren't really even after Martoma. They knew he was a small, almost insignificant, figure.

"We want Steve Cohen," Kang said. "You're in a tough situation, but I'm going to do everything I can to help you out. We are going to do this together. It's going to be teamwork."

Kang had done more of these approaches than he could count, and most had been successful. He understood the psychology of this situation, how it affected every part of a person's life, his family, his children, how it put every bit of security he might have had in doubt. Kang viewed every new cooperator as a partner, someone he would prop up through serious challenges to their mental well-being while they helped the FBI.

Rosemary was shaking. Martoma said that he wanted to be helpful but needed to consult with a lawyer. Kang left feeling confident that they would be working together.

Around 10 P.M., Kang's partner, Matt Callahan, called Charles Riely, who was at home waiting for news.

"You're not going to believe this," Callahan said. "The guy fainted."

By the end of 2011, after five years of issuing subpoenas, flipping cooperators, and wiretapping traders, the Justice Department finally had some tangible victories to show for its investigation of the hedge fund industry. Raj Rajaratnam had been sentenced to eleven years in federal prison. Dozens of other traders and executives had been convicted or pleaded guilty. In spite of all that had been accomplished, though, there was still a sense of frustration among the FBI agents and prosecutors. And that was because they still hadn't been able to get close to Cohen.

The case against Jonathan Hollander, the CR Intrinsic analyst Dave Makol tried to flip in a Manhattan Whole Foods in January 2009, had not gone forward in the end, much to Makol's irritation. Hollander had been smart about things. He didn't take SAC up on its offer of paying for his legal representation, because it struck him as a troubling conflict of interest. Instead, he hired Aitan Goelman, a white collar defense lawyer at Zuckerman Spaeder and one of the best in the business. When it came to dealing with the FBI, he wanted someone who knew exactly who he was working for.

Hollander certainly had the impression that all sorts of inappropriate stuff was going on at SAC. It seemed obvious to him that Cohen was using inside information. But since he wasn't directly involved in it, he didn't know the specifics. He met with Makol and the prosecutor Reed Brodsky and told them about a few trades he was aware of that had seemed suspicious. Elan, for one. The word inside SAC was that Cohen had "gotten a call," and then the firm had gone from being massively long to massively short Elan and had made hundreds of millions of dollars. Everyone on the trading desk was talking about it afterward. Beyond that, though, no one knew what had happened.

Hollander's career at SAC ended ingloriously. At the end of the summer of 2008, Jason Karp took his whole group for a weekend in Montauk, a surf town at the eastern tip of Long Island. They stayed in a motel together and went deep-sea fishing. Karp shared his plans for the next phase of their careers at SAC. A year earlier, Karp told them, Cohen had promised to spin off Karp's group, giving them their own capital and separate offices. Karp was done with being part of the high-pressure environment at SAC and expected to have near-total autonomy under the new arrangement. His enthusiasm was inspiring, and Hollander started to feel excited about the idea. Less than three months later, though, in the throes of the financial crisis, Cohen reneged on all the promises he'd made. Hollander and Karp were pushed out.

Even though Hollander was angry about the way he had been treated and had no sense of loyalty to Cohen or Karp or anyone else at SAC, he looked at the risk/reward ratio of the situation with Makol, just as he would with a stock trade. The government didn't seem to have enough evidence to force him to do anything he didn't want to do, so why should he cooperate with the FBI?

While the Hollander case was fizzling out, the other investigations leading toward Cohen appeared to be losing momentum as well. Donald Longueuil, the former SAC trader who destroyed his computer hard drives and scattered them in the backs of New York City garbage trucks, had pleaded guilty to securities fraud, along with his friend Samir Barai, the fund manager who had ordered his analyst to shred all their company's files. Neither of them had much information that was of use to the FBI in terms of advancing the investigation. The U.S. Attorney's Office and the SEC were preparing to charge two traders at the hedge funds the FBI raided in 2010 with insider trading: Anthony Chiasson, a portfolio manager at Level Global, and Todd Newman, from Diamondback Capital. But even though both of their funds were filled with former SAC employees, not much evidence implicating Cohen was turning up, and Chiasson and Newman were showing no signs of cooperating. Quite the opposite. They hired some of the top defense lawyers in the country and were fighting vigorously.

In the course of investigating Chiasson and Newman, however, the SEC had made a startling discovery. After going through two million pages of emails, investigators noticed that Jesse Tortora, an analyst who worked for Todd Newman at Diamondback, was emailing details about different companies' earnings to someone named Jon Horvath at SAC Capital. The SEC investigators, Joseph Sansone, Daniel Marcus, and Matthew Watkins, sent subpoenas requesting Horvath's emails. One email immediately stood out among the hundreds they got back. It was about Dell.

"I have a 2nd hand read from someone at the company—this is 3rd quarter I have gotten this read from them and it has been very good in the last two quarters. They say GMs [gross margins] miss by 50-80 bps [basis points] due to poor mix, opex in-line and a little revenue upside netting out to an EPS miss." The message continued: "Please keep to yourself as obviously not well known."

On August 26, 2008, around 1 P.M., Horvath had sent the email to Michael Steinberg, to whom he reported at SAC, and to another SAC portfolio manager named Gabriel Plotkin. It was the kind of analyst jargon that Wall Street folks used to describe companies' financial performance all the time. To an average person, it likely would have been incomprehensible. But the SEC knew what it meant. It was conveying detailed, confidential earnings information about Dell.

The SEC lawyers were intrigued. They began to wonder which other traders at SAC might have received this information.

Horvath sent the message two days before Dell released its second-quarter earnings. It appeared that Steinberg had then turned around and made $1 million shorting 150,000 shares of Dell right before the earnings announcement. All the government needed was for Horvath to flip and they would have a case against Steinberg as well. And a case against Steinberg would bring them one step closer to Cohen.

It could, after three years, put them in the inner circle of Cohen's company. A floppy-haired, low-level functionary at SAC named Jon Horvath whom they'd scarcely noticed before was about to reignite their case.

CHAPTER 12

THE WHALE

Sid Gilman bent over the security table in the lobby of the World Financial Center in lower Manhattan and emptied the contents of his pockets into a plastic dish so they could be sent through an X-ray machine. His lawyer led him through the turnstiles, into an elevator, and up to the fourth-floor conference room at the SEC's New York regional headquarters. After months of delays, Gilman was appearing for his first meeting with the government attorneys working on the Martoma case.

Throughout the fall, Charles Riely had constructed a detailed chronology of everything that had gone on before and after the Elan and Wyeth trades. Each time he got a new piece of information, he put it into the "chron" and then emailed it around to everyone involved in the investigation. The documents, on their own, told a logical story. But even as Riely and his colleagues were increasingly sure that they understood the events that led to SAC's sales of Elan and Wyeth, the government lawyers were still eager to hear from Gilman himself. It would be their first opportunity to question the only person, aside from Martoma and Cohen, who knew what had really happened in July 2008.

After months of hearing from Gilman's lawyer that his client, who was nearly eighty, wasn't physically strong enough to testify, the SEC lawyers expected a sickly, skeletal figure to stagger through the door. Instead, Gilman walked in looking alert in his suit and tie, his cheeks pink, his dark eyes bright. He eased himself into a seat with his back toward the windows and sat upright.

Riely asked about Gilman's work on bapineuzumab and how he had gotten to know Martoma. Riely then started sliding documents across the table one by one—copies of emails and calendar entries and agreements with the drug companies—and asked Gilman about each one. If Gilman claimed not to remember something, Riely would pull a sheet of paper out of his folder and show it to him to see whether it loosened his memory.

Almost from the beginning, it seemed like Gilman was being evasive.

"What about this calendar entry?" Riely asked, pointing to an appointment in Gilman's electronic calendar from July 13, 2008, which read: "Mat Martoma will call me re SAEs in bap." Riely knew from the phone records that Gilman and Martoma had spoken that evening for almost two hours.

"What are 'SAE's in bap'?" Riely asked.

Gilman slipped into avuncular professor mode, launching into a detailed explanation of Alzheimer's disease and the challenges and prospects of finding an effective treatment. He brightened up as he described the optimism he had had about bapi's potential for destroying beta amyloid in the brain, which he believed was a primary cause of cognitive degeneration. Then he finally got around to answering the question. "Serious adverse events" was the technical phrase for side effects observed during the bapi trial.

"Why would you be talking to Martoma about that?" Riely asked. "Wouldn't details about the SAE's be nonpublic information?"

"I don't know why that's in there," Gilman mumbled, his face suddenly darkening.

"Look," his lawyer interjected, "he doesn't know anything."

When Gilman was asked to explain a scientific concept or the aims of his medical research, he became animated. His memory was excellent.

He was able to summon the byzantine details of the chemistry of the different drugs on request. But if someone mentioned Martoma's name or asked about Gilman's relationship with him, he suddenly morphed into a confused old man who barely knew how to tie his own shoes.

Avi Weitzman, one of the prosecutors sitting in on the meeting, couldn't believe what he was seeing. There were huge inconsistencies in Gilman's story, which was essentially that he didn't remember a thing he had ever said to Mathew Martoma, even when there was documentary evidence right in front of him showing that he had shared inside information about bapi. How could Gilman remember so much about his research but nothing about his dealings with Martoma?

The temperature in the room seemed to get warmer as they went back and forth over the same few documents, with the SEC lawyers and the prosecutors repeating the same questions and Gilman saying he didn't know or couldn't remember. It went on like this for two hours. The government had been waiting for five months to question Gilman and had so many blind spots they expected him to illuminate. Instead, it seemed to them that Gilman was wasting their time. Riely felt like he was going to explode.

He asked Gilman again about the consultation he had had with Martoma on July 13, 2008, during which Riely was fairly certain they had discussed bapi. "What was that meeting about?" he asked.

"Oh, we were talking about Parkinson's disease," Gilman said.

Riely sighed. He asked to take a break and summoned his colleagues out into the hallway. "Look," he told them. "That thing about Parkinson's—I know it isn't true."

"How do you know that?" Weitzman asked.

Riely flipped through his files and pulled out one of Gilman's calendar entries, the one for the particular consultation they were asking about. It read: "Mat Martoma will call me re SAEs in bap." Riely then produced a corresponding email between Martoma and Gerson Lehrman Group, the expert network that had arranged the consultation. In it, Martoma said that he and Gilman would be talking about Parkinson's disease. GLG's own rules prohibited Gilman from talking about the bapi trial to the company's clients because it might violate confidentiality rules. Gilman and Martoma had evidently misled GLG about what they were planning to talk about.

Weitzman felt a wave of gratitude for Riely's thoroughness. His somewhat stiff counterpart at the SEC had just handed them the weapon they needed to prove that Gilman was lying to their faces. They would confront him with it, and he would have to fold. Weitzman grabbed the calendar entry and the email and strode back into the room.

"Look, Dr. Gilman," Weitzman said, leaning across the table. "We know you're not telling the truth. You are risking jail if you stick to this story."

Gilman shook his head as Weitzman pushed the two sheets of paper across the table, one showing his calendar entry, the other showing Martoma's communication with GLG.

Gilman's lawyer, Marc Mukasey, quickly recognized what was happening and interrupted. "Can we take a break?" he asked.

The government lawyers left the room again so Mukasey could talk with his client in private. Weitzman was sure that this was it: Gilman was about to confess everything.

A few minutes later, Mukasey joined them in the hallway. He had a slight look of surrender on his face. "Listen," he said. "You're welcome to continue this line of questioning. I understand why you think it looks bad. But he just doesn't remember it the way those documents portray it."

"Marc, that is just not credible," Weitzman said.

"You can continue asking him. I promise to keep working with him too," Mukasey said. "But he insists he doesn't remember it the way it looks."

The interview continued for two more hours, during which Gilman refused to budge, saying over and over that he didn't remember what had happened and insisting that the government was wrong. It was one of the most frustrating interviews Weitzman had ever participated in. As he walked back to the U.S. Attorney's Office afterward, Weitzman felt sure that the Elan case was dead.

Charles Riely and his SEC colleagues didn't have much time to feel bad about how poorly things had gone with Gilman because Martoma was coming in for a deposition the next morning. They had to put Gilman behind them and prepare.

Like Gilman's lawyer, Martoma's defense attorney, Charles Stillman, was in a difficult position. He was trying to gauge the intentions of the criminal prosecutors and the SEC and maximize his bargaining position with each of them. If there was a criminal case coming together that could send Martoma to jail, Stillman had to focus on that and be as defensive as possible. Stillman especially wanted to know whether the government had a wiretap. If they did, it was something like a death sentence. If it was only the SEC Martoma had to worry about, a fine was the worst-case scenario, and they could afford to be a little more helpful. Stillman was a well-known criminal defender; he had been around a long time. He prided himself on his ability to respond to situations like this.

While Stillman tried to test the prosecutors and find out how strong their case was, Avi Weitzman told him that Martoma's chances of getting a good plea deal would only decline the longer he waited to cooperate. It was a race between Martoma and Gilman: Whoever got there first was going to get the best outcome for himself. So far, Stillman had given no indication that Martoma was willing to flip.

The possibility that he might quietly go to jail to protect Cohen was not something the prosecutors had taken seriously. The crime could result in a prison term of *ten years*. Nobody took a sentence like that for someone else—especially not a person who had treated him badly. The FBI had seen countless guys turn on their best friends when the stakes were considerably lower. The longer Martoma held out, the more people involved in the investigation started to wonder if Cohen might be inducing him somehow to stay quiet.

In fact, SAC was covering Martoma's legal costs, no questions asked. It was the policy of the firm to cover the legal expenses of employees and former employees who came under investigation for things they'd done during the course of their employment. Still, it struck the prosecutors as bizarre and unfair: The person advising Martoma on whether he should cooperate against Cohen was being paid by Cohen. What's more, SAC had made it clear that the size of the defense lawyers' bills was of no concern. While some companies won't cover legal expenses without itemized receipts, Stillman's firm simply sent SAC a number each month. Their invoices had never been paid so fast.

Just before 10 A.M. on February 3, 2012, Riely went to the SEC's fourth-floor lobby to meet Martoma and bring him to the conference room. Martoma was waiting by the reception desk with Nathaniel Marmur, a partner of Charles Stillman's. Riely instantly noticed that Martoma wasn't wearing a suit, like most people who came in to meet with the SEC; he wore khaki pants and a tweedy jacket, no tie, like he was headed to a cocktail party.

He was barely through his first question when Martoma read a statement that his lawyers had prepared for him: "On the advice of counsel, I respectfully decline to answer the question at this time based on my right under the United States Constitution not to be a witness against myself." He was taking the Fifth.

The SEC lawyers had seen this tactic many times before, and there were different ways defendants handled it. Often, when Wall Street suspects took the Fifth, they acted hostile and angry the whole time, as if they were offended about having to be there. Martoma was different. He was strangely calm. His face betrayed no hint of emotion.

Riely and his colleagues studied him closely as he repeated the statement in response to each query, dozens of times. They found him impenetrable. If Martoma was innocent, they thought, he would have taken this opportunity to say so. He clearly had something to hide.

With all of their most promising leads running into obstacles, there was only one person left who had the answers the government wanted. The SEC needed to insist that Steve Cohen come in and answer questions.

It was a major decision. Bringing a billionaire in for questioning wasn't something the SEC did every day. It wasn't long ago, in fact, that SEC attorneys were openly discouraged from pestering important people on

Wall Street. The leadership of the SEC had often hinted to the staff that the wealthiest, most successful individuals in the financial world were not to be disturbed. It was part of the former SEC chairman's "hands-off" approach to regulation.

But in 2012, post–Bernie Madoff, the agency was in the midst of a transformation. This time, no one questioned the Elan team's desire to bring Cohen in for a deposition. The new director of enforcement was trying to make it easier for SEC attorneys to do their jobs. On March 12, Riely sent a subpoena requesting that Cohen appear to testify. They all knew it was unlikely that Cohen would say anything that would be helpful to them—it was likely to be one of the most carefully rehearsed and lawyered interviews they had ever done. But they had to try.

The intensifying investigation couldn't have come at a less convenient moment for Cohen. For years he had been interested in buying a professional sports franchise, trying to find a way to become the owner of a major league baseball team. It was something he had dreamed about since he was a kid. He had just spent $20 million to buy a 4 percent stake in the New York Mets, which was meant to be a first step toward full ownership. He had to prove to the governing forces of baseball that he was responsible and reputable enough.

For the previous several months, he had taken time off from running SAC to assemble a bid for the Los Angeles Dodgers, a franchise that had been driven into bankruptcy by a parking lot mogul named Frank McCourt. But with his name now appearing in the newspaper with alarming frequency in connection with the insider trading investigation, Cohen was struggling to gain the confidence of Major League Baseball, which had to approve his bid. In an effort to market himself to the city, he joined the board of the Museum of Contemporary Art, Los Angeles and teamed up with a local entrepreneur to prepare the offer. He thought that having an L.A. businessman by his side would help his case. But Cohen didn't want to be a fool, like other Wall Street moguls before him who had blown exorbitant sums to buy sports teams. He was determined to make the Dodgers work as a business. He submitted a bid of $1.6 billion.

On March 27, 2012, he was on a list of finalists to buy the team that was leaked to the media. He was the only one in the group who didn't need to borrow money for the purchase, which strengthened his position. Cohen felt certain he was going to get it.

Then, the following day, Major League Baseball announced its decision. It had accepted a $2 billion bid from Guggenheim Partners, a multibillion-dollar investment firm that had made its offer with the former Lakers star Magic Johnson, a beloved figure in Los Angeles. One of Guggenheim's most significant investors was Michael Milken. Cohen didn't usually get emotional about his investments, but he was sorely disappointed.

Charles Riely lowered himself into a chair in the SEC's testimony room and stared at the door that Steve Cohen was about to walk through. His folders and files were carefully arranged on the chair next to him. He double-checked that everything was in the right order. He knew Cohen was smooth and experienced; a transcript of a deposition he had given in the Fairfax case a year earlier showed just how naturally Cohen could respond to questions without really answering them. Riely understood that the best possible scenario was that he could catch Cohen in some small contradiction or extract a detail that they could use to put more pressure on Martoma. This was the most important moment in Riely's career. He took a deep breath.

"This is it," Riely thought. "I'm ready."

Cohen had struggled over the decision of whether to testify or take the Fifth in response to the SEC. The calculus for Cohen's legal team was simple: A subpoena from the criminal prosecutors would have been too threatening, so Cohen would have told them to "pound sand" and refused to answer their questions; but the SEC was not pursuing a criminal case, so cooperating was the smarter option. Cohen could spend a day downtown under the guise of trying to be helpful, creating the appearance that he had nothing to hide. He had to try not to lie—if he did so, he would perjure himself, and that could be used against him. But at least he could tell his investors that he was cooperating with the securities regulators, which would reassure them in the face of increasingly negative coverage in the press.

Hedge fund investors, the people whose money Cohen had such a talent for multiplying, were a predictable and self-serving group. Many of them, including university endowments and pension funds managing retirement accounts for public school teachers and police officers, were only too happy to overlook the questionable things hedge funds were doing—as long as they made money. Pension fund managers in particular had enormous, in some cases impossible, financial obligations to fulfill for their retirees, and very few ways of earning the returns they needed. Cohen had made his investors so much money over the years, it was going to take a lot to compel them to leave. And if there was one thing the Bernie Madoff case had shown, it was that even sophisticated investors could fall for the lure of easy money.

Once the government's investigation of SAC reached a certain feverish stage, however, circumstances began to change. Cohen was getting calls from anxious investors seeking an explanation as to why his name was in the newspaper every few days. Wasn't this a distraction? What was he doing to put this behind him? Finally, he had something positive that he could tell them: He was cooperating with the SEC.

Riely woke up from his meditation a few minutes later, when Cohen pushed through the door. His attorney, Martin Klotz, was with him, along with Daniel Kramer, a member of Cohen's expanding legal team from Paul, Weiss, one of the country's top corporate law firms.

Most of the attorneys who dealt with Marty Klotz had a fondness for him. Senior counsel at Willkie Farr & Gallagher, Klotz had been Cohen's, and SAC's, outside legal advisor for more than a decade. He had logged time as a prosecutor in the late 1980s and had a PhD in philosophy from Yale. His courtly demeanor and reluctance to raise his voice had won him a favored place in the defense bar. His colleagues at Willkie saw him as the intellectual in their midst, someone who could always be counted on to recommend the best opera to see at the Met that season.

On the other hand, some people viewed Klotz as the Godfather's consigliere, which made him less than trustworthy. And as was the case with many attorneys who were almost entirely dependent on one source of income, Klotz was scared of doing anything that might hurt his lucrative client.

Cohen half-smiled and took a seat next to the court reporter. His attorneys arranged themselves beside him. Riely's boss, Sanjay Wadhwa, didn't usually sit in on depositions, but this was such an important moment in the investigation that he made a point of being there.

One of the challenges of prosecuting white collar crime is the resource mismatch between the two sides, and this was on full display at the conference table. On Cohen's side sat two silver-haired professionals, each of whom boasted thirty years in the industry as well as illustrious clerkships and Ivy League degrees. They were more experienced, more cynical, and, important, were making boatloads more money, working for a client with nearly unlimited funds. On the other side, Charles Riely and Amelia Cottrell were young, smart, and hardworking, products of fine colleges themselves. But they could have been associates at Klotz's and Kramer's firms if they hadn't been working for the Securities and Exchange Commission.

Riely was determined not to be intimidated. He would treat Cohen like any other witness.

Before he could even get going, Cohen asked what time they'd be done. "I'm going to the Knicks game tonight," he announced. He didn't want to be late.

Then he raised his right hand.

"Do you swear to tell the truth, the whole truth, and nothing but the truth?" asked Riely.

"I do," Cohen said. He sat back in his chair, his dark eyes moving back and forth between Klotz and the SEC lawyers.

"Mr. Cohen," Riely said. "Do you understand that you are under oath?"

"I do," he answered.

Riely started asking questions, beginning with SAC and Cohen's role there. Cohen confirmed that he was the owner of SAC and that he also managed a stock portfolio there. He answered questions about how many employees SAC had and how they were paid. He explained that portfolio managers typically got to keep a percentage of the trading profits in their portfolios. He identified Tom Conheeney, Peter Nussbaum, Sol Kumin, Steve Kessler, and a few others as his management team.

Then, as soon as the interview moved into questions about Martoma, Cohen couldn't remember any details. He said he didn't have any role in hiring Martoma and had no memory of when he came to work at SAC.

"I'd like to talk about Elan and Wyeth and bapineuzumab," Riely said.

"Can we call it 'bap'?" Cohen asked.

"Sure," Riely said.

For the next three hours they went back and forth about bap, Wayne Holman, Martoma, why Cohen had invested in Elan and Wyeth in 2008, how large the position was, and whose advice he heeded. Cohen acknowledged that the trades were based on Martoma's research, primarily. But when it came to specifics, the greatest trader of his generation, who could track the price movements of eighty different securities at a time, claimed not to remember. He said "I don't recall" sixty-five times.

Riely had expected that it would play out this way, but he still found it frustrating. Cohen kept acting as if he didn't understand the questions, and Riely was pretty sure that the "confusion" was feigned. Cohen confirmed, again, that he had made the Elan investment based on Martoma's advice, but he couldn't or wouldn't talk about what that advice was, or why it had given him enough confidence to ignore other experts inside SAC who disagreed with Martoma's position.

None of the SEC lawyers at the table believed that Cohen would have simply taken Martoma's word for it on Elan, not with such a large and risky position. He must have had a good reason to disregard his more senior healthcare analysts. But when Riely started to probe the point, Cohen got testy. There was a round of questions about Cohen's other healthcare analysts, David Munno and Ben Slate, who had begged him not to invest so heavily in Elan and Wyeth. Cohen professed not to remember anything of the dispute.

Around 1 P.M., they broke for lunch.

The SEC lawyers retreated to Wadhwa's office to eat sandwiches and share their impressions. They all agreed that Cohen was being evasive. He had to be lying. The idea that he couldn't remember anything was ridiculous.

"We have to keep pushing him," Wadhwa said, but he could sense they weren't going to get what they needed. Disappointment was already setting in.

The deposition picked up again an hour later. After more circular talk about Munno and Slate, Riely asked about the critical day, Sunday, July 20, 2008. The day when Martoma and Cohen spoke on the phone, before Cohen gave the order to sell all his Elan and Wyeth shares. This was the conversation everyone on the SEC side of the table was dying to know about. What did Martoma tell Cohen before he decided to sell SAC's position?

Cohen was starting to look tired. Klotz asked an associate to fetch him a cup of coffee.

Then Riely placed a copy of the email Martoma had sent that Sunday morning on the table: "Is there a good time to catch up with you this morning? It's important."

"Do you remember getting this from Martoma?" Riely asked.

There was a long pause. "I believe so," Cohen replied, shifting in his seat.

"Did you speak to him?"

"Yeah, that morning he called me," Cohen said. "I remember him saying that he was getting uncomfortable with the Elan position."

One of the SEC attorneys asked why.

"I must have asked him how come, or—because he repeated back to me, 'I am just getting uncomfortable with the Elan position,'" Cohen said.

"Did he give any reasons?" Riely asked.

"He might have," Cohen answered. "I just don't remember."

They went around and around, with Cohen insisting that he didn't remember anything about why one of his traders had suddenly convinced him to undo a $1 billion investment that he had stubbornly defended in the face of significant internal opposition. One of Riely's superiors, Amelia Cottrell, watched the exchange with growing incredulity.

"When Mr. Martoma said that he was getting uncomfortable, you don't recall saying to him, 'why'?" she interjected.

Cohen said that he believed that he did ask him.

"And you don't remember any substantive response that he gave you?"

"I just don't remember," Cohen said.

Riely tried to remind himself that they had anticipated this. Steven Cohen was never going to walk into the SEC's testimony room and admit that he had received inside information from Mat Martoma. Just getting him into the room was a victory. They tried. Still, they hadn't gotten anything out of him at all.

The deposition ended at 6 P.M. on the nose. Cohen was courtside at the Knicks game by tipoff.

CHAPTER 13

KARMA

The golden ring of defense lawyering is obtaining something called a non-prosecution agreement. It guarantees that your client won't be charged with a felony, or even a misdemeanor, in exchange for fulfilling certain obligations, which might include testifying for the government. It is almost the best deal a defendant can get, and Preet Bharara's office did not give them out freely. Marc Mukasey intended to secure one for Sidney Gilman. He was confident that he could make it happen because Gilman was so important to the case against Martoma.

With this goal in mind, Mukasey called the SEC with some news. Gilman had something important to say. It was August 2012, and he suggested a date for a meeting, at 6 P.M. on a Friday. Riely and his colleagues laughed. They suspected this was yet another delaying tactic, and that Mukasey assumed they wouldn't want to meet on a Friday night, right before a summer weekend.

"Sounds great!" Riely told him.

When Gilman walked in, it was immediately clear to the SEC staff attorneys that his attitude had changed. He sat down at the conference table and announced that he was there to make a statement. He then admitted that he had given Martoma inside information about bapi. Not only that, but he had done it repeatedly. He knew he had done something seriously wrong.

The SEC investigators and the prosecutors in the room had an urgent question. The PowerPoint presentation—the one that Gilman had received from Elan two weeks before the ICAD meeting. This was critical. It was hard evidence, a *document,* with all of the confidential information that Martoma had used to make his trades. Presenting electronic evidence showing how Martoma got it would be crucial to a jury. Arlo Devlin-Brown, one of the prosecutors, asked Gilman: Did he send the presentation to Martoma? If so, how?

"Yes," Gilman said, he was sure he had sent it. The trouble was, he didn't exactly remember the conversation. He had an unformed memory of going over the slides with Martoma over the phone.

Devlin-Brown rephrased the question, hoping Gilman would remember some of the details. Finally, Gilman said he thought he had a memory of emailing it to Martoma after he asked for it.

With that, the government finally had the element it needed to seal the case against Martoma. They didn't yet have the email showing that Gilman had sent the PowerPoint to Martoma, but it had to exist on a server somewhere. Riely was already thinking about how he would track it down.

In the face of such irrefutable evidence, Martoma's only way out would be to turn on Cohen. The FBI started planning to arrest him.

Three months later FBI agents pulled up outside Martoma's house in Boca Raton. This time, they weren't there to talk. Special Agent Matt Callahan marched up to the door and knocked loudly.

Martoma looked shocked when he answered.

"Did you think you would ever see me again?" Callahan asked.

"Honestly, no," Martoma said.

Callahan had a plan. If Martoma indicated that he might be open to cooperating, then notions of charging him formally would be put on hold. But when Callahan asked him about cooperating, Martoma shook his head no. Callahan then put Martoma in handcuffs.

Rosemary's parents were visiting for Thanksgiving week. They watched with outrage as Martoma was led away and placed into the back of a dark sedan. His three children looked on, terrified and confused.

By midday, Martoma's arrest was being covered by every major news organization. The next morning, *The New York Times* ran a story on the front page: "Over the last half-decade, as federal authorities secured dozens of insider trading convictions against hedge fund traders, they have tried doggedly to build a case against one of Wall Street's most influential players," it read. "The billionaire stock picker Steven A. Cohen."

One after the other, Martoma's former colleagues saw the news and started to put the pieces together: the enormous, risky positions in Elan and Wyeth; the arguments and evasiveness surrounding them; the eerie way Cohen had listened, almost exclusively, to Martoma; the comment from a colleague about how Martoma had "black edge." Martoma's former trader at SAC, Tim Jandovitz, had left Wall Street and was living in Chicago, where he'd started a high-concept sandwich shop that was based around a special waffle bread he had developed. He hoped it would become the next Chipotle.

Jandovitz was startled when he saw the headlines about Martoma being arrested. As he read through the news reports detailing the accusations that Martoma had paid a drug researcher for inside information, all the bizarreness and secrecy that had surrounded the Elan and Wyeth trades back in 2008 made sense.

He typed out an email to a friend: "Karma is a bitch."

Now that Gilman was beginning to work productively with them, the government was feeling confident about its case against Martoma.

The prosecutors had made an unusual move in the way they filed the charges. Rather than charging Martoma through an indictment—a formal criminal charge that comes after a federal grand jury has heard evidence against the defendant—Bharara's office had charged Martoma only with a complaint. A complaint was the first step in a prosecution. An indictment meant that a grand jury had already found probable cause for the U.S. Attorney's Office to go ahead with a prosecution. The prosecutors could have gone directly to the indictment, but they hoped that delaying that step would serve as an effective pressure tactic. It was like giving Martoma a warning about what was likely coming: *Are you sure you want this? There is another way.*

Still, they didn't ask him directly to cooperate against Cohen. They didn't want to seem desperate.

"If Martoma didn't do this alone, we'd like to hear about it," Arlo Devlin-Brown told Charles Stillman, Martoma's lawyer. "He shouldn't feel like he needs to have something that's 100 percent specific. . . ."

Preet Bharara announced the arrest of Martoma at one of the biggest press conferences yet. He was a natural master of ceremonies, holding these triumphant-but-serious affairs on the ground floor of 1 St. Andrew's Plaza. To prepare, he usually turned up the air-conditioning in his office to arctic levels and blasted Bruce Springsteen.

As Bharara reviewed the charges, standing at a podium in a black suit and red tie, he maintained a somber expression that sometimes edged into a knowing smirk. "The charges unsealed today . . . describe cheating coming . . . AND going," he said. "Specifically, insider trading first on the long side, and then on the short side, on a scale that has, really, no historical precedent." He described Martoma's Elan and Wyeth trades as the most lucrative insider trading scheme in history, "allegedly resulting in an illegal windfall to the hedge fund of a quarter of a billion dollars." He paused. "That's 'billion,' with a 'B.'"

Several other people also made remarks during the news conference. Oddly, though, no one mentioned SAC by name, referring to it only as "the hedge fund" or "the hedge fund firm" where Martoma worked. Steve Cohen was in the background, evident to everyone but mentioned by no one.

Bharara left the job of publicizing Cohen's involvement in the case to the dozens of reporters in the room, who quickly ran off and did just that. News of the charges against Martoma, the fact that he had worked at SAC and the connection the case had to Cohen personally, was covered widely.

Just a few months earlier, Bharara had appeared on the cover of *Time* magazine, a close-up of his face, emblazoned with the words: "This Man Is Busting Wall St." Now it appeared to be coming true.

The winter of 2013 was bitterly cold, leaving Manhattan encased in a layer of ice that lingered into early spring. On the morning of March 8, as he was rushing to work, Sanjay Wadhwa slipped and hit his head on the sidewalk. He had just dropped his son off at daycare and was running late, as usual. There wasn't any blood, but he groaned as he pulled himself to his feet and hobbled to the office, where someone brought him an ice pack. He had an important call scheduled with Cohen's lawyer that day. They were going to finalize one of the biggest monetary settlements in SEC history.

"Are you *sure* you still want to do this?" his colleague asked.

"I'm fine," Wadhwa said. "Let's get it over with."

Marty Klotz had contacted Wadhwa a few weeks earlier to say that Cohen wanted to "settle up" the cases involving the Mathew Martoma and Michael Steinberg trades. He wanted closure, without any worry of charges against him surfacing in the future. From Cohen's perspective, it made sense to resolve the case before things got any worse—if Martoma flipped, for example. Not that there was any sign it was going to happen.

The deal Klotz had worked out would settle only the SEC's charges against SAC the company, resolving corporate liability for the illegal trades. Cohen himself, and other individuals for that matter, were still open to charges. Nonetheless, Cohen wanted to move forward.

Wadhwa picked up the phone while holding the ice pack to his head. The SEC had proposed a fine of $601.7 million for the Elan and Wyeth trades and another $13.9 million for Dell. The fines were based partly on the illegal profits the SEC was alleging in each instance, which were $275 million in Elan and Wyeth and $6.4 million in Dell. In total, it would be one of the largest settlements the SEC had ever extracted, almost four times what Raj Rajaratnam had been forced to pay. As the sole owner of SAC, Cohen would be paying the fines himself.

After Wadhwa outlined the penalties they were proposing, Klotz said that his client would agree. He knew, given all the legal scrutiny, that the alternative to paying could be much worse. Wadhwa hung up the phone and prepared to get the documents ready.

For two years, Cohen had lived with a drumbeat of press leaks and news coverage suggesting that he was the real target of the government's insider trading crackdown. Speculation centered on the question of whether he himself might be criminally charged. Now he was about to dispense with his legal problems by writing a check. He was confident that he was finally putting this nightmare behind him. Just as soon as he started making plans for how he would restore SAC's reputation and make it stronger than ever, though, momentum for a whole other case against him took on new life.

The separate team of SEC lawyers was racing to find out everything they could about the "2nd hand read" email about Dell's earnings that had gone from Jon Horvath to Michael Steinberg. It was possible that the Dell trade would still lead to charges against individuals who had traded the stock. The SEC lawyers were feeling increasingly sure, based on the evidence they were gathering, that they were going to be able to charge Steinberg with insider trading. It was a huge development, another opportunity to penetrate the layer of people who were closest to Cohen.

Anthony Chiasson and Todd Newman, two traders from the hedge funds the FBI had raided, had been convicted of insider trading the previous December. Jon Horvath had flipped and was helping the government build a case against Steinberg. Steinberg hadn't been charged yet, but it was just a matter of time.

The SEC lawyers on the Dell case had seen from the trading records that Cohen traded Dell shares at the same time Steinberg did in August 2008, right before the earnings announcement. It looked like Steinberg's trades were motivated by what Horvath had told him, which the SEC believed was based on inside information. The question was, why had Cohen traded his Dell?

On Wednesday, March 13, 2013, two days before the $600 million Elan settlement was scheduled to be signed by Cohen and the SEC, Wadhwa was sitting at his desk, contemplating what was about to happen. He had been up until 1 A.M. working and was exhausted. They were about to make history with their SAC deal, and he expected that it would get a lot of attention. And for once, the U.S. Attorney had nothing to do with it. No one else would be stealing their glory. Then his phone rang.

It was Marty Klotz. "Hi Sanjay," Klotz said. "We've been continuing to dig for the most recent documents you requested, and we discovered something that we wanted to let you know about as soon as possible. . . ." Klotz was referring to the SEC's most recent batch of subpoenas. His voice trailed off. There was a long, painful silence. "We found out that the Dell email actually made its way to Steve."

Wadhwa was now very much awake. They had been haggling with Klotz for weeks over getting access to SAC's old emails. The SEC had been asking specifically about the August 26, 2008, "2nd hand read" email, trying to determine exactly who inside the firm had received it. Based on SAC's trading records, it appeared that multiple traders had been moving in and out of Dell right around the time Horvath had sent the message warning Steinberg and others that Dell's earnings were going to be a disappointment.

SAC had been offering different excuses as to why it couldn't find the emails. As a firm policy, the fund hadn't retained copies of the email messages on its servers until after September 2008. The SEC lawyers had always found it strange that a firm of SAC's size, transacting in such tremendous volume each day, didn't keep a record of everything just in case. Klotz kept finding new backup tapes with different batches of emails on them. Each time there seemed to be a different reason why it had taken so long. The deadlines were approaching for the government to bring charges for trades from 2008. They were running out of time and Klotz knew it.

Klotz launched into an explanation as to why the Dell email reaching Cohen wasn't important, anyway. It was almost as if he were reading Wadhwa's mind.

"I think there are any number of reasons why Steve probably did not see it," Klotz said. "It was the middle of the summer, he was in the Hamptons. . . ."

Wadhwa felt like he was going to scream. SAC must take them for idiots to try to pull a stunt like this, he thought, revealing such a crucial piece of information two nights before signing a huge settlement. It was infuriating. He told Klotz that he needed to discuss the matter with his colleagues and hung up the phone.

The question of how, and when, to disclose such a significant piece of information was tricky. If he never mentioned it, and Cohen went ahead and signed the $616 million SEC settlement, there was a good chance the SEC staff would find the email later on their own, in which case they'd be justifiably angry and unlikely ever to trust him again. It could lead to bigger problems in the future. After so much work had been done to get the settlement ready, waiting to reveal it until right before was masterful, in a certain way. Klotz would gain some credibility for bringing it to their attention, while leaving them so little time to react that they might just choose to go ahead with the settlement anyway. Klotz's goal, as always, was the best possible outcome for Cohen.

That night, the SEC staff attorneys debated whether they should move forward with the settlement in light of the new information. It seemed like Klotz was trying to get away with something.

Of course there was also the possibility that SAC really had just found an email going to Cohen potentially containing inside information about Dell on a backup server no one had looked at until the day before the company was set to enter into one of the largest securities fraud settlements in the history of Wall Street. It would have been an incredible coincidence, but it was possible.

In any event, the settlement did not close off the possibility of charges against individuals at SAC, something the SEC had been adamant about throughout the negotiation. All the settlement would resolve was SAC's corporate liability for the Elan, Wyeth, and Dell trades. The agreement did not name specific people who were involved, only the companies. It was a strange omission, as Cohen owned the companies outright and made all of the major decisions. But as far as the SEC was concerned, this was only the first step. They decided to go ahead and finalize the settlement.

An SEC enforcement attorney, a key member of the Dell team named Matthew Watkins, spent most of Thursday going through all ten copies of the agreement, making every final change by hand. The following morning, March 15, 2013, the SEC blasted out a press release: "CR Intrinsic Agrees to Pay More than $600 Million in Largest-Ever Settlement for Insider Trading Case," it read.

Wadhwa and his colleagues spent the day responding to congratulatory emails and phone calls from colleagues and friends who worked in the hedge fund industry, thanking them for finally sanctioning a company that many in the business had long suspected was breaking the rules. But everyone on the case knew that this was no time to stop what they were doing. They now had an email that connected Cohen directly to inside information. They had gotten a huge fine out of him, but the goal was to see if they could charge Cohen himself and put him out of business for good. They had originally planned to go out for a celebratory lunch right after the announcement. Instead, the SEC team took the elevator down to P. J. Clarke's on the ground floor of their office building, had a quick beer, and then rushed back up to their desks. There was work to do.

That night, at 7:33 P.M., the "2nd hand read" email that had gone to Cohen came in to the SEC's Central Processing Unit in Washington. The first thing the SEC lawyers wanted to know was whether the receipt of the email by Cohen lined up with the sales of his Dell shares. Obviously, if he had sold them before he got the email, then the whole thing was irrelevant.

According to the metadata on the email, the SAC analyst Jon Horvath had sent it at 1:09 P.M. on August 26, 2008, to Michael Steinberg and Gabriel Plotkin. One of the SEC staff attorneys, Justin Smith, also noticed a new name on the email chain: Anthony Vaccarino. Apparently Plotkin had forwarded the email to Vaccarino at 1:13 P.M., four minutes after Horvath sent it. Smith excitedly typed out a message to his colleagues, alerting them to this new fact.

The SEC was not familiar with Anthony Vaccarino. They were familiar with Plotkin's name—he was a star portfolio manager, someone Cohen looked to for trading ideas, especially in large consumer companies. Vaccarino was identified on an SAC staff list as a "research trader." He worked directly for Cohen. At 1:29 P.M., Vaccarino had forwarded the Dell email to Cohen's personal and office email addresses.

The SEC rushed to get Vaccarino's phone records. Sure enough, there was a call to Cohen's cellphone from Vaccarino at 1:37 P.M. It lasted less than one minute. Two minutes later, Cohen sold 200,000 shares of Dell. He kept selling over the course of the afternoon and was out of his entire 500,000-share position by the end of the day. Two days later, Dell announced disappointing earnings—just as Horvath had predicted.

Because the SEC was only working off of phone bills, there was still uncertainty about whether Cohen had actually answered the phone when Vaccarino called at 1:37 P.M. Presumably, Vaccarino would have told Cohen about the Dell email and made sure that he looked at it. The bill showed a call occurring, but forty-eight seconds wasn't a long time. Cohen could easily say that he hadn't picked up. After several days pleading with AT&T, the SEC received a letter verifying the company's policy of billing customers only for calls that were answered. The company sent over an Excel spreadsheet showing all of the calls in question, down to the fraction of a second.

The SEC had more questions. Was it possible that someone else had ordered the sales of the Dell shares? Could Cohen have put in the sell orders before 1:29 P.M.? Was there a delay between putting in an order and the order being executed? The SEC hypothesized a likely scenario: Horvath found out important information about Dell's earnings from Jesse Tortora. Horvath then emailed the news to Steinberg and Plotkin. Plotkin then told Vaccarino, who, in turn, told Cohen. Cohen then sold off all of his shares before the bad news became public. Any other explanation involved a more convoluted set of assumptions. Occam's razor again.

Everything they had learned about Cohen suggested that he was fanatical about his stocks. He had built SAC into the most sophisticated and powerful information-gathering operation in the financial industry. He had an incredible memory and a voracious appetite for new intelligence that might drive his trading. He hated it when his portfolio managers made a move without telling him first. In fact, he was known to berate people on the trading floor for doing just that. Surely, they reasoned, he'd be up to date on anything his portfolio managers, like Steinberg, were doing with their Dell positions and why.

Still, Klotz argued that Cohen hadn't necessarily seen the "2nd hand read" email. He was doing everything he could to delay and distract them and waste their time.

Steven Cohen was not in hiding. He was eager to project confidence and reassure his investors about SAC's future, and he made a point of being visible during the early months of 2013. He attended the World Economic Forum in Davos in January and made a rare appearance at a hedge fund conference in Palm Beach, in part to show the world that he wasn't daunted by the enormous payment he had just agreed to hand over to the SEC.

At the end of March, he received a call from the art dealer William Acquavella. Steve Wynn, the casino owner and prodigious art collector, was ready to sell Picasso's *Le Rêve*; seven years had passed since Cohen's original deal with Wynn had had to be canceled due to Wynn's expensive bout of clumsiness. During the intervening period, Wynn had devoted significant resources to restoring the painting. Might Cohen still be interested in buying it? Cohen and his art advisor rushed to Acquavella's gallery the next morning.

Cohen's art collection was world-renowned. In 2005, he'd made several significant purchases, including a painting by Van Gogh and one by

Gauguin, which he had allegedly bought for $110 million. In 2006 he acquired a $137.5 million de Kooning. In 2012, he had paid $120 million for four bronze sculptures by Henri Matisse, and he owned dozens of other masterpieces, including canvases by Pollock, Monet, and Manet. Gallery owners loved him for his willingness to pay whatever it took to acquire the best. As in other areas of his life, Cohen could usually buy whatever he desired. But, thus far, *Le Rêve* had eluded him.

After the accident, Wynn had sent *Le Rêve* to Terrence Mahon, one of only two art restorers in the United States seen as capable of repairing the painting in such a way as to not diminish its value. Mahon had set about realigning the threads of the canvas from his studio on Park Avenue South, sewing them together using an interface of acupuncture needles. He was then able to gently apply paint over the newly merged threads.

"Fortunately, there wasn't a lot of damage once the tear itself was realigned," Mahon said. "There was minimal paint loss. It wasn't like there was a hole or void in the canvas. The space I had to fill up with new paint was only about the width of a pencil tip."

It was work that required a jeweler's eye and the steady hand of a vascular surgeon. Mahon completed the assignment on December 11, 2006, at a total cost of $90,493.12. Then the painting began its reputational laundering and was put on display at William Acquavella's gallery on East Seventy-ninth Street. Then Acquavella called Cohen.

"In three minutes we had a deal," Cohen's art advisor said. "This is a painting that has haunted Steve for nearly a decade."

"When you stand in front of it, you're blown away," Cohen said of the piece.

When news of the purchase, for $155 million, appeared, it immediately caught the attention of the prosecutors, FBI agents, and SEC attorneys who were still trying to assemble cases against Cohen after several years of investigations. What defense lawyer would possibly allow his client to make a purchase of such ostentation and scale when there was a criminal investigation going on? It was almost as if Cohen was trying to antagonize the government.

After the Picasso sale, Richard Zabel, Preet Bharara's deputy, started making jokes about Cohen's art collection around the office. "I want his pickled shark," he said, referring to Cohen's $8 million Damien Hirst installation. "I want to put his shark up in the office."

Cohen was acting like a man who was celebrating, while the government was far from finished with its investigation. The $616 million he paid the SEC was nothing, Cohen seemed to be saying. He could find that in the cushions of his Maybach.

CHAPTER 14

THE LIFE RAFT

Early in the morning, before the sun rises over Manhattan, the sidewalks of the Upper East Side are illuminated by little pools of light that spill out of the lobbies of gracious limestone buildings. Just before 6 A.M. on March 29, 2013, at the corner of East Seventy-eighth Street and Park Avenue, a group of armed FBI enforcement agents were gathered near one of the building entrances.

Inside the building, in a co-op apartment on the eighth floor, Michael Steinberg was sitting on the couch with his hands resting in his lap. Typically, the FBI liked to surprise people when agents came to take them into custody, but Steinberg's lawyer, Barry Berke, had found out ahead of time that his client would be arrested that day. Steinberg had left his family behind in Florida, where they were visiting his wife's relatives for Spring Break, and flown home to New York in order to be there. Berke, head of the litigation department at Kramer Levin Naftalis & Frankel, joined him at his apartment at 5 A.M. They intended to make the arrest as friction-free as possible. Steinberg dressed in khaki pants and a navy V-neck sweater and made a point not to wear a belt or shoelaces—potential instruments of suicide, which Berke had advised him were not permitted in federal detention. Steinberg unlocked the front entrance. Then he and Berke waited.

At 6 A.M., the FBI agents banged on the door.

Steinberg stood by and watched as a group of agents entered his apartment and started searching every room. They swiftly ascertained that no one else was home. Then Steinberg was handcuffed, walked out of the building, and steered into the back of a gray Ford. It was still dark out. The only surprise for Steinberg that morning was that there was a *Wall Street Journal* reporter standing out on the street, recording the whole thing on her phone. Steinberg wasn't the only one who had gotten a tip ahead of time.

Steinberg's attorneys had been trying to negotiate a surrender for weeks. They had strongly suspected that he was going to be arrested, and they offered to bring him in voluntarily, but the FBI was adamant that Steinberg be handled just like any other defendant. Steinberg, of course, wanted to avoid a humiliating and traumatic scene in front of his wife and kids. Berke had called Antonia Apps, the lead prosecutor on the Dell case, and told her that his client was going to start checking in to a hotel at 5 A.M. every morning and waiting there until 7 A.M., the window when the FBI usually carried out arrests, and that they could come and pick him up there. "If you or your colleagues are looking for Mike Steinberg any time starting tomorrow, I'll give you the hotel and room number," Berke told her.

"Thanks," Apps said. "But I don't need that information this week." She hesitated a moment and then said: "Call me next week."

It went on like that for six weeks, with Berke calling to check whether "they would be needing Mike's hotel information"—that is, whether he was going to be arrested that week. Then, at the end of March, Apps called him. "He needs to be here on Friday," she said, and hung up the phone quickly. Steinberg and Berke were both on vacation, but they dropped everything and rushed back to New York.

On a purely financial basis, Steinberg's case was minuscule. Under normal circumstances, the government probably wouldn't have even bothered to charge him. He was alleged to have made only $1.4 million on his illegal trades—a tiny amount compared to the $276 million Martoma case. But the arrest sent an important message. It was the first time that someone close to Cohen was dragged out of his home in handcuffs. Unlike most of the others charged until that point, Steinberg was like Cohen's son.

"We got your guy," Preet Bharara seemed to be saying to Cohen. "We're coming for you next."

Steinberg was ferried downtown to 26 Federal Plaza to be processed; his fingerprints were taken, and he was interviewed by pretrial services. An indictment was unsealed, charging him with conspiracy and securities fraud. He relinquished his passport and was released on $3 million bail, which he secured by pledging his apartment as collateral. Almost immediately, the pressure to cooperate started. Apps called Berke as soon as the charges were filed.

"We think Steinberg should talk to us," she said. "We'd be very interested in anything he had to say about people who are senior to him at SAC."

To Berke it was clear that she was referring to Cohen. Everyone knew that the U.S. Attorney was desperate to charge him. But from Berke's perspective, cooperation wasn't an option. Steinberg was adamant that he was innocent, and cooperating required a guilty plea.

Berke thrived on situations like this. The first one in his family to go to college—to Duke, followed by Harvard Law School—Berke had grown up middle-class in Philadelphia, where he watched his father lose his small linen supply company after a series of tax audits that Berke didn't understand at the time but seemed profoundly unfair. The family had lost nearly everything, and the experience had left him wary of the government. Berke took pride in this kind of fight.

"He can't make a deal," Berke told Apps. "He didn't do anything wrong."

The day of Steinberg's arrest, the SEC's Dell team found themselves back inside 1 St. Andrew's Plaza to meet with their counterparts at the U.S. Attorney's Office. Everyone involved in the Dell case, both the prosecutors and the SEC investigators, had been summoned for an urgent meeting. George Canellos, the acting head of the SEC's enforcement unit, was in New York for only half a day. The meeting had been arranged in part to accommodate his schedule.

The purpose was to discuss how the investigation would move forward in light of the new information the government had about Cohen receiving the "2nd hand read" email about Dell. Securities fraud had a five-year statute of limitations. The Elan trade had happened in July 2008, the Dell trade in August of the same year. That gave them three and four months, respectively, to charge Cohen—or anyone else—with crimes in those cases. They had no time to waste.

Canellos role-played the white collar defense lawyer, pointing out weaknesses in their cases. He loved doing this, playing the role of the contrarian. It had earned him a reputation outside of the SEC as an enforcer who was at times reluctant to file aggressive cases because he empathized a bit too much with the defendants. Still, his colleagues found his argumentative style to be helpful. There was nothing worse than walking into a settlement meeting or a courtroom only to find that your opponent had a defense worked out that you hadn't seen coming. George could always be counted on to show them exactly what their defense-lawyer opponents were likely to focus on.

Just because someone sent Cohen an email didn't mean that he actually *read* it, Canellos pointed out, let alone acted on it. And what does "2nd hand read" mean, anyway? In all likelihood, yes, whoever got that email from Horvath understood exactly what it was referring to. It was all about context. But in isolation, the phrase was open to multiple interpretations, and you could be sure that Cohen's lawyers would exploit this to the maximum.

They made a list of everyone they wanted to talk to, every person at SAC who had any connection to the Dell email, as well as SAC's upper management and compliance staff. Because they had so little time, they needed to establish priorities. They needed to know more about how things worked at the firm, who had the authority to green-light a trade, who made sure that Cohen was kept apprised of important stock news.

They discussed the benefits of sending subpoenas to the various executives versus asking them to submit to interviews. They went over all the evidence they would need to prove a case in a trial.

For the criminal prosecutors, the debate was an exercise in frustration. In spite of the extensive amount of evidence they had connecting SAC to insider trading, they were afraid it would be next to impossible to successfully prosecute Cohen himself without evidence that was more specific, ideally a witness who could testify that Cohen knew exactly what he was doing. Preet Bharara, along with other top prosecutors around the country, had become increasingly sensitive to the possibility of losing big cases, especially ones that attracted a lot of news media attention. Ambitious young prosecutors from Ivy League law schools did not want to be associated with high-profile failures, especially when they were trying to build their careers and reputations. Bharara had watched prosecutors in the Eastern District lose a closely watched fraud case against two Bear Stearns hedge fund traders a few years earlier, in 2009, a case that had similarly seemed to be a surefire winner. It was one of the first major criminal cases to arise out of the financial crisis, and the two fund managers were acquitted after just six hours. The government was harshly criticized for choosing the case in the first place and for the way it was handled. It was a disaster, and it sent a message to the Justice Department that when it came to pursuing crime on Wall Street, it was much safer to file cases that were close to a sure thing, rather than risk losing after a big trial. To make a criminal case against Cohen that would be unbeatable in court, Bharara's prosecutors felt they needed a witness or a wiretap linking him explicitly to the Dell or the Elan trade, something that clearly, irrefutably, showed Cohen *knew* he was trading based on inside information. Basically, they needed Steinberg, or Martoma, to flip.

While they waited, and hoped, for that to happen, they were considering filing a corporate fraud case against SAC. The prosecutors had two high-ranking employees—Steinberg and Martoma—and all of the other evidence they'd gathered that they could use to argue that SAC's whole culture was rotten.

The debate was very different at the SEC. With the agency's lower standard for proving a civil case, they had a viable argument for charging Cohen. They wanted to put him out of business. The SEC investigators knew that Cohen had the "2nd hand read" email in his in-box at the time he sold his Dell shares. That, on its own, was practically enough. SEC rules expressly bar someone from trading a stock while in possession of inside information. Wadhwa felt certain they could persuade a jury once they put the whole story together. "We're going to get him," he thought.

Steven Cohen's lawyers had been immersed in subpoenas, document requests, memos, and strategy sessions for four years now. In early spring, they embarked on an urgent new project, putting together a defense presentation they intended to make to the U.S. Attorney. They organized the presentation, approximately 130 pages long, into a black binder. They were going to use it to build a life raft.

On the morning of Thursday, April 25, 2013, men and women in dark suits began filing into a large conference room on the eighth floor of 1 St. Andrew's Plaza. The jockeying that went on for the chairs at the table closest to the action was a reflection of the hierarchy of those attending the meeting. Richard Zabel, Preet Bharara's deputy, sat at the center of the "government" side of the long table. Surrounding him were the prosecutors, the securities unit chiefs, the head of the asset forfeiture unit, and the leader of the office's criminal division. Several FBI agents were there as well as the SEC lawyers working on the Dell and Elan cases. There were so many government attorneys, seventeen in all, that someone had to get extra chairs from down the hall.

A couple of weeks earlier, in anticipation of this moment, Bharara had asked his prosecutors to prepare a detailed memo outlining all the evidence the government had against Cohen. The memo was to include any evidence of knowledge that Cohen had about the trades in Dell and Elan, as well as any evidence from other cases that could be used against him. Antonia Apps and Arlo Devlin-Brown locked themselves up for a week putting it together. In addition to the evidence from the Dell and Elan cases, the memo contained example after example of Cohen receiving what seemed to be inside information from his traders and analysts and doing nothing to find out if the information was clean. Clearly, the prosecutors felt, Cohen's employees felt comfortable giving him inside information. Some had told the FBI that they regarded it as part of their jobs. And Cohen had never, that the prosecutors found, referred an instance of suspicious trading by an employee to the SEC.

When the memo was finished, it went to Bharara, who reviewed it carefully. Then he and Zabel spent hours with Apps and Devlin-Brown going over it. They outlined possible defense arguments and asked the prosecutors what their responses to those arguments would be. There was a mountain of evidence they could use to make a case against Cohen, everyone agreed, but it wasn't enough to be certain of a victory at trial. Their chances of winning might not even be fifty-fifty. The evidence was too circumstantial.

A criminal charge against SAC, on the other hand, was a case they could easily win. They would start putting that case together while they waited for Martoma to come to his senses and decide to cooperate. Martoma had a young family and a long prison term in his future. As his trial date approached, they hoped that the benefits of working with the government would become clearer and he would give them the evidence they needed against Cohen.

The next step was to request a meeting with Cohen's lawyers. It was important to hear their point of view and give them an opportunity to talk the government out of moving forward. It was also a chance to get a preview of what Cohen's defense would be. This was the moment when Marty Klotz and the rest of Cohen's $10,000-an-hour legal team would prove just how clever they were.

Klotz showed up looking slightly disheveled, as usual. Michael Schachter, his partner from Willkie Farr & Gallagher, took the seat next to him. Daniel Kramer, Michael Gertzman, and Mark Pomerantz, all partners at Paul, Weiss, sat next to them. Ted Wells, star trial lawyer at Paul, Weiss, was also in attendance. He didn't speak, but the message was clear: If this case reached a courtroom, Wells, who was known to cry during his own closing arguments, would be their adversary.

Klotz led the presentation. His mission was straightforward: He was there to keep Steve Cohen from going to jail. He took the assignment as seriously as he would have if Cohen had been a member of his own family.

In 1988 Michael Milken's lawyers, when faced with a similarly daunting set of legal pressures, had taken the cynical tack of arguing that Milken was an American hero whose junk bond empire provided fuel for the U.S. economy. They described Milken as a "national treasure," a "genius," and a "national resource" and publicly argued that Milken's work building the junk bond market had created value for companies and communities around the country. This argument actually had some validity. Milken had ushered in new methods for companies to borrow money and expand, especially companies considered too small or too risky to obtain traditional loans; his innovations had contributed to economic growth in ways modern-day hedge funds never had. Milken also launched a public relations campaign, offering interviews to news outlets he was sure would be friendly. In many ways, Cohen was Milken's equivalent, a financier who came from middle-class roots and rose up to embody the Wall Street of his time, partly through methods that regulators suspected were illegal. In Milken's case, his defense had proved to be a colossal miscalculation, an expression of hubris that only hardened the prosecutors' resolve to take him down.

Cohen's attorneys were smart enough not to follow that example. They didn't suggest that Cohen was a saint or a creator of jobs or that he had somehow lifted up his fellow Americans. Rather, they focused on the government's weak spot: its crippling fear of losing a big case. What Klotz wanted to do was create doubt. He and his colleagues were shrewd enough to know that, in the end, the government's calculus was a matter of risk assessment and vanity as much as anything else. Klotz would get the prosecutors thinking hard about what it would be like to suffer a humiliating defeat at trial. As soon as that happened, the newspaper headlines about Preet Bharara would change from "This Man Is Busting Wall St." to something much less flattering.

A Willkie associate distributed the black binders they had prepared to everyone in the room. Inside was a presentation divided into three sec-tions: "Plotkin," "Cohen," and "Elan." Klotz looked out at the crowd of faces. "Thank you all for giving us this time to come and talk to you today," he said in his gravelly voice. Then he started talking, and he didn't stop for almost four hours. He walked them through page after page of trading records and emails. The government officials present had never endured anything like it.

The argument Klotz made regarding Dell contained three elements: that it was highly unlikely Cohen had read the "2nd hand read" Dell email; that whether or not he had read it wasn't relevant anyway; and finally, that even if Cohen had read the email and made a trade based on its contents, it was far from clear that it would constitute insider trading because Cohen knew so little about the original source of the tip.

The argument Klotz was making was deceptively simple. He was not making the case that Cohen had his own, brilliant, reasons for selling his shares of Dell. Rather, Cohen's own lawyer was saying that the most successful trader of his generation was winging it every single day. Maybe he read a critical email, maybe he didn't. Who knew? Cohen lived in a swamp of information so deep that there was simply no way to prove that any single email was even read, let alone acted upon. He was making decisions independent of his own highly paid analysts and experts, based on his gut. There was basically no method to what he did; it was all chaos.

"There is no evidence that Steve read the '2nd hand read' email or that he spoke to anyone about the email," Klotz continued. "There isn't a single witness who would testify that they discussed the email with Steve." He added, "Steve only reads a very small percentage of his emails."

He flipped to a printout of a screen shot of Cohen's email in-box. Cohen had spam filters that diverted the junk messages from his overwhelming stream of communications—and even after that, he received at least twenty thousand emails a month, or almost a thousand emails per business day. He looked at just 10 percent of them. Cohen read only about 21 percent of the emails he got from his research trader, Anthony Vaccarino, who had forwarded the "2nd hand read" email to Cohen, Klotz added. The example Klotz showed of Cohen's email box in Microsoft Outlook included a message from Wayne Holman about scheduling a golf game and dinner as well as research reports from various brokerage firms about oil prices and the Fed minutes.

Halfway down, the message from Vaccarino was clearly visible: "FW: DELL," it said in bold type.

The government lawyers tried not to chuckle out loud when they noticed that the message directly above the Dell email was a marketing message from Amazon—"Up to 60% Off Art Magazines." Apparently the spam filters didn't always work.

Cohen, Klotz pointed out, also received a similar number of instant messages on a daily basis. Cohen's desk had seven monitors on it. His Microsoft Outlook messages appeared on the far left one, behind multiple other screens, further increasing the likelihood that he never saw the Dell message. He would have had to "turn to the far left of his seven screens, minimize one or two computer programs, scroll down his emails, double-click into the '2nd hand read' email to open it, read down three chains of forwards to read the '2nd hand read' email, before issuing an order to sell shares of Dell." All of it, according to Klotz, taking place in less than half a minute.

This idea that Cohen could run his business in such a haphazard style didn't seem plausible to most of the investigators in the room. They had been studying Cohen for six years and understood him to be a rapacious consumer of information. They believed that SAC had been structured to ensure that Cohen had access to every bit of trading data being gathered by his portfolio managers and their aggressive, ambitious teams. He was controlling and demanding. The suggestion that he ignored 80 percent of the messages from his own research trader, whose sole job was to alert him to critical market information, struck them as absurd.

But as a glimpse into Cohen's potential defense arguments, it was powerful.

Klotz reminded everyone in the room of the convoluted journey the "2nd hand read" email had taken before being sent to Cohen. "Steve does not remember reading it," Klotz said. "He may not have read it."

Klotz then revisited some of the facts surrounding the email's transmission: On August 26, 2008, two days before Dell reported its earnings,

Cohen owned 500,000 shares. Steinberg, on the other hand, was short Dell stock. As soon as Steinberg learned that Cohen was long Dell, he and Horvath started to debate whether and how to tell Cohen that they had the opposite bet. Steinberg spoke with Cohen about their opposing views on the stock on that morning, when the earnings release was still two days away. Then Steinberg urged Gabe Plotkin, who was also long Dell, to discuss his own research with Horvath via email. At 12:54 P.M., Plotkin and Cohen spoke on the phone for seven minutes. Shortly after, Horvath sent the "2nd hand read" email, which Plotkin forwarded to Vaccarino, who then sent it to Cohen.

Vaccarino had then called Cohen, a call that lasted around a minute. At 1:39 P.M., right after hanging up the phone, Cohen started selling. By the time the market closed that afternoon he had gotten rid of all 500,000 shares of Dell that he owned.

Shortly after 4 P.M. on August 28, Dell made its earnings announcement. The stock went way down. Cohen averted losses of $1.5 million.

Klotz then started attacking the legal underpinnings of the case. It was far from clear that a trade made by Steve after he received the "2nd hand read" email would even constitute insider trading, he argued. The Dell information had passed from a Dell investor relations employee to another trader named Sandeep Goyal, to Jesse Tortora to Horvath to Steinberg to Plotkin to Vaccarino to Cohen. Klotz and his colleagues from the defense bar believed that Cohen was too far from the original source of the information, and too ignorant of the circumstances, to be criminally liable for any securities fraud.

"A number of people I've spoken to say that isn't a legitimate extension of insider trading," Klotz said.

"Are any of these people federal judges?" Rich Zabel, the most senior member of the Justice Department at the meeting, asked. "Give me a break."

Zabel, who had a gray goatee that made him look a bit wolflike, had grown up in the shadow of the hedge fund industry. He was the son of William Zabel, the founder of the law firm Schulte Roth & Zabel, which had a huge number of hedge fund clients. He understood how rich hedge fund guys operated, and he wasn't afraid to express his cynicism about their motives. But where his bluntness would normally have sparked laughter, there was only awkward silence. Much as they didn't want to admit it, the government attorneys knew that Cohen's distance from the Dell leak was a serious weakness.

Klotz then launched into a hypothetical story about his son-in-law, an employee of Best Buy, the electronics chain. "You could ask him, 'How are the flat screen TVs selling?' and he'd tell you how they were doing," Klotz said. "That would be a '2nd hand read from someone inside the company.' And that would be totally legitimate. There's nothing in this Dell email to distinguish it from me talking to my son-in-law."

Klotz glanced at the faces of the government lawyers around him. They appeared unmoved. Inside, though, the prosecutors knew he had a point. It would be difficult to convict Cohen on the basis of the email alone.

Three hours in, Klotz finally turned to Elan, the smallest portion of the binder, a reflection of the level of threat that Cohen's lawyers evidently felt the trade represented, given that Martoma wasn't cooperating. The core of Klotz's argument was that there were multiple reasons why it made sense for Cohen to sell his Elan shares, none of which had anything to do with any inside information that Martoma might have obtained. He showed a chart of Elan's stock, which had gone from about $19 in March to over $30 in July. On that alone, he said, it was a good idea to sell. Several analysts had issued reports that month arguing that the stock had peaked and that it was time to get out. SAC was sitting on an unrealized profit in the stock of around $80 million. Then, Klotz said, Cohen got a call from Martoma, who said that he was "no longer comfortable" being long the stock. Selling was the only prudent thing to do.

When Klotz finished, Zabel just shook his head. "I'm sorry, I just don't buy it," he said, reflecting the thoughts of many people in the room.

Typically, defense lawyers presented their strongest arguments in meetings like this, and to Zabel it all sounded weak. Klotz's arguments were abstract, not built on actual assertions of anything. Cohen *may* not have read the email. He *might* not have had time to react to it. In Zabel's view, it was a bit like saying, "I might have been in the bank, and I might have had a mask, and I might have had a gun, but that doesn't mean I robbed the bank."

Still, hearing Klotz lay it all out, much the way he would in front of a jury, was a hard dose of reality. After years of agonizing work, they didn't quite have the evidence they felt they needed to convict Steve Cohen. Not in a criminal case, anyhow. More than a dozen people at the FBI, the SEC, and the U.S. Attorney's Office had worked for almost a decade to line up a row of pins, and Klotz had just kicked them all over. Their only remaining hope was that Steinberg or Martoma would cooperate.

Klotz gathered his materials and stood up. He was going to sleep comfortably that night.

"Thanks very much for giving us this time," he said.

Zabel rushed to Bharara's office to tell him what had happened.

The two groups departing the meeting had different impressions of what had just transpired. Cohen's lawyers felt that they had made a powerful case against a criminal indictment of their client. Their confidence was not misplaced. The criminal prosecutors who attended the meeting were more convinced than ever by the time it was over that they didn't have the evidence they needed to charge Cohen with securities fraud. Instead, they turned their attention to their Plan B, indicting Cohen's firm rather than Cohen himself. Legally, when any employee acting within the scope of his employment committed a crime, that crime could be attributed to the company he worked for. Charging SAC wasn't the most satisfying outcome, but the prosecutors could do it and still leave open the possibility that Martoma would flip and give them a case against Cohen later.

The U.S. Attorney's Office was often criticized for not penalizing Wall Street firms that committed fraud, and Bharara could point to the prosecution of SAC as a response to that. It would send a strong message to Martoma, too, that time was running out for him to change his stance. A few days later, Apps and Devlin-Brown started sending out grand jury subpoenas. One was sent to Cohen, others to SAC's top executives. These were not signs of an investigation being quietly wrapped up. Rather, the case had gathered force and veered into a new, more serious phase. The prosecutors were hoping that they'd have two historic cases in the end, one against Cohen and another against his company.

Klotz called the head of the securities unit at the Southern District to say that Cohen would be taking the Fifth in response to the subpoena. They were going to war.

With news of the grand jury summonses being reported in the newspaper, SAC's investors, after years of ignoring the signs, finally started withdrawing their money, and a torrent of capital flowed out the door. Since the beginning of the year, almost $2 billion had been redeemed out of the roughly $6 billion the fund managed that didn't belong to Cohen and his employees. SAC's largest outside investor was the Blackstone Group, a giant private equity fund run by the billionaire Stephen Schwarzman. Blackstone had $550 million with SAC. Executives at the firm had been watching as the investigation developed, debating what to do. Schwarzman had strong views about the government. He felt that the Obama administration was going out of its way to vilify Wall Street, and he didn't want to abandon Cohen just because the government was going after him, but this new indication that Cohen was preparing for battle with the Justice Department pushed Blackstone to submit a redemption notice. The risk of their money getting tied up in litigation was now too high to ignore.

It was as if the country's biggest investors, its wealthy individuals, its major pension funds, and its educational endowments, had regained their senses. By taking their money out, they acknowledged that perhaps SAC's enormous returns year after year had been too good to be true.

Inside the SEC, the staff attorneys and their bosses within the enforcement division were debating what to do about their own case. The agency's renowned enforcement division was being co-managed by Andrew Ceresney, a former partner at Debevoise & Plimpton who was new at the job, and George Canellos, a longtime enforcement official. Klotz and the rest of Cohen's legal team came in with their binders and put on the same presentation for both of them that they had at the U.S. Attorney's Office, arguing that the agency should not file charges.

The SEC lawyers who had investigated the Dell case for the previous three years felt they had enough evidence to charge Cohen with insider trading. The burden of proof that the SEC had to meet was lower than that for the criminal prosecutors, who had to prove guilt beyond a reasonable doubt. For a civil case, the SEC only needed to prove the facts by a preponderance of the evidence—essentially, that it was more likely to be true than not. The task ahead of them was convincing their bosses, Canellos and Ceresney, that they should move forward. If those two agreed, then the staff needed to go to the SEC's five-person commission and persuade a majority that they should proceed.

Ceresney's instinct was that they should file the case. Canellos was more circumspect, arguing that they didn't have the evidence to win. Ceresney was like an excitable puppy, while Canellos was the cautious one who worried about how an embarrassing loss against the most famous hedge fund manager in the world might damage the agency. Two SEC trial lawyers, the ones who would actually present the case in court if it went that far, pointed out the problems with the evidence they had, which was largely circumstantial. They said that Cohen's lawyers would surely argue that the sequence of events—the forwarding of the "2nd hand read" Dell email, the phone call between Cohen and his research trader—hadn't left him enough time to go through all the steps to sell his shares.

Klotz and his partner Schachter repeated the same points they had raised to the U.S. Attorney's Office: Cohen hadn't necessarily read the email. Cohen would fight. It would go to trial. The SEC wouldn't have *one single witness* to put on the stand to contradict Cohen's position. Schachter also attacked the legitimacy of the AT&T phone records the SEC possessed showing that Cohen had spoken with Vaccarino right before he sold his Dell; he insisted that there was no way to prove that Cohen had actually answered the phone. The SEC had spent months consulting with phone company experts proving that he *had* answered the phone, but Schachter still managed to consume precious hours drawing them into a debate about it.

The SEC staff spent the Memorial Day weekend locked in a tense debate with their supervisors about how to proceed. Sanjay Wadhwa had driven to Providence, Rhode Island, with his wife and three-year-old son. Matt Watkins was in West Virginia visiting his relatives. Justin Smith passed the long weekend in Massachusetts. All of them spent a good portion of the time on the phone or trying to locate pieces of evidence that the higher-ups wanted to see. Long emails flew back and forth, followed by heated phone calls.

Slowly, the SEC staff attorneys started to detect a shift in Ceresney's view. He was starting to waver.

No one wanted to acknowledge it, but the arguments made by Cohen's lawyers over the previous few weeks seemed to be having an effect. By the end of the Memorial Day weekend, Ceresney suddenly didn't think they had a strong case anymore. The heads of the SEC's vaunted enforcement division had gone from robust confidence in their case to a state of retreat.

The SEC staff attorneys were in despair at the prospect of not filing any charges against Cohen. They couldn't believe that after all this, their bosses were on the verge of backing down. They started trying to research other ways they could penalize Cohen. They believed his company was corrupt and that they had to get him out of the market. There were other types of violations besides insider trading, ones that could spring from negligence or recklessness in managing your employees. There had to be *some* mechanism to shut SAC down.

One after the other, black SUVs pulled up on Centre Street in lower Manhattan to drop SAC's senior executives in front of the U.S. Attorney's Office. Half a dozen of them had come for interviews with Arlo Devlin-Brown and Antonia Apps, in which they answered detailed questions about how the firm worked. Everyone to whom the prosecutors had sent a subpoena came in to talk. Everyone, that is, but Cohen.

Even without him, the process had been illuminating. The prosecutors had learned of many situations where questionable trading seemed to be happening at SAC. In one case, a trader was recommended for a job at SAC because he had rented a summer house with the CFO of a publicly traded company, and he had gotten good at predicting the company's quarterly earnings. In another instance, a portfolio manager had learned about a negative research report that was about to be released about a company called Medicis Pharmaceutical and shorted it before the report came out. It was the only case the prosecutors had found where SAC's own compliance department had sanctioned someone for insider trading. The internal punishment was a fine.

Everything they had learned about how SAC operated made perfect sense to the prosecutors once they interviewed Steven Kessler, SAC's head of compliance. The compliance department at a hedge fund was crucial, as it was tasked with enforcing the rules. Unlike Sol Kumin, Tom Conheeney, and the other SAC executives they met with, Kessler did not seem like a very sophisticated person. He was one of the last ones to come in, and when he did, he began the meeting with a scripted presentation about SAC's compliance department and how robust it was. He boasted that SAC had launched a pilot program to catch inappropriate trading by searching firm emails for certain keywords, but it hadn't started until four years after the trades the government was looking at had happened. Once he started answering questions, Kessler didn't prove to be any more impressive.

"How many times have you ever reported suspicious activity of insider trading at SAC to law enforcement?" Devlin-Brown asked.

"Zero," Kessler replied.

The exchange revealed something about the way Cohen had chosen to run his company. Both Kessler and to some extent Peter Nussbaum, SAC's general counsel, were quiet, low-energy guys whose voices could easily have been drowned out. The firm's president, its chief recruiter, and the head of trading, on the other hand, were all big and broad-shouldered, jocular and confident, the kind of cool guys that Cohen probably wished he was. Cohen seemed to the prosecutors like someone who had probably been picked on as a kid. Now that he was immensely wealthy, he could bully other people. As the prosecutors saw it, the people he was most likely to want to push around were in compliance and legal.

At the SEC, the teams working on Dell and Elan sat down together to see if they could combine the evidence they had gathered in both investigations into one charge that would shut SAC down. A few similarities between the cases stood out. Both the Dell situation and the Elan and Wyeth trades had happened under Cohen's direct supervision. There was a clear pattern showing that Cohen was more than willing to ignore signs that information he was getting from his traders might be illegal.

Wadhwa went to Ceresney and Canellos with an idea: Why didn't they drop the idea of insider trading and instead charge Cohen with "failure to supervise," with having neglected to properly monitor his traders? It was a weaker charge than insider trading, but in the end, if their goal was to bar Cohen from the securities industry, it could be enough. The evidence, Wadhwa's staff thought, was definitely strong enough to support the charge. Plus, it didn't carry the same risk of losing a trial. They could bring the case in an internal SEC court, where the stakes would be lower. At this point, the SEC leadership was leaning toward not filing any case at all, and failure to supervise was better than nothing.

Much to the relief of the SEC staff, Ceresney and Canellos said yes.

When Wadhwa called Klotz to inform him of the case they planned to bring, Klotz seemed relieved, too.

"Okay, fine," he said. He asked only that Cohen be given a day to inform his employees. Cohen didn't want his traders reading about it on their Bloomberg terminals.

The SEC's enforcement chiefs arranged a phone call with Rich Zabel, the Deputy U.S. Attorney, to update him on their plans. Rather than congratulating them, though, Zabel seemed annoyed. He was exasperated that the SEC was pushing ahead with its own case without waiting for them, and he said so. As soon as the SEC filed something, Cohen's lawyers could start to extract information about the government's evidence. Bharara still planned to charge SAC Capital Advisors with insider trading. His prosecutors were working to get the papers ready. Cohen was hanging out there, and there was still a possibility that Martoma would flip. In the past, the criminal prosecutors and the SEC had tried to coordinate the timing of their filings to avoid interfering with one other. It was essential that they maintain a unified front. Not only was the SEC violating that implicit agreement to work together, they were racing ahead with a weak case—failure to supervise instead of insider trading.

"I don't understand," Zabel said. "We've been moving in lockstep. Why would you do this?"

The SEC enforcement chiefs defended themselves by saying that they were worried about the statute of limitations deadline on the Elan trades, which was only a few days away. They went forward on their own and charged Cohen with failing to supervise his employees. The SEC announced the case with a news release. There was a storm of media attention.

Six days later, on the morning of July 25, an alert went out from the U.S. Attorney's Office to members of the news media: "1:00 P.M.—A press conference will be held on a securities fraud matter." Bharara was ready to unveil his indictment of SAC Capital Advisors, with all of the pageantry and stagecraft that such a significant legal action required. Around lunchtime, camera crews started setting up tripods along the back wall of the ground-floor atrium at 1 St. Andrew's Plaza. The room grew so crowded that people had to stand in the aisles. At 12:59 P.M., Preet Bharara stepped out from behind a dark curtain and took his familiar spot behind the podium. "Today, we announced three law enforcement actions relating to the SAC group of hedge funds," he said, against a soundtrack of popping camera flashbulbs. Bharara outlined three sets of charges that his office was making against Cohen's company: insider trading and wire fraud charges; civil money laundering charges seeking forfeiture of assets tied to the illegal trading; and a guilty plea of another portfolio manager at SAC, named Richard Lee (not Richard C. B. Lee)—the eighth SAC employee charged with insider trading so far.

"When so many people from a single hedge fund have engaged in insider trading, it is not a coincidence. It is, instead, the predictable product of substantial and pervasive institutional failure," Bharara said. "SAC trafficked in inside information on a scale without any known precedent in the history of hedge funds." The indictment painted a devastating portrait of Cohen and his company. Bharara described the scope of illegal trading at SAC as "deep" and "wide," spanning more than ten years and involving at least twenty different securities from different industries, resulting in illegal profits of "at least" hundreds of millions of dollars.

Still, the key question went unaddressed: What about Cohen? For Bharara, indicting SAC had crystallized an important point: Now more than ever, they needed Martoma to cooperate. That was the only thing, at this point, that would allow them to put the man responsible for everything behind bars.

Once he finished with his prepared remarks, Bharara said that he would take a few questions from the dozens of reporters in the room. "Do you plan to criminally indict Steve Cohen?" a woman shouted.

A hint of irritation could be detected on Bharara's face. He knew, of course, that rather than focusing on the triumph of his SAC Capital case, the media would fixate on the lack of charges against Cohen. The press had its familiar storyline, about catching the "big fish," and reporters would be eager to cast the indictment of SAC as a failure. Bharara intended to make it clear that they were not yet done. Steven Cohen was still a target, and they planned to continue to investigate and, eventually, to bring him to justice. "Today, we're bringing the charges that I've described," Bharara said, hoping that he was making himself clear. "I'm not going to say what tomorrow may or may not bring."

Then a second reporter asked essentially the same question. "Sometimes when you bring a case, that opens up doors to bringing other cases in the future," Bharara said. "You'll have to wait and see."

As Bharara ended the press conference, which was broadcast live on CNBC, everyone on SAC's trading floor stared at Cohen, who was trying to pretend that it was just another typical trading day.

"A lot of people were thinking Steve was just going to walk away," said one person who was there. "Assistants were asking if they should box up their belongings."

Cohen made an announcement over the company's PA system: "We're going to be okay," he said, trying to sound reassuring. "We're going to get through this."

Privately, though, Cohen was in a state of shock. He withdrew to East Hampton for the weekend with Alex and their four youngest children, the eldest of whom was home visiting from university. Through most of the investigation, Alex had tried to protect the kids from the news coverage and had banned any discussion of it at home. Cohen had been terrified of how they would react to the cartoonish depictions of him in the press, and he had avoided talking to them about it. But now, with the Manhattan U.S. Attorney broadcasting to the world that their father was the financial world's Al Capone, he couldn't keep it hidden any longer.

His daughters climbed to the second floor of the seven-bedroom house, where Cohen spent most of his time in his office staring into his trading station, to talk to him.

You are going to be reading and hearing a lot of stuff about me that isn't very pleasant, Cohen told them. He struggled with what to say; he was bitter about what was happening. His friends had started making jokes that he "looked good in stripes," but he didn't find them funny.

"People will have different opinions," Cohen said to his daughters, "and some are going to be untrue."

The girls were understandably anxious. Was their father in trouble? Did he do something terrible?

"People in the company have done things that are wrong, and they're going to pay for what they did," Cohen told them. "I didn't do anything wrong."

PART
FOUR

CHAPTER 15

JUSTICE

Every weekday morning for the rest of the summer, Steve Cohen set-tled into the backseat of his black Maybach for the twenty-three-minute drive from his home in Greenwich to SAC's offices in Stamford. He made a point of being there by 8 A.M., as he had always done. He took up his post behind his screens as if everything were normal. And he did the only thing he knew how to do: He traded. He was largely able to do this because major investment banks like Morgan Stanley, JPMorgan Chase, and Goldman Sachs, the ones that had earned hundreds of millions of dollars in commissions from Cohen over more than a decade, refused to abandon him during his time of darkness, even though his company had been branded a criminal enterprise and Cohen himself was still at risk of criminal prosecution. It was virtually unprecedented in the financial industry. Mainstream Wall Street looked at the agency that stood for law and order and ethics in their field and at the most profitable trader they had ever worked with and then pointed at Cohen and said, "We choose you."

"They're an important client to us," Goldman Sachs's president, Gary Cohn, said days after the U.S. Attorney for the Southern District of New

York declared SAC a "magnet for market cheaters" and said that the company had "trafficked in inside information on a scale without any known precedent" in the history of hedge funds. "They're a great counterparty."

During discussions with Cohen's lawyers prior to the indictment of SAC, the U.S. Attorney's Office had made it clear that, in order to resolve the case, Cohen would have to shut his hedge fund down. Cohen would still have close to $10 billion of his own money, however, which he would be allowed to trade and invest as a private family office. The government could not stop him from trading his own money. Until he was convicted, Cohen and his army of traders would still command respect from Wall Street's major investment banks and have access to the best IPO allocations. The $10 billion number was important to Cohen. It sent a signal to the world that nothing had really changed.

Then, in the second week of September, Cohen's lawyers got a call from Anjan Sahni, the co-chief of the securities unit at the U.S. Attorney's Office. Sahni and his colleagues wanted to talk about settling the case against SAC. Not much had happened during the month of August, after the indictment. The prosecutors noticed, though, that business at SAC had gone on as if nothing unusual had occurred. There were no visible crises in the market, no layoffs or margin calls. Wall Street had absorbed criminal charges against one of the largest hedge funds in the world with barely any disruption.

Settling the case was the only resolution that made sense; a trial was a risky proposition for both sides. For the government, losing the SAC case would have led to humiliation, a heavy blow to morale at the office. Mathew Martoma's trial was approaching, and the FBI still hoped that he would decide to cooperate, in which case prosecutors would need all of their resources to develop that case.

For Cohen, the calculation was similar. The idea that he would submit himself and his employees to months of discovery and take the stand to answer questions under oath about his trading activities if he didn't have to was laughable. He was a trader without nerves, but a long, drawn-out court battle that threatened to expose all his secrets was one risk he did not have the stomach for. Plus, if he ended up being charged himself, he needed to reserve all his legal firepower to defend himself. In the end, after all the calculations, the case against SAC Capital came down to a question of how big a check Cohen would have to write in order for it to be over.

Cohen's lawyers made an opening offer of $100 million to $150 million. Bharara didn't even take it seriously, it seemed so far from the figure he had in mind. The co-chief of the securities unit reminded Klotz and Cohen's other attorneys that there were two very relevant trials coming up: those of Michael Steinberg, which was starting in November, and Martoma, in January. The cost of settling was only going to increase if Cohen dragged the negotiations out until both of those trials ended with convictions. Sahni didn't have to mention the obvious point that if either of them decided to cooperate before then, the argument would become even more forceful.

Two months later, on November 4, Bharara announced that they had a deal. The terms of the settlement were large and sweeping and intended to deliver a powerful message that Wall Street was not above the law. In the twenty-first century, when the financial industry had largely taken over the economy, the SAC case was supposed to prove that Wall Street excess had a price, that, even when up against the most powerful transgressors, the law can win. SAC had agreed to plead guilty and pay $1.8 billion—the company managed to negotiate credit for the $616 million it had already committed to pay the SEC, so in reality the new fine was $1.2 billion. The settlement would also include a guilty plea by SAC, an admission, in court, that the firm had done everything the government was accusing it of.

Again, comparisons with Michael Milken, in many ways Cohen's precursor, seemed appropriate. In 1989, Milken's firm Drexel Burnham Lambert had pleaded guilty to securities fraud and agreed to pay a $650 million fine. The SAC deal was similarly impressive. For Americans who were still confused and upset about why nobody had been held legally responsible for the crimes that led to the financial crisis of 2008, the case against Cohen's company was something different: a clear, unequivocal victory for the forces of fairness and integrity.

Or at least that was the idea.

All that was left was for SAC to register its guilty plea before a federal judge a few days later. While TV networks beamed news of the settlement onto trading floors around the world, Cohen sat glowering at his desk in Stamford. He wasn't happy about it, but he had known this day might be coming, and he had an aggressive crisis PR firm on retainer ready to go into counterattack mode the second Bharara made his announcement. "The tiny fraction of wrongdoers does not represent the 3,000 honest men and women who have worked at the firm during the past 21 years," SAC's public relations handler said in a statement. The last line read: "SAC has never encouraged, promoted or tolerated insider trading."

Bharara couldn't believe it when he read it. SAC had just signed a guilty plea admitting that it had, in fact, been built on a culture of insider trading. Cohen had admitted as part of the agreement that his company had fostered a culture of securities fraud for over a decade. The chief of Bharara's securities unit called Cohen's lawyers and ordered them to retract the statement, which they did. Then they released a new one that stated: "We greatly regret this conduct occurred."

On November 8, one of the highest-priced teams of defense lawyers in the country filed into a courtroom at 500 Pearl Street in lower Manhattan, wearing their best pinstripes and shiny cuff links. The spectator's gallery was packed with reporters, prosecutors, SEC attorneys, FBI agents, law students, and curious gawkers, all crammed in on benches like passengers on a train. Tabloid photographers lurked outside. Incredibly, Cohen didn't have to show up in court himself. He would be paying the $1.8 billion out of his own funds, but he was barely going to notice that the money was gone.

The judge, Laura Taylor Swain, placed a stainless steel coffee cup on the desk in front of her and peered down at the herd of lawyers assembled below. The room fell silent.

"Mr. Nussbaum, it is my understanding that you need to remain seated today," she said, blinking through her glasses.

A hundred heads turned to look at Peter Nussbaum, SAC's legal counsel, who was sitting, uncomfortably, at the defense table.

"That is my preference, yes, your honor," said Nussbaum, wincing a little. He was doubled over in pain from an emergency appendectomy three weeks before which had been exacerbated by extreme stress. He stood halfway up to be sworn in and then do what he had come here for, to surrender on behalf of Cohen.

"Do you understand the charges that SAC Capital is pleading guilty to?" the judge asked.

"Yes."

"Are you under the influence of any drugs or alcohol?"

"I've taken some antibiotics for my condition," he said.

"Do you want me to read the indictment out loud?" Swain asked, holding up a forty-page document.

"No thank you, your honor," Nussbaum said.

Laughter rippled through the gallery. In an instant, Swain had brought out just how odd the whole ceremony was, a burial without a body.

Nussbaum knew the charges by heart. His employer of thirteen years was about to admit that it had been run like a criminal empire for more than a decade, amassing hundreds of millions of dollars in illegal profit and making its founder one of the richest men on earth.

Judge Swain described the agreed-upon penalty in the case, $900 million in criminal fines and $900 million in civil forfeiture, as well as a five-year probation period during which a compliance monitor to be approved by the Justice Department would watch over the fund's activities. The hedge fund would be shut down.

Nussbaum sighed and looked up at the judge. "On behalf of SAC I first want to express our deep remorse for the misconduct of each individual who broke the law while employed at SAC," he said. "This happened on our watch, and we are responsible for that misconduct.

"We have paid and are paying a very steep price," Nussbaum continued. "We are chastened by this experience, but we are determined to learn from it and emerge from this as a better firm."

The judge stared at Nussbaum. A few droplets of sweat had appeared on his forehead.

"How does SAC Capital plead?" she asked.

Nussbaum pulled himself halfway out of his chair.

"Guilty," he said.

"Are the defendants pleading guilty because they *are* guilty?" the judge said.

"Yes, your honor."

With a tap of her gavel, Judge Swain said, "We are adjourned."

It took a while for the two hundred or so people in the courtroom to squeeze their way through the single door in the back. Outside on the curb, SAC's group of defense lawyers waited, unable to find the black Escalade that was supposed to whisk them away. They stumbled around as a pack of photographers and TV reporters swarmed around them like gnats, trying to corner them for a statement.

Finally the lawyers spotted their car and ran over to it. They climbed in, the doors closed, and it sped off.

A man with a backpack exiting the building looked after them, bewildered. "Who's the crook they're following?"

Almost two weeks later, on November 20, Michael Steinberg's trial began. The prosecutors had never felt confident that he would choose to cooperate—he was intensely loyal to Cohen, for one thing, and because his trades were so small, the leverage the government had against him was weak. Still, they had hoped that some sense of honor or civic-mindedness, perhaps the entreaties of his wife, might bring him around to their side.

As Antonia Apps strode into the courtroom and took her place behind the prosecution table on the first day of trial, however, it was clear that it wasn't going to happen. All the prosecutors could try to do was punish Steinberg. Apps turned toward the twelve men and women seated in the jury box.

"Members of the jury," she began. "Michael Steinberg got stolen business information and then used that information to make money—lots of money—by trading in the stock market." Steinberg was sitting with his lawyers at the defense table with a pained look on his face. "He got secret financial information from people inside companies before that information was made available to the public. He did it to get an illegal edge over ordinary investors who played by the rules. And when Michael Steinberg traded on that illegal inside information, he broke the law."

Apps was known as someone who, when presented with the choice between going out for drinks with her colleagues and staying late preparing for a trial, almost always chose the latter. Tall and fit, she was a former national figure skating champion who had left a lucrative partnership at a white shoe law firm to prosecute securities cases at the U.S. Attorney's Office. She *wanted* to be here.

Her job was to take a vastly complicated case and turn it into the simplest story possible: Michael Steinberg was a rich Wall Street guy who had cheated. "He wanted to make big money for himself and for the hedge fund for which he worked," Apps said. "That, ladies and gentlemen, is called insider trading, and it's a serious crime."

In an environment where the average person harbored unfocused but intense anger toward Wall Street, Steinberg was a juicy target. Privileged, arrogant, he lived on another plane from most Americans. He was not Steve Cohen, but he was close.

The job of saving Steinberg from this characterization fell to his defense lawyer, Barry Berke. Where Apps was meticulously rehearsed, Berke was willing to improvise, with the affect of a congressman who knew how to turn on the charm. Berke had wanted to be a defense attorney since he was in law school at Harvard, when he had stumbled into the glare of TV news cameras on the courtroom steps after defending a wrongful conviction case as a student.

He loved that moment in the spotlight. "This better not be the last time there are cameras for one of my cases," he had thought.

Berke smoothed his tie and turned toward the jury, gripping the sides of the podium. To test out his arguments, Berke had staged two mock trials and recorded the proceedings so that he and his partners could analyze their performances. He had researched every juror on the case, scouring their social media footprints for any sign of their views about Wall Street or the government. He knew the facts of the case better than anyone. As in the Martoma defense, SAC was paying the bills.

He flashed the jurors a smile and launched into a parable that was meant to illustrate the core of Steinberg's defense: that Horvath, Steinberg's former underling, was only testifying against Steinberg to save himself. Not everyone in the room understood the point he was trying to make with the parable, which involved a farmer falling into a well, but Berke went ahead anyway. "He needed to point the finger at somebody to get a deal," Berke said, referring to Horvath. "So he pointed it at Mike Steinberg."

Berke's first task was to undermine Horvath and portray him as a dishonest person who was trying only to save himself. His second job was subtler and, given the political environment, far more difficult. He had to humanize Steinberg. He had to show the jury that Steinberg was a generous, warm family man, not simply another greedy hedge fund millionaire who spent his summers in East Hampton. It was not going to be easy.

Berke tried to explain what it was that Steinberg did for a living in the plainest terms possible. "SAC is a fund," he said in his most obsequious voice. "It's kind of like a mutual fund. . . ."

There was some snickering in the room. Describing SAC as similar to a mutual fund was sort of like describing the New York Yankees as a group of kids who played baseball.

"He worked hard to become a portfolio manager," Berke continued. "He was someone who was known as successful, steady. . . . He was dependable, and he was paid well for it."

Steinberg's wife, Elizabeth, had taken it upon herself to try to push back against what she felt were unfair perceptions of her husband. She had encouraged a group of supporters to attend the trial, and they filled almost the entire left side of the courtroom. She had even instructed them on how they should look so it wouldn't backfire on her husband. "Dress conservatively," she wrote in an email to the group. "We request that women wear no jewelry or furs, and no designer scarves, handbags, etc."

Liz herself wore a black sweater, black slacks, and flat shoes, like an Italian widow, and sat in the front row between Steinberg's parents and her own. Behind them were several more rows of men and women in dark clothes—assorted uncles, aunts, and cousins and another dozen or so friends, several of whom were regulars in the Manhattan society pages. Sandy Heller, Cohen's art advisor and Steinberg's childhood friend, was in attendance, along with his twin brother, Andy, who ran his own hedge fund. Other defendants in insider trading cases had tried to do the same thing; the idea was to show the jury that this was not some amoral, greedy trader but a good neighbor who donated to charity and had people who loved and believed in him.

If Steinberg was resentful that he was here, while Cohen was free to do as he pleased, he didn't show it. He had refused multiple offers to cooperate. Apps had made it clear that the government was interested in *anything* he had to say, no matter how insignificant it seemed. But Steinberg had refused. And based on conversations he had had with some of the top criminal defense lawyers in the country, he thought that he had a shot at getting acquitted.

"I know there are strong views today about Wall Street," Berke said to the jury, preparing for the finale of his opening argument. "I don't have to tell you, this case is not a referendum on Wall Street, as you know. This case is really about one question. That's this guy, Michael Steinberg." He implored them to find Steinberg not guilty of all the charges. Then Berke collapsed into his chair.

When Horvath was led into the courtroom three days later, he looked out of place, like a little boy wearing his father's suit. He had a deep tan, and his hair was spread like a fringe across his eyes. Steinberg's wife glared at him as he walked past.

By this point, Steinberg had already suffered some damage. On the second day of trial, Apps had lingered over slides showing how much money Steinberg had made in 2007 and 2008, when his bonus was well into the millions of dollars. It was sure to seem like an unimaginable fortune to the jurors, a group that included a former postal worker, a motel bookkeeper, and a tennis court attendant. Then Jesse Tortora, Horvath's source on the Dell tips, spent two days testifying about how he'd obtained inside information from a friend who used to work at Dell and given it to Horvath, who shared it with Steinberg.

With a cool, detached manner, Apps asked Horvath what he was hoping to gain by agreeing to testify against Michael Steinberg.

"I'm hoping to avoid jail time," Horvath said.

Shortly before 3 P.M. on the eighth day of the trial, the moment Berke had been waiting for arrived: He would have the opportunity to cross-examine Horvath. Privately, he called it the "snitch cross."

So far, Apps's approach had been effective. While Horvath was far from a sympathetic character, he sounded like he was doing his best to describe events the way he remembered them. He was a weasel, but a believable weasel.

A large team of attorneys, associates, and paralegals had helped Berke prepare for this; private investigators had tracked down Horvath's friends and family members; they had subpoenaed his files from his previous jobs; Berke's firm had even hired a forensic computer expert, who had taken Horvath's laptop from SAC and re-created the Google searches he had conducted from that machine. They learned, for example, that after he was arrested, Horvath researched document-shredding companies. Berke was armed with six hundred pages of arguments and evidence to counter every possible excuse or explanation Horvath could put forth.

Berke stood up and strode toward the podium. He immediately focused on Horvath's claim that Steinberg had ordered him to get inside information at SAC.

"He told you, according to your testimony, he wanted you to get 'edgy proprietary information,'" Berke said. His tone was hostile. "Is that your testimony?"

"Yes," Horvath said.

"What did you say?" Berke asked. "What did you say?"

Horvath said he didn't think he had responded to Steinberg.

They went back and forth, with Berke pressing him about whether he had said anything in response to Steinberg's directive. He seemed to be trying to get Horvath to admit that it wasn't clear what Steinberg had been asking. The stakes were higher than usual, because Steinberg was not expected to take the stand himself. Horvath's credibility alone would determine Steinberg's future.

Berke questioned him for five days. At one point, on the second day of the cross-examination, he goaded Horvath into saying, of Steinberg, "He didn't explicitly tell me to go out and break the law!" At that, Steinberg smiled for the first time since the trial began.

"Isn't it true," Berke said, "that you're telling a lie by falsely accusing Mr. Steinberg?"

Without looking up, Horvath shook his head, no.

By the time Berke was finished, Horvath had been severely weakened as a witness. Apps was able to undo some of the damage when her opportunity for redirect arrived. She walked Horvath back through the core facts of the case: Steinberg had told him to get illegal information; Steinberg knew that the information Horvath was giving him came from someone inside Dell; they shorted the stock before the earnings announcement; Horvath never concealed the source of the information from Steinberg.

When she was done, on December 13, the government rested its case.

When the jury started deliberating a few days later, Berke was feeling good about Steinberg's chances. It was one of his strongest trials, he thought. Nothing undermined a prosecution's case like showing its key witness to be untrustworthy, and he felt that he'd done that on several fronts. A scenario in which Steinberg was acquitted, which had seemed laughable at the outset of the trial, was suddenly very real.

The courtroom emptied out, aside from Steinberg, his wife, their parents, and the two sets of lawyers. For Berke and his team, the possibility that this might be the first case to topple Preet Bharara's perfect 76-0 record for insider trading convictions was exhilarating.

What the lawyers, family members, and news reporters who were standing by for the verdict didn't know as the hours ticked by was that, inside the overheated jury room, the jurors had reached an impasse. Halfway through the second day of deliberations, two of the jurors were not convinced that Steinberg explicitly knew that Horvath was giving him inside information about Dell. The jurors had struggled throughout the trial, which included thirteen witnesses over five weeks, to understand all the financial jargon, the references to "edge" and "channel checks" and gross margins. Several felt that Horvath was dishonest, someone who did whatever it took to "save his own skin," in the words of one juror. The jury forewoman, a massage therapist from Manhattan named Demethress Gordon, counted twenty-eight times that she felt Horvath was lying. As she later put it, she "didn't believe anything he said."

Still, ten of the jurors argued with Gordon and the other holdout, the fact that Horvath was dishonest didn't mean that Steinberg didn't know what was going on.

Gordon had written down notes throughout the trial. She prided herself as a judge of character. She was one of the ones who was resisting voting to convict. She was just not convinced of Steinberg's guilt.

After an hour of fruitless back-and-forth, a different juror suddenly had an idea. The juror asked Gordon to get up and walk through the doorway in the jury room, as part of a demonstration. Gordon did it. Then the other juror said: "I told you to go through the door, but I didn't tell you explicitly *how* to go through the door."

It was like two wires connecting. Gordon knew how to walk through the door without being explicitly told how to do it. It was the same as being ordered to get "edgy" information. Horvath understood what that meant without having it spelled out.

The other holdout, a seventy-one-year-old woman, was swayed by the demonstration as well. She had been struck by Steinberg's instruction to Horvath after receiving the "2nd hand read" email, when he told his underling to keep the information "especially on the down low." That seemed to indicate a clear understanding that the information was illegal. Both pieces together seemed to indicate guilt.

At 2:59 P.M. on December 18, 2013, the jury took a vote. They voted unanimously to convict.

The clerk told the judge that the jury had reached a verdict. Suddenly, the courtroom, where people were lounging around, grew tense. Both sets of lawyers started sending out emails, letting people know that a verdict was imminent. People flowed into the room, filling the empty seats. Steinberg's brother rushed in and took a spot at the front. His wife sat between her parents, clutching both of their hands.

Berke was looking less hopeful. The verdict had come down relatively fast, which was usually bad news.

The jury filed into the room at 3:15 P.M. and took their seats in the jury box. Then, out of nowhere, a scream rang out. Steinberg had slumped forward in his chair, unconscious. It was his wife, Liz, who had screamed, and she reached out for her husband over the heavy oak barrier separating the spectators from the well of the courtroom. She was sobbing. Steinberg's mother started to cry as well. Berke had his arm around Steinberg, trying to cradle his head.

"Okay, let's get the jury out," said Judge Richard Sullivan, jumping out of his chair.

The jurors were ushered out of the room. They had already handed over the envelope containing their decision to Sullivan's clerk. The prosecutors looked stricken. The trial had not gone smoothly for the government, and the prospect of an embarrassing loss was looming. Steinberg's friends and relatives, meanwhile, looked like they were praying. His mother and mother-in-law clung to one another in the first row, swaying back and forth.

After several minutes of silence during which Steinberg was tended to by the court nurse, he resumed his seat at the defense table. The jurors came back into the room, their eyes fixed on the floor in front of them.

It appeared that Steinberg had had a premonition. The jury found him guilty on all counts.

CHAPTER 16

JUDGMENT

The Christmas holidays were not relaxing for Arlo Devlin-Brown. He was living in his office, preparing exhibits, going over witness lists, staying until 10 P.M. before trudging home to the Upper West Side, where he lived with his wife and two children. He was deep into preparations for the Mathew Martoma trial, which was starting right after New Year's. He knew the government had a strong case, but he didn't want to be over-confident.

No one in the U.S. Attorney's Office could quite believe that it had come to this, with Martoma going to trial rather than cooperating. The hope among the prosecutors was that with Martoma suddenly facing a long, public court proceeding, he would finally succumb to the pressure to flip and help them make a case against Cohen.

In late December 2013, a few days after Steinberg was convicted, Devlin-Brown's phone rang. Martoma's lawyer, Richard Strassberg, was on the line. Strassberg was calling to make an offer—one that he wanted the prosecutor to seriously consider. Devlin-Brown caught his breath for a moment. Maybe this was it, the call they had all been waiting for. Maybe Martoma was ready to talk.

"I cannot represent that Mat had agreed to this," Strassberg began. "But would you potentially be interested in a guilty plea to a 371 with a five-year cap?"

Fuck, Devlin-Brown thought.

Martoma wasn't going to cooperate. "371" was a reference to the conspiracy statute in the criminal code. Strassberg was trying to find out whether the U.S. Attorney's Office might agree to let Martoma plead guilty to a charge of conspiracy to commit fraud, the lowest of the charges he faced, and a maximum of five years in prison. It was not a suggestion that Martoma might help them, only that he might plead guilty to get a reduced sentence. Strassberg was eager to try the case, but he knew that the trial would be excruciating for Martoma's family, sort of like watching their loved one being waterboarded in public. The odds were against them. A last-minute deal would spare them weeks of stress and humiliation.

Devlin-Brown couldn't tell how serious the proposal was, especially if Strassberg was saying that Martoma hadn't even agreed to it yet. Bharara was unlikely to go for it, anyway. The news that this was Martoma's final offer would be a crushing disappointment to everyone in the office. Leaving aside the fact that it was not at all what Bharara had been hoping for, U.S. Attorneys didn't like to make favorable deals with defendants on the eve of a trial. It looked bad. Judges didn't like it. And on a personal level, Devlin-Brown found it irritating. He and his colleagues had spent months working seven days a week preparing for what was expected to be one of the most high-profile trials of the year. Why hadn't Strassberg approached him with this idea sooner? Still, he agreed to discuss the offer with the higher-ups in the office. That afternoon, he and the securities chiefs talked it over.

The next day, Devlin-Brown called Strassberg back. The answer was no. There would be no deal. They were going to trial.

On January 7, 2014, Mathew and Rosemary Martoma arrived at the courthouse by chauffeured SUV. A blizzard had left mountains of snow on the street, and Rosemary navigated the slippery sidewalk in four-inch heels. The trial was expected to go on for several weeks, so they had pulled their kids out of school and booked a suite at the Intercontinental Hotel near Times Square so the family could be together. Mathew and Rosemary's arrival at the courthouse was documented by a pack of news photographers and TV cameras.

Shortly before they were supposed to begin opening statements two days later, Roberto Braceras, Strassberg's partner at Goodwin Procter, stood behind the defense table facing the judge, trying not to lose control of his anger. In one hand he held that day's business section of *The New York Times*. His hand was trembling. On the front page was a headline: "Ex-SAC Trader Was Expelled from Harvard Law School."

For several weeks the two sets of lawyers had been waging a fierce battle behind the scenes. And now it was splashed all over the newspaper.

That morning, the government had filed a motion with the judge requesting permission to admit evidence of Martoma's expulsion from Harvard Law School during the trial. Not just the expulsion itself, but the entire sordid tale of how Martoma doctored his transcripts, tried to cover it up, and then created a fake company to try to get himself readmitted. On the surface, the Harvard story had no connection to the question at the heart of the case—whether Martoma had paid a doctor to get non-public drug trial results and then traded stock on the basis of the information. There were some weaknesses in the prosecution's case, though, that the Harvard story could potentially compensate for, a piece of ammunition they wanted to hold in reserve. The FBI still had not been able to recover the missing email with the PowerPoint presentation containing the drug trial results that Gilman said he had sent to Martoma. It was an important piece of evidence that would have proven that Martoma had received the bapi results a week before they were publicly released. Devlin-Brown believed that Martoma might have been able to make that email disappear. His attempted email-doctoring at Harvard proved he had the technical expertise and the temperament to pull something like that off—or at least to try.

As soon as Strassberg and Braceras learned that Devlin-Brown was seeking permission to introduce the Harvard backstory, they filed their own motion arguing against it. They also filed a separate motion asking to keep the whole debate under seal and out of the public court docket. They knew that the revelation of the Harvard story would be devastating to Martoma's case. District Judge Paul Gardephe dealt Martoma a major setback when he ruled that the Harvard documents would be made public. Not only would Martoma be publicly humiliated, but it constrained his lawyers in their defense. Even Strassberg had to admit that pushing the Harvard evidence into the case was a brilliant tactical move on the part of the prosecutors. If he so much as suggested that Gilman was lying about sending the PowerPoint to Martoma, the jury would hear everything about Harvard. It was like having handcuffs on.

"Your Honor," Braceras said, "as we anticipated, there were a number of stories both on television and in the newspaper. . . ." He pointed to a pile of other papers on his desk, including the *New York Post,* which had its own sensational headline. Braceras wanted Gardephe to ask the jurors if any of them had read the Harvard coverage.

Braceras was a seasoned partner of Strassberg's from Goodwin Procter's Boston office. Fit and well-groomed, he had a self-deprecating style that was disarming. As he made his argument, Martoma's wife and parents sat in the first two rows of the courtroom, their heads hanging. Their darkest family secret, and their greatest shame, was now on display. For Martoma, this was almost more painful than being charged with insider trading.

Gardephe expressed sympathy but ultimately refused to interrogate the jurors about whether they'd read the Harvard stories. They were already under orders not to look at any of the press about the case. He had told them at the outset to avoid the Internet. He had been a federal judge since 2008, and he believed that the jury system was based on trust.

The opening argument was one of Devlin-Brown's favorite parts of a trial. In a case like this, it was sometimes all that mattered. The U.S. Attorney's Office had a formula for it, a system that was passed down through generations of prosecutors. It started with what they called "the grab"—a quick, two-minute summary of the case, meant to capture the jury's attention. The grab could begin in one of two ways. The first was with a big thematic idea, as in, "This is a case about greed." Devlin-Brown preferred what he called the "It was a dark and stormy night" beginning, which dropped the jurors right into a dramatic scene. Just like in a movie.

On this day, his version began with, "It was July of 2008." He spoke in a gentle, even voice. "Mathew Martoma, the defendant, was one of about a thousand people packed into a crowded Chicago convention hall waiting for an expert on Alzheimer's disease to take the stage." Sidney Gilman, he explained, was at an international Alzheimer's conference to unveil the results of a hotly anticipated drug trial. The results of the trial could herald a major medical breakthrough, and a tremendous profit, for the drug companies involved. Everyone at the conference was anxiously waiting to hear from the doctor. Except for Martoma. "You see, Mathew Martoma, he already knew what Dr. Gilman was going to say," Devlin-Brown said. "He had corrupted Dr. Gilman, through real money and phony friend-ship, and Dr. Gilman had already shared the presentation with him." After Gilman finished presenting the results, shares of Elan dropped 40 percent. "A lot of people lost money. But not Mathew Martoma. The hedge fund where Mathew Martoma worked made a *lot* of money."

Devlin-Brown was a natural performer, the son of a former Broadway actress. He went to Columbia University and, like many of his colleagues, Harvard Law School, where he took every opportunity to speak in front of others, from debate to moot court to singing in the law school's a cap-pella group. The joke in Devlin-Brown's family was that he ran away from home and became a lawyer instead of joining the circus.

"This case will contain some science, but it is not a science test," he told the jury. "There is also a sophisticated hedge fund, but this case is not about finance. This case is about cheating."

As he sketched out the government's case, Rosemary leaned forward in her seat, sliding her glasses on and off her face, assessing the prosecu-tor as an adversary. Her husband sat stiffly in his chair at the defense table five feet away with a blank look on his face. It was as if the whole spectacle was so painful for him that his soul had departed his body, leaving be-hind an empty shell in a pressed suit.

By the time Strassberg rose for his opening, it was clear that it would be difficult for him to change the picture Devlin-Brown had painted. They faced a significant challenge with Gilman as the main witness. How could you discredit an eighty-one-year-old doctor, the former head of a university medical department, without something irrefutable? He had to be careful about how he presented Martoma's side of the story.

"A little more than ten years ago, there was a big hit on Broadway—*The Exonerated*—about people who'd been convicted of horrible crimes," Strassberg said, starting to pace. His hair was combed back with a glint of pomade, and he wore a tailored gray suit with a pink tie. His shoes were gleaming. "In each of those cases, the prosecutor was wrong," he continued. "They had put innocent men and women on death row, until hard evidence exonerated them." As he got warmed up he started to wave his hands in the air. "I stand before you, not in some play, but in real life. The prosecution has rushed to judgment and in that rush to judgment, they have charged an innocent man."

Devlin-Brown listened to him with slight bemusement. Comparing Martoma to a wrongfully convicted death row inmate? It seemed a little over-the-top. But, given their resources, it was likely Martoma's lawyers had tested the idea with a high-priced jury consultant and concluded it might work.

The jury would hear no wiretaps, only the deeply conflicted account of an aging doctor who was desperate to get immunity for himself, Strassberg continued. "Dr. Gilman felt pressure to tell a story the prosecutors wanted to hear," he said.

Then he moved on to the unfairly maligned integrity of his own client. "In many ways, Mathew was the quintessential American success story," Strassberg said. Born to Indian immigrants in Florida, he grew up in the shadow of the Kennedy Space Center, where he was part of a minority Christian community. He graduated from public high school and attended Duke University. "As he was getting his MBA he met Rose," Strassberg said, gazing beatifically at Rosemary. She beamed at the jurors, right on cue. "They married in 2003 and in short order produced three kids, Joshua, Ava and David, all under age nine.

"The stakes here could not be higher," he said, walking the length of the courtroom and sweeping his arms in the air. "The case will not add up! The pieces will not fit! What's important is that you, the jury, don't rush to judgment. You will find that Mathew did not commit these charges. He has been falsely accused!"

Both openings were strong. But already, it seemed that Strassberg was overplaying his hand. He was in salesman mode, peddling a story to the jury that required assumptions that defied common sense. Defending Martoma was going to be the fight of Strassberg's career.

Five days after opening arguments, the jurors had their first glimpse of Dr. Sidney Gilman. As he was led into the courtroom, around 11:45 A.M., a hush fell over the room. Martoma's family had followed the conventional wisdom and attempted to recruit friends to attend the trial. Martoma's parents, Rosemary's parents, and a handful of cousins and aunts appeared, bundled in sweaters and looking like they might freeze. Rosemary appeared in court each day in a different eye-catching outfit. But the group of supporters was much sparser than what Steinberg had enjoyed. Where the Steinberg crowd had looked robust and well-off, Martoma's tiny army seemed almost tragic.

Gilman's eyes were dark and bright, with deep, pronounced bags under them, and his hair was snow-white, each strand visible where it sprouted from his head. Rosemary looked at him coldly as he shuffled by in a charcoal suit, looking so frail that he might shatter at the touch.

Gilman was far from the perfect witness. For one thing, his memory was wobbly. Devlin-Brown had heard that Martoma's defense lawyers had thoroughly investigated Gilman in an attempt to find information they could use to discredit him. They'd even sent a private investigator to Ann Arbor to interview Gilman's tailor—the tailor refused to talk to them, citing "tailor privilege." Someone had also tracked down Gilman's estranged son in Connecticut. Devlin-Brown's hope was that by putting Gilman on the stand relatively late in the trial, the basic narrative of what happened would already be clear in the jurors' minds. All Gilman would be doing was confirming what they already knew.

He wore hearing aids in both ears and his eyesight was faltering, which gave him an air of confusion. When Devlin-Brown asked him to identify Martoma in the courtroom, there was a long pause while Gilman fumbled to get his glasses on and peered out into the sea of attorneys.

"He's wearing a dark suit and a grayish tie," Gilman said, squinting in Martoma's direction.

There was laughter in the room. The description could have referred to almost any man in the room.

But while Gilman looked fragile, and unsteady, his mind appeared sharp as a blade. He described his decision to "step down" from the University of Michigan in November 2012, right after Martoma was charged, rather than wait to be fired for betraying the ethical standards of his profession. "I had given a great deal to that university, and I am suddenly ending my career in disgrace," he said. The university had scrubbed any mention of him from its website and buildings. Many of his former colleagues had renounced him. The only work he was doing now was seeing patients in a free medical clinic in Ann Arbor. He had been banned from the University of Michigan campus, his lifelong academic home. From his side of the room, Strassberg studied the doctor. This was going to be harder than he thought.

On January 21, 2014, New York City officials were in a state of alarm over an approaching winter storm. Seven to ten inches of snow was predicted, and the news prompted a kind of siege mentality, with schools and train service being closed early or canceled. Judge Gardephe announced that court would be closing early, at 2 P.M., so that people could get home safely. Devlin-Brown rushed to get through Martoma's trip to Michigan to view the final drug trial results.

He projected a copy of one of Gilman's Microsoft Outlook calendar entries onto the overhead. "Dr. Gilman, could you please read the entry at 12:30 to 1:30 on Saturday, July 19, 2008?" said Devlin-Brown.

Gilman read off of one of the sheets of paper in front of him. " 'Mat Martoma will visit me in my office,' " he said.

"How did the planned meeting with Mr. Martoma in your office come about?" Devlin-Brown asked.

Gilman said Martoma had told him he was going to visit some relatives near Ann Arbor and that his uncle had died a couple of months before. Could he drop by while he was in town? Devlin-Brown asked him to describe the meeting.

"I do not recall all the details," Gilman said. But he remembered getting a phone call from Martoma on his way over from the airport. He also remembered opening the door for him when he arrived and offering him lunch. And he remembered showing Martoma the bapi PowerPoint slides on his computer.

"Did you have any understanding as to whether what you were doing was violating the law?" Devlin-Brown asked.

"My understanding was that I was disclosing inside information and that was against the law," Gilman said. "I understood I was committing a crime."

The question of why someone like Gilman, with so much to lose, would have entered into such an entanglement with Martoma was one of the major riddles of the case, and a challenge for the prosecution. They needed the jury to focus on Martoma's behavior, not Gilman's. Their strategy was to demonstrate that Gilman was himself a victim. As Devlin-Brown led the doctor through the deepening of his relationship with Martoma—the phone calls, the meetings, Martoma's expressions of fascination and affection—a picture emerged of an intellectual seduction, in which a lonely older man fell under the sway of a charismatic young trader. Gilman was a workaholic who was estranged from his own son. He was lonely and isolated from the rest of the world. Martoma, then, became something of a surrogate child.

By the time they reached Gilman's last day of testimony, Devlin-Brown was feeling confident that he had accomplished what he needed to. Gilman came off as a sympathetic character, someone who had lost everything he had and who didn't have any reason to lie. The evidence the government had presented confirmed the outlines of the prosecutors' story. It was devastating for Martoma.

During the doctor's final minutes on the stand, Devlin-Brown asked, once again, why he had transgressed with Martoma as opposed to the many other investors he spoke with.

Gilman sighed. "He was personable," he said. "And he, unfortunately, reminded me of my first son. In his inquisitiveness. His brightness. My first son was very bright also." There was a long pause. "And he committed suicide."

If Martoma's lawyers came into the trial at a severe disadvantage, now they were doubly constrained. The prosecutors couldn't have asked for things to go much better with their star witness. Gilman was a natural teacher, and he charmed an audience. Strassberg was in a hole that would be almost impossible to climb out of. Bullying a decorated, elderly physician who had lost a son to suicide during a cross-examination was not likely to endear him, or his client, to the jury.

Despite Gilman's apparent frailty, he exuded a stubbornness that was evident in the unflinching way he stared back at Strassberg, as if daring him to take his best shot.

"Good afternoon, Dr. Gilman," Strassberg said.

"Good afternoon, sir," Gilman replied frostily.

"My name is Rich Strassberg, and I represent Mr. Martoma. We've never met before, is that right, Dr. Gilman?" There was a pause. Strassberg leaned forward a little. "Can you hear me?"

"It would help if you speak into the microphone so that I hear you better," Gilman said loudly.

"Are you aware that we asked your lawyer to meet with you but we were refused? Are you aware of that?" Strassberg said.

"I couldn't hear what your opening statement was to me, sir."

Six seconds into his cross-examination, Strassberg was visibly exasperated. Gilman seemed unable to understand every other thing he was saying, interrupting the flow of his questions. Strassberg started again. He placed his mouth right up near the microphone, and his voice took on a high-pitched, condescending tone, as if he were speaking to a two-year-old. "Dr. Gilman, I'm going to be asking you some questions this afternoon, and I want you to let me know if there are any questions that you don't understand," he said, seething with irritation. "*Okay?*"

Strassberg's plan was to show the jury that Gilman was an old, confused man who had been pressured into lying by the government. But he had underestimated the person he was dealing with. Gilman still had some fight in him. Far from being driven into submission by Strassberg's tactics, he knocked the veteran trial lawyer off his balance. Every time Strassberg opened his mouth, Gilman bristled.

After Strassberg demanded for the umpteenth time to know whether Gilman had heard him, the doctor snapped, "You're slurring your words."

Strassberg tried to steady himself and stick to his theme: The doctor was old and forgetful. He ran through a list of a dozen chairmanships, consultations, calendar entries, email exchanges, asking Gilman along the way if he recalled this detail or that one, if he could remember what he said to whom at a particular time or what was discussed during a specific meeting, jumping back and forth in the timeline. Many of the things Strassberg flashed up onscreen Gilman claimed never to have seen before. "I do not recall, sir," he said, over and over.

"Are you aware, Dr. Gilman, that you had over four hundred consultations with over three hundred clients, as reflected in this log?" Strassberg asked at one point.

"That is possible," Gilman said.

Strassberg tried to suggest that Gilman had been driven purely by pecuniary interests—he made huge sums of money consulting for his Wall Street clients: $340,000 in 2006, $420,000 in 2007, and $425,000 in 2008, amounts that dwarfed his salary from the University of Michigan, as if Gilman were working more for Wall Street than for science. The defense lawyer charged that Gilman was lying about sharing information about bapi with Martoma. Through three straight days of questions from Strassberg, though, Gilman held firm on the major elements of his story.

Trial lawyers in the midst of a high-profile case must draw upon an almost inhuman reservoir of stamina. The fat black binders of exhibits and evidence piled in front of Strassberg seemed to be reproducing and spreading across the tables and onto the floor. Looking exhausted, Strassberg finally turned to the subject of B. J. Kang, the FBI agent who approached Gilman back in 2011 and tried to get him to flip. Strassberg asked Gilman about what he said when the FBI first approached him and whether he had told the truth.

"Dr. Gilman, you also told the agents in this meeting that you wanted to cooperate with their investigation," Strassberg said. "Do you remember that?"

"Yes," Gilman said.

"And it's fair to say that in the entire interview that happened between the FBI agents and you, they never mentioned any other client but Mathew Martoma, correct?"

"I believe that's correct," Gilman replied.

As Strassberg moved on to his next set of questions, Gilman started to fidget in his seat. There was something more he wanted to say. He asked the judge if he could return to the previous question because he hadn't answered fully.

"No, Dr. Gilman," Strassberg snapped. "Your Honor, I would ask that Dr. Gilman answer the questions that I am asking."

But Judge Gardephe was intrigued. He told Gilman that he could answer again. The doctor took a deep breath.

"The agent also mentioned that I am only a grain of sand, as is Mr. Martoma," Gilman said in a clear voice. "They are really after a man named Steven A. Cohen."

There were gasps in the courtroom. The prosecutors, the judge in his robes, the bus drivers and actuaries in the jury box—it was as if they were all playing a role in the prosecution of Martoma, when the real story was about Cohen. He was the target, the one the FBI wanted, the person Martoma was supposed to have testified against in order to save himself. The lawyers and the judge had taken pains to keep Cohen's name out of the proceedings, but Gilman was too old, and had too little left to lose, to care about any of that. For a moment, he yanked back the curtain and showed everyone what was really going on.

Though Cohen's complicity in Martoma's crime was never addressed directly in the trial, his name came up repeatedly. When Chandler Bocklage, Cohen's research trader and "right-hand man," in the words of Martoma's lawyers, took the stand for the defense, he said: "I personally think that Steve is the greatest trader of all time." Every time Cohen's name was mentioned, Devlin-Brown grew more annoyed. His goal, for the moment at least, was to convict Martoma. Having a villain popping up in the background was muddying their case.

Judge Gardephe had repeatedly told both sets of attorneys not to bring Cohen's name up for the same reason. He was a billionaire who had made most of the money and the decisions at SAC and who was paying for Martoma's defense. It was strange, but for the purposes of Martoma's trial, it was his duty to try to eliminate distractions. "General questions about how Steve Cohen conducted his trading, I think, are very dangerous," Gardephe said during a discussion out of earshot of the jury. "They represent a risk of opening the door to a broader examination of how Steve Cohen did business. And I think we all agree that that is not a path we want to go down."

During closing arguments, Devlin-Brown's co-prosecutor, Eugene Ingoglia, again walked the jurors through the timeline, from Martoma's career at SAC to his cultivation of Gilman as a source and, finally, to his visit to see the slides from the big ICAD presentation in Gilman's office in Michigan. "Steven Cohen and Mathew Martoma talked for twenty minutes on Sunday," Ingoglia said. "How do we know what they talked about? Right after the phone call, Martoma emails Cohen the lists of the total number of shares in every account. The next day, over four days, they sold all of their shares. In secret."

Then it was Strassberg's turn. He stood up and looked at the jury. "Steven Cohen is not on trial," he said. "Steven Cohen is not even alleged to be a co-conspirator. Mathew is not Steven Cohen. Steven Cohen is not here. What Mr. Cohen did is Mr. Cohen's business."

It was true, of course. But coming from the mouth of a lawyer who was being paid by Cohen, it was suspect. Martoma had taken advice about whether he should cooperate with the government and testify against Cohen from a lawyer whose fees were being paid by Cohen. It was largely because of Martoma's refusal to cooperate, the prosecutors believed, that

Cohen was not on trial himself. To some, a system that allowed such an arrangement seemed corrupt.

Strassberg's closing statement lasted more than two and a half hours. After about forty-five minutes, the jurors began to look put out as he repeated the same points over and over. Then he inhaled deeply. "Mathew's hopes, his family's hopes, will be forever altered by what happens here," he said. "This has been hell for Mathew, his wife, his kids, and his parents. He is not a grain of sand, he is not a means to make a case against Steven Cohen." As he talked, tears rolled down Rosemary's cheeks.

When the jurors returned to deliver the verdict at 1:51 P.M. on the third day of deliberations, it was immediately obvious what they were about to say. Not one looked toward Martoma's side of the courtroom. Rosemary sobbed as the foreman read the result: guilty on all three counts.

Martoma's parents looked stunned as they shuffled out a back door and into the cold. For Martoma's father, hearing the word *guilty* after every count felt like three bullets going through his heart.

When the stories were written the next day, it appeared that a very rich man who controlled one of the largest hedge funds in the world had parted with a negligible fraction of his wealth and skated free from personal culpability. Steve Cohen would continue trading stocks and buying art. All that was left for the prosecutors to do was to make an example of Martoma and claim victory even though they had not reached their ultimate goal.

To an outside observer, the Martoma case had never made much sense. Martoma had been given ample opportunity to testify against his former boss in exchange for a lighter sentence, and he had refused. Instead, he went through a humiliating trial and now faced more than ten years of jail time. Why? It was the question that surrounded his case for three years. Federal prosecutors who had pursued Steven Cohen for almost a decade were certain that Martoma had information to incriminate him. People charged with crimes like Martoma's who were facing long sentences almost always flipped. Why hadn't Martoma played along?

There was always the possibility that he didn't have any incriminating information about Cohen. But, even still, whatever he did have would likely have brought him a reduced sentence. The puzzling thing was, he didn't even *try*. There were three theories that were most commonly discussed.

The first was honor. Perhaps Martoma simply could not accept the idea of being an informant. Such a principled stand was highly unusual in white collar cases, and for someone with Martoma's history it seemed particularly implausible. Could this be the moment when he suddenly chose the righteous path?

The second was fear. Perhaps Martoma believed he would face some kind of retribution if he crossed Cohen. This, too, was hard to accept. Martoma had already left the financial industry, and for all his ruthlessness as a businessman, there was no evidence that Cohen had ever employed the loyalty enforcement methods of an actual gangster.

Another hypothesis, the one that was mentioned most often by those involved in building the case, was material self-interest, or that Martoma harbored a desperate hope that Cohen would repay his loyalty. There was no evidence to support this theory, but it was easier to grasp than the others. Money, in the end, is what drives most people on Wall Street, and the case had left Martoma financially ruined. The government ordered him to forfeit his and Rose's house in Boca Raton, $3.2 million in an American Express Bank account in Martoma's name, $245,000 in an ING Direct account in Rosemary's name, as well as $934,897 that was left in the Mathew and Rosemary Martoma Foundation. It turned out that, after establishing the foundation as a nonprofit in 2010 and depositing $1 million into the account, the Martomas had received a tax benefit for the gift and then barely gave any of the money away. That same year they charged $22,826 in travel and other expenses to the foundation. Everything that was left in the account would be going to the government.

Rosemary argued that she and the children were at risk of ending up on the street. Neither of their families had the resources to help them, she pleaded to the judge through various court filings.

The logistics of Cohen funneling resources to the Martomas would be tricky, to say the least. (It would also be illegal, the most blatant form of witness tampering.) Government accountants would quickly seize on any mysterious sources of income. Even though there was no evidence, observers of the case couldn't resist speculating that something was going on. Rosemary didn't exactly quell the rumors when she said, in tortured legalese: "There is not, and never was, and never will be, any discussion of Steve Cohen taking care of us." It sounded to some like a line that had been fed to her by a lawyer. For now, Martoma's motivations remain a mystery.

During the weeks leading up to the sentencing hearing, the Martoma family fell into a state of anguish. Their nightmare had finally come true. Among the most painful blows was a letter from Stanford stripping Martoma of his business degree for having lied on his application.

Nonetheless, Rosemary threw herself into asking friends, colleagues, and relatives to send letters of support to the judge determining Mathew's sentence. Mathew put aside his pride and asked his former ethics professor at Duke, Bruce Payne. Payne felt bad for his former student, someone he'd once considered a friend, though he also knew that Martoma had deceived him when he asked him to write recommendation letters to Stanford's business school without disclosing what had happened at Harvard. This was too great a transgression. Payne told Martoma he couldn't do it.

Largely due to Rosemary's efforts, however, plenty of others did send letters, dozens of cousins, uncles, and aunts, many of whom were medical doctors, some from as far away as India. Their letters featured several recurring themes: that Mathew's incarceration would unfairly punish his three young children, that Rosemary was a fragile person who would be devastated if Mathew were sent away, and that she wouldn't be able to care for their children on her own. Some argued that Martoma had already suffered enough. There were allusions to an ailment Rosemary suffered that made her weak—it sounded practically Victorian, and didn't fit the forceful personality who had been so deeply involved in Martoma's defense. The prosecutors were dismissive when they read about it. As Devlin-Brown later pointed out, there weren't any letters from a doctor or a psychiatrist confirming the diagnosis.

Martoma's father, Bobby, wrote an impassioned thirteen-page letter, including photos of Martoma as a young child, smiling and wearing a pin-striped suit and necktie. After describing his searing paternal disappointment when Martoma didn't attend Harvard for his undergraduate education, Bobby wrote: "Almost 22 years later, today, I feel, maybe I pushed him too far to accomplish my dream. We pressed him to excel until he maxed out."

Rosemary knew the odds were against her husband. Strassberg and Braceras had tried, as sensitively as possible, to prepare her for what was coming. Jail terms in insider trading cases were often severe. Rajaratnam had been sentenced to eleven years, for example, and a Galleon trader named Zvi Goffer had gotten ten. Still, she clung to the hope that Mathew might be spared. She prayed for it every day.

At 3:30 P.M., on September 8, 2014, Martoma again stood before Judge Gardephe, waiting to hear what would happen to him. According to the sentencing guidelines, he faced up to nineteen and a half years in prison.

The judge recapped the damning narrative: the phone call between Gilman and Martoma on July 17, 2008, when they reviewed the Power-Point slides; Martoma's flight to Detroit and his meeting with Gilman in his office; the twenty-minute phone call with Cohen the next day; SAC's secret sales of all of its Elan and Wyeth shares the next week. While the government never named Cohen in the case, he was central to the story of Martoma's crime.

"Given this sequence of events," Gardephe said, "it is much more likely than not that Cohen did, in fact, receive material, non-public information from Martoma." For the purposes of sentencing, Martoma could be held responsible for all of it.

"Mr. Martoma has been ruined by this prosecution," the judge said.

And yet, he added, in order for his case to deter others, "I find that a substantial sentence of imprisonment is necessary."

Rosemary hung her head. Gardephe paused. He seemed genuinely saddened by what he was about to do. "I intend to impose a sentence of nine years' imprisonment."

It took a moment for this to sink in. Nine years. Rosemary started to cry.

There was a long moment of quiet after the judge left. Then Rosemary took Mathew's hand and they walked out of the courtroom.

Martoma's parents had stayed quiet for months, pushing bravely through a crowd of photographers on their way in and out of the courthouse every day, never saying a word. Staggering out into the bright sunlight after the verdict, however, they exploded with rage.

"He was framed!" shouted Lizzie Thomas, Martoma's mother, at the base of the courthouse steps. Her eyes were blazing. She couldn't take it anymore.

"I'm his father," Bobby Martoma said, standing beside his wife. "If the prosecution knew, when the two agents approached in Boca Raton, three years ago—if they knew that Mathew was guilty, why did they tell him that they wanted to recruit him as an informant? What was the reason?" Bobby went on, "If he was guilty, they should have said, 'You are guilty, we are going to proceed with the case! Instead they said, 'We want to recruit you.' . . .

"He was framed," Bobby continued. "Who made the money? Somebody made $275 million, and they put all the blame on Mathew! Today the judge put all blame on him. That judge, there was no justice from that judge. This was nothing but a mockery. This is the U.S. system."

"Who made the money?" Lizzie interjected. "My son made $9.3 million out of that, and $3 million went for the tax."

Why, then, someone asked, didn't Mathew cooperate with the prosecutors and help himself? Why didn't he help them get the man who made the money, Steve Cohen?

"You want me to tell you?" Bobby answered, jabbing his finger in the air with righteous anger. "Because he believes in the Ninth Commandment. You know what is the Ninth Commandment? Thou shall not bear false witness against thy neighbor."

"The person who made the money is on a yacht," Lizzie said, in apparent reference to photographs Cohen's wife had posted online that summer of their sailing trip around Greece. "And my son is going to jail."

"This is not justice," Bobby said.

EPILOGUE

On May 11, 2015, eight months after Mathew Martoma was sentenced, Christie's hosted a special themed evening sale for the world's top art collectors at its headquarters at Rockefeller Center. The auction was called "Looking Forward to the Past," and it was built around a carefully selected group of twentieth-century masterpieces, a mix of contemporary and slightly older works that in another era might have lived in major museums. The big prize of the evening was a Picasso painting called *Les Femmes d'Alger* that was expected to sell for $140 million. In all, the night was anticipated to be a record-breaking sale, a coda to a worldwide boom in the art market fueled largely by Wall Street money and exploding wealth in Asia. One of the paintings going up for sale was from Cohen's collection, *Paris Polka*, by Jean Dubuffet, which had an estimate of $25 million.

While his former employee Martoma was appealing his conviction and preparing for a new life behind bars, Cohen had been anything but quiet. With assurances from his legal team that the threat of criminal charges was all but gone, he started to move aggressively to show the world that he was still as powerful as ever. He made a trip to Davos and sat courtside at Madison Square Garden, in full view of the television cameras. On November 10, the day Martoma was supposed to start serving his prison term, Cohen made news by spending $101 million at Sotheby's to buy an Alberto Giacometti sculpture called *Chariot*.

"Steve is a very serious, very astute collector," William Acquavella, one of Cohen's art dealers, told *The New York Times*. "He also has just the right instincts, ones that can't be learned from reading art history books."

Cohen had been working to cleanse his reputation on Wall Street as well, trying to create distance between himself and the legal scandal. As required by the criminal settlement with his company, Cohen had closed SAC and turned it into a private family office that invested only his own money, close to $10 billion. It was important to him, that $10 billion figure.

In April 2014, three months after Martoma was convicted, Cohen changed his firm's name from SAC Capital Advisors to Point72 Asset Management, a reference to its address at 72 Cummings Point Road in Stamford. He also removed his top associates and advisors who had helped guide him through his legal troubles. Steven Kessler, SAC's head of compliance, left, as did Tom Conheeney, SAC's president. Sol Kumin, Cohen's director of business development, who had been involved in hiring many of the traders who were implicated in insider trading, also moved on and started his own hedge fund. Cohen looked for a new head of compliance, and a recruiter contacted several prosecutors and FBI agents who had been involved in the investigation of SAC.

Eventually, Cohen hired a former Connecticut U.S. Attorney to be Point72's general counsel and announced plans for a six-person "advisory board" that would be made up of high-profile business leaders who would advise the firm on management and ethics issues. In a bit of dark comedy, Cohen started a program for college students called the Point72 Academy, a "highly-selective and rigorous 12-month training program" that purported to teach investment strategies to young people seeking careers in finance.

The SEC's case against Cohen for failing to supervise Martoma and Steinberg was still unresolved. The agency wanted to bar him from the securities industry for life, but Cohen was fighting it. He hired the defense lawyer David Boies to join the legal team working on the SEC case. He told friends that he expected to run another hedge fund in the not-too-distant future, something that would likely be impossible if the SEC won its case. In the meantime, Cohen's "family office" was earning him hundreds of millions of dollars a year. He was still trading billions, he was still buying art—eight years and every resource the government could direct at him couldn't stop him.

Over the course of the three years in which I conducted the reporting for this book, I was in and out of contact with Cohen's office, attempting to arrange an interview with him. I called and wrote letters and had meetings with his representatives. There had been hints that he might eventually speak to me, but he never came through. I was determined to talk to him. I knew that he would be at Christie's that evening in the spring of 2015, so I went to see him there.

The night of the auction, the Christie's building was overflowing with women of multinational identity whose cheekbones could have sliced a wheel of Brie and men who looked too rich to possibly care about the financial crisis in Greece, which was dominating international news headlines. It was a feverish atmosphere. A glamorous game was about to be played, one whose winners would be parting with enormous sums of money.

Around 6:30 P.M. Cohen's former trader David Ganek glided through the lobby with his shirt unbuttoned to the middle of his chest, looking as if he had just stepped off of a yacht. Then, just minutes before the auction's 7 P.M. start time, Cohen walked in.

He was short and slightly pear-shaped, in a gray zip-neck sweater and khaki pants, and he appeared to be by himself. His cheeks were pink, and he was smiling his gap-toothed smile as he waded into the crowd. He looked like a kid who had just entered a large toy store. It was an assertion of power, arriving five minutes before the scheduled start time of one of the most hotly anticipated art auctions of the season. Cohen knew they couldn't begin without him.

I stepped in front of him as he entered the hallway leading to the table where the bidders collected their paddles. "Hi," I said, introducing myself. By this point, I had done hundreds of interviews with his former colleagues, employees, and confidants. I felt like I knew him as well as anyone did.

"Oh, it's you," Cohen said. He froze.

"I'd really like to talk to you," I said, grabbing his hand and shaking it.

"I bet you would like to talk to me, I bet you would," he said. He started looking around for a way to escape.

"You won," I said. "I think you have a great story to tell."

"I don't think I can talk to you," he said, moving away. "But never say never. . . ."

As he slipped off into the crowd, I squeezed in one last question: "Are you buying or selling tonight?"

"Oh, *selling*," he said. "Selling."

He walked up the stairs to the packed gallery, where the auction was about to begin. Toward the end of the auction, another of Alberto Giacometti's bronze sculptures, *L'homme au doigt* (Pointing Man), came on the block. It is widely considered one of the artist's greatest works.

For Cohen, who had just come through a challenging time, the sculpture was a sign of his own future, which was brightening again after several years under a legal shadow. The government had made its best effort to bring one of the wealthiest men in the world to justice and left him largely in the same condition he had been in before. Cohen was a survivor, a symbol of his time in history in more ways than he would likely want to acknowledge. Free from fear, he could buy anything he wanted. After several rounds of aggressive bidding, he placed the winning bid for the Giacometti, at $141.3 million. It was the most money anyone has ever paid for a sculpture at auction.

After Preet Bharara led the investigation into hedge funds that turned him into a national celebrity, the legal system delivered a stunning rebuke. In December 2014, an appeals court overturned the convictions of

Todd Newman and Anthony Chiasson, from Diamondback and Level Global, respectively, funds that had strong ties to SAC. The judges reprimanded Bharara's office for being too aggressive in charging traders who were getting inside information indirectly, from friends or employees, rather than from the company insider himself. In what came to be known as the "Newman decision," the court said that in order for a trader to be prosecuted for trading on material nonpublic information, he or she had to be aware of the benefit the original leaker of the information had received. In many of the insider trading rings, traders got earnings or revenue numbers from other traders, knowing that they originated with someone inside the company and little else. The court also ruled that the benefit the leaker received in exchange for sharing the information had to be something tangible, akin to money. Friendship or favor-trading on its own was not enough.

"Yesterday's decision took an eighteen-wheeler truck and drove it through the insider trading laws," said Richard Holwell, the federal judge who presided over the Raj Rajaratnam trial. "It pushes so far back that it's going to sweep within it activity that, until yesterday, most people working on the Street would say, 'That's wrong.'"

Bharara was outraged by the decision. He felt that it didn't reflect how things work on Wall Street, where information can be as valuable as cash, exchanged between friends and colleagues in return for goodwill and unspoken promises of future gifts. He appealed the Newman decision to the Supreme Court. When the Court declined to take up the case, Bharara felt compelled to dismiss charges against seven people, including Michael Steinberg; after having his life turned upside down, Steinberg was free. In addition to Steinberg, his former analyst Jon Horvath, Horvath's friend Jesse Tortora of Diamondback Capital, and the other key witnesses in the case had their guilty pleas dismissed. It was yet another measure of vindication for Cohen, essentially legalizing the don't-ask-don't-tell information-gathering model employed at SAC. Bharara said that the decision will affect only about 10 percent of the cases his office filed, but he believes that a large category of insider trading will now go unpunished and that the precedent creates yet another advantage for wealthy and well-connected people with access to valuable information. It basically grants permission to trade on material nonpublic information, as long as you don't know too much about where it came from.

"This creates an obvious road map for unscrupulous behavior," Bharara said. "I think people have to ask themselves whether that is good for the markets, whether that is good for the integrity of the markets." (Two years after the initial Newman decision, in December 2016, the Supreme Court ruled unanimously in an unrelated insider trading case that the Newman ruling had gone too far, and that valuable information given to a friend or a relative *did* count as an improper benefit, offering some relief to the Justice Department.)

In February 2015, David Ganek sued Bharara and the FBI and charged them with violating his constitutional rights and illegally raiding his fund Level Global, which had shut down as a result of the legal scrutiny. Many lives and businesses were unjustly damaged in the course of the government's pursuit of Cohen, Ganek believes, including his own. Both his fund, Level Global, and the fund where Todd Newman worked, Diamondback Capital, closed under the pressure of the investigation; after the Newman appeal, both companies' settlements with the DOJ (in Diamondback's case) and the SEC were reversed and the fines they had paid were refunded. (Ganek's case was dismissed in October 2017. It was "a great day for ambitious, attention-seeking prosecutors, who are now being rewarded with total immunity even when they lie and leak," Ganek said.)

The charges that the SEC filed against Cohen in 2013, accusing him of failing to supervise Steinberg and Martoma, were quietly settled in January 2016. The appeals court ruling in the Newman and Chiasson case had weakened the SEC, and the agency resolved the case with only one significant sanction against Cohen, which barred him from managing outside investor money for two years. The deal leaves him free to return to the hedge fund business in 2018. "I wouldn't be surprised if he got $2.5 billion the day he opens up," said one hedge fund investor, Don Steinbrugge of Agecroft Partners.

"People are going to be lining up out the doors," said another, Brad

Alford of Alpha Capital Management, who previously had money with SAC. "It's a layup."

The case Biovail filed against SAC and other hedge funds in 2006 alleging stock manipulation was also dismissed. Biovail was charged with fraud by the SEC, and the company later paid SAC Capital $10 million to settle vexatious litigation claims. Separately, the lawsuit filed by Fairfax against SAC and other hedge funds was dismissed in 2013. It is currently under appeal. The case filed by Cohen's ex-wife, Patricia, against him was dismissed in May 2016; the district judge found that there was "no evidence that Steven concealed any assets from Patricia during the divorce." In late 2017, Mathew Martoma's appeal of his conviction was turned down. He is currently serving his nine-year sentence in Florida.

Meanwhile, many of the prosecutors and regulators involved in building the case against Cohen and SAC moved on to careers in the private sector. Lorin Reisner, the head of Bharara's criminal division who helped negotiate SAC's $1.8 billion fine, became a partner at Paul, Weiss, the same law firm that supplied Cohen's legal defense team. Antonia Apps, the prosecutor who tried the Steinberg case, left the government for a partnership at Milbank, Tweed, Hadley & McCloy, another corporate law firm where she does white collar defense work. Bharara's deputy, Richard Zabel, announced that he was taking a job as general counsel at a hedge fund called Elliott Management, which is run by the prominent billionaire political donor Paul Singer. After twenty-five years with the FBI, B. J. Kang's former supervisor, Patrick Carroll, joined Goldman Sachs as a vice president in its compliance group. Arlo Devlin-Brown, who led the Martoma prosecution, became a partner at Covington & Burling.

The most startling move of all, might have come from Amelia Cottrell, a senior enforcement attorney at the SEC who oversaw the agency's Martoma investigation. At the end of June 2015, she shocked her colleagues by announcing that she was joining Willkie Farr, the firm where Cohen's longtime defense counsel Marty Klotz worked. It turned out that leading the most powerful case the government assembled against Cohen was the best possible audition for a job working for his consigliere.

The financial industry has evolved to be so complex that large parts of it are almost completely beyond the reach of regulators and law enforcement. Wall Street's most successful enterprises are constantly pushing into the frontier; every time the law looks like it's catching up, they move farther away. There is a perception that in the years after the Michael Milken era, and especially since the financial crisis of 2008, it has become almost impossible, due to a lack of will or expertise, to prosecute corporate criminals who operate at the highest levels. The fear of suffering embarrassing losses after long, expensive trials has led to a kind of paralysis in law enforcement. The Justice Department was unable, or unwilling, to bring any senior Wall Street figures to face criminal charges for the widespread fraud that swept the financial system prior to 2008. Instead, it extracted billions of dollars in fines from the world's largest banks. In 2015, in response to criticism regarding the lack of individual prosecutions, the Justice Department announced aggressive new policies on financial crime that would focus on holding individuals accountable, although as of this writing, little seemed to have changed.

The hedge fund industry created unprecedented fortunes for a new generation of Wall Street inventors whose primary innovation was to find ways to make more aggressive bets in the stock market. Cohen was a pioneer, the creator of a trading empire designed to gain an edge over less sophisticated investors. Years later, after paying some of the largest fines in the history of financial crime—and seeing a dozen of his employees implicated in insider trading—Cohen emerged from the crisis that engulfed his company as one of the world's wealthiest men. In the end, the evidence against him that the government spent nearly ten years assembling was never presented to a jury. All that was left was for Cohen to spend his billions and to plan for his return.

On November 8, 2016, Donald Trump was elected president, vowing to usher in a new era of financial deregulation. The general counsel for Point72, Cohen's private investment firm, was appointed, briefly, by the incoming Trump administration to recruit candidates for the new Justice Department during the tumultuous transition, and Trump fired Preet Bharara from his post as U.S. Attorney for the Southern District of New

York. Trump named hedge fund managers and bankers from Goldman Sachs to key economic policy posts, and the Justice Department began to deemphasize the prosecution of corporate crime. In this environment, the Steven Cohens of the future are likely to thrive.

At the time of this printing, Cohen was making preparations to launch a new hedge fund in 2018. According to news reports, marketers Cohen hired were expecting that he could raise up to $10 billion.

CAST OF CHARACTERS

At the time of the events depicted

SAC CAPITAL ADVISORS, STAMFORD, CONNECTICUT

THE EXECUTIVES

Steven A. Cohen, Founder and Owner

Peter Nussbaum, General Counsel

Solomon Kumin, Chief Operating Officer

Tom Conheeney, President

Steven Kessler, Chief Compliance Officer

CR INTRINSIC, AN ELITE RESEARCH-DRIVEN UNIT OF SAC

Matthew Grossman, head of CR Intrinsic

Mathew Martoma, portfolio manager

Jason Karp, director of research

David Munno, portfolio manager

Benjamin Slate, portfolio manager

Jonathan Hollander, analyst

Timothy Jandovitz, healthcare trader

SIGMA CAPITAL, A UNIT OF SAC BASED IN MANHATTAN

Michael Steinberg, portfolio manager

Jon Horvath, analyst working for Michael Steinberg

Gabriel Plotkin, portfolio manager

Richard Grodin, portfolio manager; co-founder of Stratix Asset
Management

Richard Choo-Beng Lee, technology analyst working for Grodin;
co-founder of Spherix Capital

OTHERS AT SAC

Wayne Holman, healthcare portfolio manager; founder of Ridgeback
Capital Management

Phillipp Villhauer, head trader

David Ganek, portfolio manager; co-founder of Level Global
Investors

Richard Schimel, financial-stock trader; co-founder of Diamondback
Capital; was married to Steven Cohen's sister Wendy

Larry Sapanski, energy trader; co-founder of Diamondback Capital

Donald Longueuil, portfolio manager

Noah Freeman, portfolio manager

Ken Lissak, executive during early days; independent trader

Dr. Ari Kiev, psychiatrist and "trading coach"

THE DELL TRADE

Todd Newman, portfolio manager, Diamondback Capital

Anthony Chiasson, co-founder with David Ganek of Level Global
Investors

Jesse Tortora, analyst under Newman at Diamondback Capital

Sam Adondakis, analyst under Chiasson at Level Global Investors

Sandeep Goyal, analyst, Neuberger Berman

Chandradip "Rob" Ray, Dell employee

GRUNTAL & CO., NEW YORK

Ronald Aizer, head of options department

Jay Goldman, Steven Cohen's friend; founder of J. Goldman and Company

MATHEW MARTOMA'S LAWYERS

STILLMAN & FRIEDMAN, NEW YORK

Charles Stillman, partner

Nathaniel Marmur, partner

GOODWIN PROCTER, NEW YORK

Richard Strassberg, partner and co-chair of Securities Litigation and White Collar Defense

Roberto Braceras, partner

MICHAEL STEINBERG'S LAWYERS

KRAMER LEVIN NAFTALIS & FRANKEL, NEW YORK

Barry Berke, partner and co-chair of Litigation Department

STEVE COHEN'S LAWYERS

WILLKIE FARR & GALLAGHER, NEW YORK

Martin Klotz, senior counsel, Litigation Department
Michael Schachter, partner

PAUL, WEISS, RIFKIND, WHARTON & GARRISON, NEW YORK

Theodore V. Wells Jr., partner and co-chair, Litigation Department
Michael Gertzman, partner and co-chair, Litigation Department
Daniel Kramer, partner and co-chair, Securities Litigation and
    Enforcement Group
Mark Pomerantz, of counsel

BOIES, SCHILLER & FLEXNER, NEW YORK

David Boies, chairman

FAIRFAX AND BIOVAIL CASES

KASOWITZ BENSON TORRES & FRIEDMAN, NEW YORK

Michael Bowe, partner

THE NEW YORK FIELD OFFICE, FEDERAL BUREAU OF INVESTIGATION

WHITE-COLLAR CRIME UNIT

Patrick Carroll, B. J. Kang's supervisor
David Chaves, David Makol's supervisor
B. J. Kang, special agent, C-1 squad
David Makol, special agent, C-35 squad
Matthew Callahan, special agent

James Hinkle, special agent
Tom Zukauskas, special agent

THE SECURITIES AND EXCHANGE COMMISSION

HEAD OFFICE, WASHINGTON, D.C.

Mary Schapiro, chair, 2009–2012
Mary Jo White, chair, 2013–2017
Andrew Ceresney, director, Enforcement Division, 2012–2016
George Canellos, deputy director, Enforcement Division, 2012–2013;
    co-director, Enforcement Division, 2013–2014

NEW YORK REGIONAL OFFICE

Sanjay Wadhwa, assistant regional director for enforcement
Amelia Cottrell, branch chief
Charles Riely, staff attorney
Matthew Watkins, staff attorney
Joseph Sansone, head of the SEC's Market Abuse unit
Daniel Marcus, staff attorney
Justin Smith, staff attorney
Neil Hendelman, analyst
Thomas Smith, staff attorney
Michael Holland, staff attorney

THE U.S. ATTORNEY'S OFFICE FOR THE SOUTHERN DISTRICT OF NEW YORK

Preet Bharara, U.S. Attorney
Richard Zabel, Deputy U.S. Attorney
Lorin Reisner, head of criminal division at the Southern District of
    New York
Antonia Apps, assistant U.S. attorney

Arlo Devlin-Brown, assistant U.S. attorney

Avi Weitzman, assistant U.S. attorney

Andrew Michaelson, special assistant U.S. attorney on loan from the SEC

Joshua Klein, assistant U.S. attorney

Raymond Lohier, chief of the commodities and securities fraud task force

Reed Brodsky, assistant U.S. attorney

Eugene Ingoglia, assistant U.S. attorney

Harry Chernoff, assistant U.S. attorney

Christopher Garcia, chief of the commodities and securities fraud task force

Marc Berger, chief of the commodities and securities fraud task force

Anjan Sahni, deputy chief of the commodities and securities fraud task force

ACKNOWLEDGMENTS

This book would not have been possible without the help and support of many people, from researchers to editors, employers and colleagues, fact-checkers and friends. I owe my deepest debt of gratitude to the many sources and subjects who shared their time and their insights as I sought to learn as much as possible about insider trading investigations at several hedge funds and endeavored to reconstruct events that occurred over the course of the last ten years.

This story began, for me, as a magazine feature assignment at *Bloomberg Businessweek,* which was my journalistic home through most of the reporting process, when many of the events depicted later in the book took place. Josh Tyrangiel, *Bloomberg Businessweek*'s editor, always had high standards that one felt motivated to try to meet. He and his deputy and successor, Ellen Pollock, were both tolerant of my long periods of distraction and generous with opportunities to write ambitious stories for the magazine. Bryant Urstadt, a *Businessweek* features editor and also a friend, first urged me to take on the SAC Capital case as a subject. I am also grateful to many other friends and colleagues from that period, including my editor Brad Wieners, as well as folks at Bloomberg Media.

Since leaving *Businessweek* I have had the privilege of working as a staff writer at *The New Yorker,* for David Remnick, who is a role model in so many ways. I'm also blessed to count Henry Finder, Vera Titunik, Susan Morrison, Nick Thompson, and many others as editors and colleagues.

My book landed in the hands of Andy Ward, one of the most patient and exacting book editors in the industry. From the moment I walked in to Penguin Random House to meet with Susan Kamil and Tom Perry, who referenced *All The President's Men* during our first conversation, I knew that I was collaborating with publishers who understood and appreciated the importance of this story. Sally Marvin and London King have been both wise and energetic in their publicity guidance, and Kaela Myers, Melissa Sanford, Evan Camfield, and Joseph Perez were also incredibly helpful.

My agent, Gail Ross, has been a tireless supporter and advisor, as has her partner, Howard Yoon, who was a crucial source of editorial advice. Hugo Lindgren was an invaluable editor, advisor, and friend. Theodoric Mayer and Nadine Sabai were crack research assistants at different stages, and Andy Young played the important role of fact-checker. I am fortunate to have many friends and colleagues who were willing to read pages, offer reporting advice, listen and/or generally set an example through their own work, including Katrina Brooker, Steve Fishman, David Glovin, Suzy Hansen, Alexandra Jacobs, Patrick Radden Keefe, Kate Kelly, Peter Lattman, Devin Leonard, Duff McDonald, Bethany McLean, Miranda Purves, Anita Raghavan, Andrew Rice, Maria Russo, Gabriel Sherman, Jennifer Stahl, Nick Verbitsky, David Voreacos, and others. This book is also dedicated, in part, to Peter Kaplan, who taught me about being a journalist.

I am grateful for my family, including my parents, Frank and Rowena; my sister Amanda; my relations-in-law, including Carlota and Patsy; and, most important, the people who share four walls with me, Seth, Wyatt, and Lola, whom I love more than anything and who somehow tolerated it all.

New York City, November 2016

NOTES AND SOURCES

I began reporting this story on November 20, 2012, the day that Mathew Martoma was arrested, and that reporting continues to this day. This book is based on hundreds of interviews with more than two hundred people, as well as voluminous court transcripts, exhibits, deposition testimony, SEC interview notes, notes taken by FBI agents during witness interviews—known as 302s—diary entries, written correspondence, and other documents. Additionally, many of the cases and characters herein were covered in detail by the press, by reporters who did fine work at *The New York Times*, Reuters, Bloomberg News, *The Wall Street Journal*, *Institutional Investor*, *Fortune*, *Vanity Fair*, *New York*, CNBC, and *The New Yorker*, as well as in books, among them Anita Raghavan's *The Billionaire's Apprentice*, which is the definitive retelling of the Raj Rajaratnam case. James B. Stewart's *Den of Thieves*, which is a crucial account of the insider trading that overtook Wall Street during the Michael Milken era, was also an important resource.

Many of the people I was writing about, or who were witnesses to the events I describe, were facing the possibility of criminal prosecution or regulatory sanction at the time I was conducting interviews; others had signed nondisclosure agreements with their employers—which is standard in the financial industry—or worked for departments of the government that forbade them from speaking openly about their work. For those reasons and due to the sensitive nature of the subject matter, the vast majority of the interviews were conducted on a background basis, which meant that I could use the information, including character's states of mind and dialogue, but that I could not attribute it to a source by name. It should not be assumed that my reporting of a character's state of mind or dialogue or any other fact means that that individual was the source; in some cases, such passages are drawn from documents, transcripts, witnesses, or people who were briefed on what occurred. In order to write certain passages, I was forced to rely on memories of events that took place many years in the past. I made a great effort to corroborate facts and versions of events conveyed by different people with multiple sources and documents wherever possible. Every effort was made through reporting and rigorous fact-checking to make sure the story as depicted is as accurate and complete as possible. It is also worth noting that the legal cases involved dramatic twists and surprises; some people who were convicted or pleaded guilty later saw their convictions or guilty pleas reversed, and some who looked like they might be charged never were.

Nearly every person mentioned in this book was given an opportunity to comment. Steven Cohen did not cooperate in the reporting process, in spite of multiple requests over a three-year period, one of them conducted through an in-person encounter at Christie's. Cohen tried to prevent members of his closest circle from speaking with me, and at one point, a press representative working for Cohen threatened to have me followed. Cohen (still) exerts tremendous influence on Wall Street and beyond, and people are generally afraid of him.

In spite of many obstacles, dozens of people did choose to speak to me as I worked on this book, for their own reasons and because it was understood that this is a story of public interest and historical significance. This book would not have been possible if it weren't for them.

PROLOGUE: THE FLIP

ix **"They're gonna guide down":** David Glovin, Patricia Hurtado, and Bob Van Voris, "Chiesi Told Rajaratnam She 'Played' Friend Like 'Piano,'" Bloomberg News, April 4, 2011.

ix **an $800 million Internet company:** "Akamai Reports Fourth Quarter 2008 and Full Year 2008 Financial Results," company press release, February 4, 2008.

ix **"I played him like a finely tuned piano":** *U.S. v. Rajaratnam,* No. 09 Cr. 1184 (RJH), Government Exhibit (hereafter GX) 532T, transcript of call between Rajaratnam and Chiesi, July 24, 2008.

x **to Kenya for a birthday safari:** Anita Raghavan, "Power and Pleasure," *Forbes,* September 23, 2010.

x **Super Bowl party on Star Island:** Robert A. Guth and Justin Scheck, "The Man Who Wired Silicon Valley," *The Wall Street Journal,* December 30, 2009.

x **Six days after that phone call:** *U.S. v. Rajaratnam,* GX 44, "Galleon Tech Profit from Trades in Akamai Technologies Beginning on July 25 2008."

x **Raj, who was short 875,000:** *U.S. v. Rajaratnam,* GX 42, "Galleon Tech Daily Closing Position in Akamai Stock," June 1 2008–July 30 2008.

x **Chiesi, made $2.5 million:** *U.S. v. Rajaratnam,* GX 45, "New Castle Profit from Trades in Akamai Securities Beginning on July 25 2008."

xi **"It's a conquest":** *U.S. v. Rajaratnam,* GX 543T, transcript of call between Raj Rajaratnam and Danielle Chiesi, from July 30, 2008.

xi **Raj shorted 138,550 shares:** *U.S. v. Rajaratnam,* GX 42.

xi **Kang had wires going on Rajaratnam's friends:** David Glovin and Patricia Hurtado, "Chiesi Swaps Cell for Halfway House," Bloomberg News, May 18, 2013.

xii **SAC Capital Advisors:** From here on, the more common reference "SAC Capital" or "SAC" will be used to refer to Cohen's company, SAC Capital Advisors.

xii **"Ali Far?":** *U.S. v. Ali Far,* No. 09 Cr. 1009 (RPP), Ali Far Sentencing Memo. Far was an electrical engineer by training. Born in Iran, he moved to the United States as a teenager in 1978, in the midst of the Iranian Revolution. After graduating from Berkeley, he worked at Plantronics, a Silicon Valley firm that made computerized phone headsets, among other things, while studying for his master's degree at night. He became a semiconductor analyst at Prudential Securities, impressing Rajaratnam, who hired him at Galleon. His career there was bumpy, though, and in 2008 he left.

xii **Far's wife, two daughters, mother, and mother-in-law cowered in the background:** *U.S. v. Far,* Far Sentencing Memo, letter from Far's mother, Esmat Akhavain.

xiii **Lee was a technology analyst:** *U.S. v. Richard Choo-Beng Lee, et al.*, No. 09 Cr. 0972 (PKC), Richard Choo-Beng Lee Sentencing Memo, November 18, 2015. Before becoming an analyst at SAC, Lee worked at Monolithic Memories, a chip company in Silicon Valley that eventually became Advanced Micro Devices, as well as at Sun Microsystems.

xiv **Far placed a call to his partner:** *U.S. v. Choo-Beng Lee, et al.*, Richard Choo-Beng Lee Sentencing Memo.

xiv **"I know people":** *U.S. v. SAC Capital Advisors, et al.*, No. 13 Cr. 541 (LTS), Sealed Indictment, July 25, 2013; some details of Lee's call to Cohen.

xv **"We heard he's wearing a wire":** *Fairfax Financial Holdings Ltd. and Crum & Forster Holding Corp. v. SAC Capital Management LLC, et al.*, MRS-L-2032-06; Superior Court of the State of New Jersey, videotaped deposition of Steven A. Cohen, February 22, 2011. More details on this conversation from Matthew Goldstein, "Cohen Said to Have Warned Friend About Possible Federal Investigation," *The New York Times*, December 23, 2013.

xvii **Before earning anything for his or her investors:** Nina Munk, "Greenwich's Outrageous Fortunes," *Vanity Fair*, July 2006.

xvii **Paul Tudor Jones and Ken Griffin:** Tudor Jones founded Tudor Investment Corp.; Griffin founded Citadel Investment Group. See Sebastian Mallaby, *More Money Than God* (Penguin, 2010).

xvii **a more traditional Wall Street career:** One of the most alluring aspects of the hedge fund business was the fact that a hedge fund manager could easily expand his or her annual bonus from millions a year to tens of millions or more just by bringing in more investor money and making the fund larger, often with little extra work. Most hedge funds charge a management fee of 2 percent of assets, which is intended to cover expenses and salaries, as well as 20 percent of the profits generated by the fund at the end of the year. A fund managing $300 million of other people's money, then, would take $6 million in fees, plus its 20 percent cut of the profits. If the fund grew to $3 billion in assets, the management fee would jump to $60 million. If a fund of that size returned just 6 percent that year, it would generate $180 million in profits, $36 million of which the fund managers could keep. All of this could be done by only a handful of employees.

xvii **the twenty-five highest-paid hedge fund managers:** Mallaby, *More Money Than God*, p. 3. See also "The Top 25 Moneymakers: The New Tycoons," *Institutional Investor's Alpha*, April 24, 2007.

xvii **almost $3 trillion in assets around the world:** "HFR Global Hedge Fund Industry Report: Year End 2015," *Hedge Fund Research*.

xix **Trading on it is also usually illegal:** Recent court decisions have loosened the definition of what constitutes illegal insider trading; for more, see Jon Eisenberg, "How United States v. Newman Changes the Law," K&L Gates LLP, May 3, 2015.

1. MONEY, MONEY, MONEY

4 **Established in 1880, Gruntal had survived:** Richard Behar, "The Shabby Side of the Street," *Fortune,* March 3, 2003.

5 **Aizer had implemented a strategy called "option arbitrage":** The options department at Gruntal had been started in 1964 by Carl Icahn. Icahn and Aizer, and Cohen for that matter, had much in common. Even though Icahn was several years older than Aizer, they were all kids who'd spent their youths admiring the skyline of Manhattan from the outer boroughs and plotting to triumph over their middle-class upbringings. At the time, if someone wanted to trade a stock option, they had to call up a broker at Gruntal or a handful of other firms, explain what kind of bet they wanted to make and over what time horizon, and basically accept whatever price they were given. By 1968, Icahn's department at Gruntal was bringing in commissions of $1.5 million and was one of the most profitable at the firm. Icahn left that year to start his own company. Connie Bruck, *The Predators' Ball* (Penguin, 1989), p. 151.

7 **so he could study the stock tables:** Jack D. Schwager, *Stock Market Wizards* (HarperCollins, 2001), p. 269.

7 **the area became partial inspiration:** Judith S. Goldstein, *The Great Gatsby: Inventing Great Neck: Jewish Identity and the American Dream* (Rutgers University Press, 2006), p. 3.

9 **Cohen would stumble home early in the morning with fistfuls of cash:** Bryan Burrough, "What's Eating Steve Cohen?" *Vanity Fair,* July 2010.

9 **The culture at Wharton:** Several Wharton graduates of the era were indicted (see "Wharton Producing Its Share of Criminals on Wall Street," *Boca Raton News,* September 26, 1988), the most famous being Bruce Newberg, a classmate of Cohen's who received his bachelor's degree in 1979 and an MBA from Wharton in 1980. Newberg went on to become a star trader for Michael Milken at Drexel Burnham and was indicted for racketeering and securities fraud as part of the takedown of the junk-bond king's empire in 1989. Milken also had an MBA from Wharton.

10 **He thought he had no chance of competing:** "I was dead on arrival at Penn," Cohen says. "All these prep-school kids, they were ready, they had read all the books. Me, well, it was a real struggle." Burrough, "What's Eating Steve Cohen?"

10 **"I'd just stand there and stare":** Burrough, "What's Eating Steve Cohen?"

11 **Gruntal's CEO:** Howard Silverman ran Gruntal from 1974 to 1995.

11 **Silverman drove sports cars:** Lawrence Van Gelder, "Long Islanders: Driving Hard on Wall Street," *The New York Times*, May 3, 1987.

12 **She and Cohen ended up talking for hours:** Some details about Cohen and Patricia's first meeting from Steve Fishman, "Divorced, Never Separated," *New York*, March 28, 2010.

13 **But in fact there was a tiny wedding:** *Patricia Cohen v. Steven A. Cohen, et al.*, Complaint Under the Racketeer Influenced and Corrupt Organizations Act, No. 09 Civ. 10230 (WHP), December 9, 2009; the date of marriage was December 7, 1979. Another divorce filing has the date of marriage as December 12, 1979.

14 **The pace of mergers and acquisitions increased:** Between 1981 and 1988, more than 1,500 publicly traded American companies were taken private. Mallaby, *More Money Than God*, p. 113.

15 **He abandoned Aizer's riskless options strategy:** "It occurred to me that I was more right than wrong on the direction of stocks," Cohen later said. "So I thought, Why hedge them? Why not just buy stocks?" Burrough, "What's Eating Steve Cohen?"

15 **Cohen was making $5 to $10 million a year:** Burrough, "What's Eating Steve Cohen?"

17 **This brought him one step closer to his dream:** *Patricia Cohen v. Steven A. Cohen, et al.*, Statement of Facts, 2009.

18 **"I heard there might be a restructuring going on":** In the Matter of: Trading in the Securities of RCA Corporation, SEC File No. HO-1793.

18 **he'd been telling people that a Wharton classmate had told him:** *Patricia Cohen v. Steven A. Cohen, et al.*, Statement of Facts, 2009.

18 **General Electric announced a takeover of the broadcaster:** "General Electric Will Buy RCA for $6.28 Billion," *Los Angeles Times*, December 12, 1985.

18 **Cohen made $20 million:** *Patricia Cohen v. Steven Cohen, et al.*, First Amended Complaint, No. 09 Civ. 10230 (WHP).

18 **Three months later, an envelope from the SEC arrived:** Date of subpoena April 23, 1986, per Cohen SEC deposition testimony, In the Matter of: Trading in the Securities of RCA Corporation.

19 **The SEC wanted Cohen to come in and testify:** In the Matter of: Trading in the Securities of RCA Corporation.

19 **"Don't worry":** In the Matter of: Trading in the Securities of RCA Corporation.

19 **The SEC accused Levine:** James B. Stewart, *Den of Thieves* (Simon & Schuster, 1991), p. 294.

19 **Around 6 P.M. on June 5, 1986:** "Investment Banker Pleads Guilty to Insider Trading," Associated Press, June 5, 1986.

19 **Gruntal had arranged for Cohen to be represented by Otto Obermaier:** After representing Cohen in 1989, Obermaier was appointed U.S. Attorney for the Southern District of New York by President George H. W. Bush, replacing Rudy Giuliani. Obermaier held the post until 1993. "Otto Obermaier Is No Rudy Giuliani," *BusinessWeek,* July 27, 1992.

21 **"taking the Fifth":** The Fifth Amendment to the Constitution, also known as the privilege against self-incrimination, provides that no person can be forced to be a witness against himself. For more on implications of taking the Fifth in SEC investigations, see Tom Hanusik, "Averse to Adverse Inferences? Rethinking the Scope of the Fifth Amendment Protections in SEC Proceedings," *Securities Regulation & Law Report,* 41 SRLR 574, The Bureau of National Affairs, March 30, 2009.

22 **The testimony was over in twenty minutes:** Cohen SEC deposition testimony, In the Matter of: Trading in the Securities of RCA Corporation.

22 **Patricia and the children would cower:** "He used to come home beat up, impatient, at the end of his wits," Patricia says. "He could be demanding, hypercritical, and a screamer." Fishman, "Divorced, Never Separated."

22 **"I'm just a stock trader":** SEC testimony of Brett K. Lurie, In the Matter of: Trading in the Securities of RCA Corporation.

23 **He had many short positions:** Peter Lattman, "SAC Capital's Cohen Opens Up," *The New York Times,* February 15, 2011.

25 **Cohen moved out:** *Steven A. Cohen v. Patricia Cohen,* No. 11 Cv. 1390, filed March 21, 1991; per Order to Show Cause for Modification Upward of Child Support, apartment was located at 120 East End Avenue, 10A.

25 **Around half of that, $8.75 million, had been invested in a real estate deal:** *Steven Cohen and SAC Trading Corp. v. Brett K. Lurie and Conversion Trading Corp.,* No. 9891/87, affidavit by Brett K. Lurie, May 12, 1987.

25 **which he said was worth $2.8 million:** Mr. and Mrs. Steven A. Cohen Statement of Financial Condition, July 1, 1988.

25 **Cohen made more than $4 million that year:** *Steven A. Cohen v. Patricia Cohen,* Cohen's 1989 earnings of $4.3 million per 1989 form 1040, filed as an exhibit to Affidavit in Opposition, filed August 9, 1991; according to Patricia's divorce filings, she believes that Cohen made $20 million in 1989 and $12 million in 1988. Cohen disputed this.

25 **$80,000 in Bergdorf's bills:** *Steven A. Cohen v. Patricia Cohen,* Affidavit in Opposition, filed August 9, 1991.

2. WHAT STEVIE WANTS, STEVIE GETS

27 **Gruntal had earned a reputation as a less than reputable firm:** While the company was run by Howard Silverman from 1974 to 1995, Silverman's two sons operated a firm that cleared all of Gruntal's trades for the New York Stock Exchange, an arrangement that was legal but had the appearance, at a minimum, of a conflict of interest. At the same time, the son of another deputy of the firm, Edward Bao, cleared all the firm's trades for the Amex stock exchange. Richard Behar, "The Shabby Side of the Street," *Fortune,* March 3, 2003.

27 **Cohen started SAC with around $23 million:** The number cited in some published accounts is $25 million; former employees I spoke with say it was $23 million or $24 million.

28 **especially those who'd played college sports:** Jack D. Schwager, *Stock Market Wizards* (HarperCollins, 2001), p. 274.

29 **Steinhardt came into stock trading:** Raised by a single mother in a gritty neighborhood in Brooklyn, Michael Steinhardt had both a brilliant investing sense and an unpredictable temper, which fueled his desire to make money. "I had an overriding need to win every day," he once said. "If I was not winning, I suffered as though a major tragedy had occurred." Sebastian Mallaby, *More Money Than God* (Penguin, 2010), pp. 55–56.

29 **George Soros and Paul Tudor Jones:** The industry was dominated by a handful of men who had become semi-celebrities on Wall Street: Julian Robertson, who ran the Tiger fund and was known for breeding new hedge fund managers; George Soros, who was seen as an intellectual and, along with his partner Stanley Druckenmiller, ran the Quantum Fund, which made bets on broad economic forces; and the Memphis cotton trader Paul Tudor Jones, who started Tudor Investment in 1983 and who in 1988, at age thirty-three, was reported to be the highest-paid individual on Wall Street, with $80 to $100 million in earnings. Each had his own strategy for making money, usually based in a strong idea about investing. Alison Leigh Cowan, "Where the Money Is: Wall St.'s Best-Paid People," *The New York Times,* June 4, 1988.

30 **to almost $100 million:** SAC Capital Advisors marketing presentation, May 1, 2012.

32 **He signed up for a dating service:** Bryan Burrough, "What's Eating Steven Cohen?" *Vanity Fair,* July 2010.

34 **Cohen, who showed up thinking:** *Steven A. Cohen v. Patricia Cohen,* Index No. 62593/90, Affidavit in Opposition, November 9, 1995.

34 **"A lot of these things occurred":** Alex and Steven Cohen appearance on *The Cristina Show*, July 29, 1992.

35 **Kiev's other area of expertise was success:** The son of a Bronx rabbi who'd gone to Harvard, Kiev wrote several books on depression and had been at the forefront of research into antidepressants, running clinical trials of Prozac and Zoloft. William Grimes, "Ari Kiev, Psychiatrist to Traders, Dies," *The New York Times*, Nov. 30, 2009.

36 **some of his favorite phrases:** Ari Kiev, M.D., *Trading to Win* (John Wiley & Sons, 1998).

36 **"You need to trade to *win*":** Schwager, *Stock Market Wizards*.

38 **Cohen called Kenny Lissak with some shocking news:** The story of Lissak's firing comes from Lissak, and was corroborated by several other people who were there at the time.

40 **SAC generated far more revenue:** A version of this story is also recounted by Gary Sernovitz, "Edge and the Art Collector," *n+1*, January 16, 2013.

42 **once housed heirs to the Rockefeller and J. Pierpont Morgan fortunes:** Nina Munk, "Greenwich's Outrageous Fortunes," *Vanity Fair*, July 2006.

42 **Paul Tudor Jones was one of the first:** Munk, "Greenwich's Outrageous Fortunes."

44 **raised his bid to $14.8 million, and bought the house in cash:** Looking back on the incident, Steinberg said in an interview: "The property was magnificent—it was just a big beautiful home. I thought it was perfect the way it was, and he tore it apart." Steinberg ended up buying another Greenwich mansion, which had previously been owned by Donald Trump, for $15 million.

45 **They built a nine-foot stone wall:** Marcia Vickers, "The Most Powerful Trader on Wall Street You've Never Heard Of," *BusinessWeek*, July 20, 2003.

45 **It took 283 dump-truck loads:** Matthew Purdy, "Our Towns: In Greenwich, More Is Just Too Much," *The New York Times*, December 5, 1999.

45 **"I feel that it's not a home":** Purdy, "Our Towns: In Greenwich, More Is Just Too Much."

3. MURDERERS' ROW

46 **returns were getting harder to find:** "It's hard to find ideas that aren't picked over, and harder to get real returns and differentiate yourself," Cohen said. "The days of big returns are gone." Susan Pulliam, "The Hedge-Fund King Is Getting Nervous," *The Wall Street Journal*, September 16, 2006.

49 **He had recruited Lee from a brokerage firm:** *U.S. v. Choo-Beng Lee, et al.*

51 **One of the things SAC looked for in new traders was personal connections:** James Sterngold and Jenny Strasburg, "For SAC, a Shift in Investing Strategy Later Led to Suspicions," *The Wall Street Journal*, July 24, 2013. See also *U.S. v. SAC Capital Advisors*, No. 13 Cr. 541, filed July 25, 2013, Sealed Indictment.

53 **The art market offered a way to transform wealth:** A version of this idea was expressed by Jonathan Jones, "Art and Money: The Sharks Behind the Showpieces," *The Guardian*, October 12, 2011.

53 **"It is not even cool to be a billionaire anymore":** Rebecca Mead, "The Daredevil of the Auction World," *The New Yorker*, July 4, 2016.

55 **paying $8 million for a shark:** Carol Vogel, "Swimming with Famous Dead Sharks," *The New York Times*, October 1, 2006.

55 **4,360 gallons of formaldehyde:** Roberta Smith, "Just When You Thought It Was Safe," *The New York Times*, October 16, 2007.

55 **the casino magnate Steve Wynn had bought it:** Account of Wynn cocktail party: Nick Paumgarten, "The $40-Million Elbow," *The New Yorker*, October 23, 2006.

55 **"This is the most money ever paid for a painting":** "Steve Wynn to Keep Picasso He Damaged," Associated Press, October 18, 2006.

56 **the collectors Victor and Sally Ganz:** Geraldine Norman, "Life with Picasso," *The Independent*, September 27, 1997.

56 **"terrible" ripping sound:** Nora Ephron, "My Weekend in Vegas," *The Huffington Post*, October 16, 2006.

56 **the sale was off:** Paumgarten, "The $40-Million Elbow"; some details from *Stephen and Elaine Wynn v. Lloyd's of London*, No. 07 Civ. 00202, filed January 10, 2007.

57 **Martoma would have a portfolio of about $400 million:** *U.S. v. Martoma*, January 20, 2014, Timothy Jandovitz testimony.

57 **base salary of $200,000 and a signing bonus of $2 million:** *U.S. v. Martoma*, GX 570, introduced January 13, 2014, Mathew Martoma SAC job offer from June 2, 2006.

58 **He fit the new SAC image:** *David Kaplan, et al., v. SAC Capital, et al.*, No. 12 Civ. 9350 (VM) (KNF), filed September 3, 2014, Elan Shareholder Second Amended Complaint.

58 **he stayed up late working another shift, reading research reports:** *U.S. v. Martoma*, Mathew Martoma Sentencing Memorandum, Exhibit 1, letter from Rosemary Martoma.

59 **he volunteered in the Alzheimer's wing:** Patrick Radden Keefe, "The Empire of Edge," *The New Yorker*, October 13, 2014.

59 **Bapi had a less complex structure:** *U.S. v. Martoma*, January 17, 2014, testimony of Dr. Sidney Gilman.

59 **an "expert network" or "matchmaking" firm:** Laurie P. Cohen, "Seeking an Edge, Big Investors Turn to Network of Informants," *The Wall Street Journal*, November 27, 2006.

61 **"We thought it was kind of ridiculous":** Steve Bodow, "Investing; It's Not What They Know, but Whom," *The New York Times*, December 23, 2001.

61 **$1.2 million annual subscription:** *U.S. v. Martoma*, GLG SAC Subscription Agreement, GX 630, introduced January 16, 2014.

61 **"Are any of these docs in your database?":** *U.S. v. Martoma*, GX 262, email sent on August 30, 2006; also *David Kaplan, et al., v. SAC Capital, et al.*, Elan Shareholder Second Amended Complaint, filed September 3, 2013.

61 **"I am Chair of the Safety Monitoring Committee":** *U.S. v. Martoma*, GX 660, January 16, 2014; Gilman email to Noopur Batsha dated August 23, 2006.

4. IT'S LIKE GAMBLING AT RICK'S

65 **accusations of each side rifling through the other's garbage:** Michael Orey, "Corporate Snoops," *BusinessWeek*, October 9, 2006.

65 **Biovail, a Canadian drug manufacturer:** The company specialized in taking established drugs, such as the commercially successful antidepressant Wellbutrin, and getting licenses to produce them in new form, with time-release delivery mechanisms it had developed that made the drugs more efficient.

66 **Biovail's CEO, Eugene Melnyk:** For more details, see Leonard Zehr, "Biovail and the Analyst's Secret Account," *The Globe and Mail*, June 22, 2002.

66 **a piece in *BusinessWeek*:** Marcia Vickers, "The Most Powerful Trader on Wall Street You've Never Heard Of," *BusinessWeek*, July 20, 2003.

67 **The SAC call came a few minutes before:** The SAC trader was never accused of any wrongdoing with regard to ImClone. Vickers, "The Most Powerful Trader on Wall Street You've Never Heard Of."

67 **Biovail filed a lawsuit against SAC:** *Biovail Corporation v. SAC Capital Management, et al.*, No. 06 Cv. 01413, filed February 23, 2006.

67 **from close to $50 to $18 in Canadian dollars:** Jenny Anderson, "Claiming Stock Manipulation, Biovail Sues Hedge Fund," *The New York Times*, February 23, 2006.

68 **"SAC places extreme pressure on its traders":** *Biovail Corporation v. SAC Capital Management, et al.*

68 **the SEC launched its own investigation:** Stunningly, the Biovail suit against SAC was dismissed in 2009 by a judge in New Jersey. In February 2010, SAC sued Biovail, which had been taken over by Valeant Pharmaceuticals, accusing it of vexatious litigation. Valeant and SAC settled the case in November 2010, with

Valeant agreeing to pay $10 million to SAC to compensate it for legal expenses. On March 24, 2008, the SEC sued Melnyk and Biovail, accusing the company of engaging in accounting fraud. The company paid $10 million to settle the charges and another $128 million to settle a class-action lawsuit filed by its shareholders. "Biovail Settles with SAC Capital," *The New York Times*, November 4, 2010.

68 *60 Minutes* **aired a segment about the litigation:** Leslie Stahl, "Betting on a Fall: On One Company's Lawsuit Against a Hedge Fund," *60 Minutes*, CBS News, March 24, 2006.

68 **"When you see a tidal wave coming":** Stahl, "Betting on a Fall."

69 **"never ending quest to poison my relationship":** *Steven A. Cohen v. Patricia Cohen,* Index No. 62593, Affidavit and Affirmation in Opposition, November 9, 1995.

70 **a sleazy place:** Richard Behar, "The Shabby Side of the Street," *Fortune*, March 3, 2003.

71 **who made close to a billion dollars that year:** Peter Lattman and Ben Protess, "$1.2 Billion Fine for Hedge Fund SAC Capital in Insider Case," *The New York Times*, November 4, 2013.

72 **Bowe hoped to prove that the hedge funds were insider trading:** *Fairfax Financial Holdings Ltd. and Crum & Forster Holding Corp. v. SAC Capital Management LLC, et al.,* Fairfax Appeal Brief.

72 **"Save yourself!":** Bethany McLean, "A Wall Street Battle Royal," *Fortune*, March 6, 2007.

73 **Traders at various hedge funds shorted the stock:** *Fairfax Financial Holdings Ltd. and Crum & Forster Holding Corp. v. SAC Capital Management LLC, et al.* In 2012, a New Jersey state judge dismissed Fairfax's case against SAC and the other funds. Fairfax refiled the case in 2013. See David Voreacos, "SAC Dismissal from New Jersey Lawsuit Appealed by Fairfax," by Bloomberg News, June 4, 2013.

78 **Spitzer launched an investigation of research departments:** "SEC Fact Sheet on Global Analyst Research Settlements," Securities and Exchange Commission, April 28, 2003.

78 **The classic case was Henry Blodget:** "SEC Sues Goldman Sachs for Research Analyst Conflicts of Interest," SEC press release, April 28, 2003.

79 **The hedge funds demanded service in return:** Many services the banks provided could be paid for in what were called "soft dollars"—basically IOUs that were repaid in the form of trading commissions.

80 **gambling at Rick's:** This phrase comes from a scene in the film *Casablanca*, when Captain Renault, a regular patron of Rick Blaine's nightclub and gambling den, Rick's Café, must find an excuse to shut the place down: "I'm shocked, shocked, to find that gambling is going on here."

5. EDGY, PROPRIETARY INFORMATION

82 **he majored in philosophy in college:** *U.S. v. Michael Steinberg,* No. 12 Cr. 121 (RJS), filed May 2, 2014, Michael Steinberg Sentencing Memorandum, letter from Rebecca and Kenneth Roban.

82 **Steinberg was put in charge of the portfolio on his own:** *U.S. v. Steinberg,* November 21, 2013, testimony of SAC CFO Dan Berkowitz.

83 **Each had been worth more than $20 billion:** Kate Kelly, Serena Ng, and David Reilly, "Two Big Funds at Bear Stearns Face Shutdown," *The Wall Street Journal,* June 20, 2007.

83 **To Horvath, it was clear what his boss wanted him to do:** *U.S. v. Steinberg,* testimony of Jon Horvath. During the trial, Steinberg's defense lawyers disputed this account, and the charges against Steinberg were later dismissed for unrelated reasons as a result of an appeals-court ruling.

84 **FBI Special Agent David Makol:** The son of a forklift driver who grew up in Springfield, Massachusetts, Makol had had obsessive work habits that brought him into the office at 5 A.M. most days. His first big case was the Martha Stewart investigation, based on allegations that she covered up a sale she made of four thousand shares of ImClone Systems in 2001 after getting a tip from the company's founder, Sam Waksal, who was a social friend. From there, Makol moved on to the Reebok–Adidas case, in which a young Goldman Sachs analyst traded options in Reebok after learning in advance that Adidas was taking it over; he placed the trades through the account of his aunt, a sixty-three-year-old retired seamstress in Croatia. For more, see Susan Pulliam, Michael Rothfeld, and Jenny Strasberg, "The FBI Agent Who 'Flips' Insider-Trading Witnesses," *The Wall Street Journal,* January 20, 2012.

84 **he agreed to cooperate:** Susan Pulliam, "Wired on Wall Street: Trader Betrays a Friend," *The Wall Street Journal,* January 16, 2010; also David Glovin and David Voreacos, "Dream Insider Informant Led FBI from Galleon to SAC," Bloomberg News, December 2, 2012.

85 **Slaine agreed to make recordings of his conversations:** *U.S. v. David Slaine,* No. 09 Cr. 1222 (RJS), January 9, 2012, government's Sentencing Memorandum; Slaine's evidence led to prosecutions of Zvi Goffer and Craig Drimal, both Galleon traders, as well as to the prosecution of many others. *U.S. v. Goffer,* No. 11 Cr. 3591 (2d Cir. 2013).

86 **the amount of the profit he got to keep:** *U.S. v. Steinberg,* GX 2004, Sigma Capital Management, LLC 2007 Year-End Payout Calculation.

86 **Steinberg sent a strong message to Horvath:** *U.S. v. Steinberg,* GX 2064, Jon Horvath performance review 2007.

86 He relocated to the East Coast: *U.S. v. Steinberg*, testimony of Jesse Tortora.

87 Then Tortora invited a few others to join: Including his friend Sam Adondakis, an analyst at David Ganek's fund, Level Global.

87 He told Tortora never to email him: *U.S. v. Steinberg*, testimony of Tortora.

87 "Rule number one about email list": *U.S. v. Steinberg*, GX 327, testimony of Tortora.

87 home prices in ten major U.S. cities: Ben Rooney, "Home Prices: Down Record 11%," *CNN Money*, March 25, 2008.

87 almost $17 billion in assets: *U.S. v. Mathew Martoma*, No. 12 Cr. 0973 (PGG), testimony of Dan Berkowitz.

88 SAC's returns had averaged 30 percent: Katherine Burton and Anthony Effinger, "How Hedge Fund Manager Steve Cohen Averaged 30% Returns for 18 Years," *Bloomberg Markets*, April 25, 2010.

88 SAC had doubled in size: *U.S. v. Martoma*, testimony of Berkowitz.

89 He had purchased the work in 2005: Colin Gleadell, "Saatchi Sells Another Key Work in His Collection," *ArtNews*, May 10, 2005.

89 Damien Hirst's shark: Carol Vogel, "Swimming with Famous Dead Sharks," *The New York Times*, October 1, 2006.

92 Between 2000 and 2007: Kelly, Ng, and Reilly, "Two Big Funds at Bear Stearns Face Shutdown."

92 It was the worst June: Alexandra Twin, "Stocks: Mixed Day, Brutal June," *CNN Money*, June 30, 2008.

93 "I want to buy 750,000 to 1 million Elan": *U.S. v. Martoma*, GX 302.

6. CONFLICT OF INTEREST

95 He sent a similar note for Wyeth: *U.S. v. Mathew Martoma*, No. 12 Cr. 0973 (PGG), GX 305.

96 "I spoke to Steve about it": *U.S. v. Martoma*, GX 302.

96 He and his first wife, Linda: Michael Betzold, "The Corruption of Sid Gilman," *Ann Arbor Observer*, January 2013.

97 Gilman's mother, who had taken her own life: According to "Not My Father's Keeper: Unveiling the Skeletons in Dr. Sid Gilman's Closet," a book proposal by Todd Gilman that was submitted to publishers in 2014.

97 he and his father stopped speaking: Gilman, "Not My Father's Keeper."

97 "The man worked himself to distraction": Patrick Radden Keefe, "The Empire of Edge," *The New Yorker*, October 13, 2014.

97 He led research projects: Betzold, "The Corruption of Sid Gilman."

97 **He barely knew what a hedge fund was:** *U.S. v. Martoma,* testimony of Dr. Sidney Gilman, cross-examination.

98 **"It paid well":** *U.S. v. Martoma,* testimony of Gilman.

98 **For a thirty-minute phone call:** *U.S. v. Martoma,* cross-examination of Gilman.

98 **hundreds of thousands of dollars a year consulting:** *U.S. v. Martoma,* January 23, 2014, cross-examination of Gilman. "Outside consulting" brought in $340,000 in 2006, $420,000 in 2007, $425,000 in 2008; earlier, during direct testimony, Gilman said it was $200,000. See also Jenny Strasburg, "Doctor's Alleged Role Highlights Ties Between Investors and Medical Field," *The Wall Street Journal,* November 20, 2012.

98 **"He was not a flashy guy":** Tim Greenamyre, a former student of Gilman's, who runs the Institute for Neurodegenerative Diseases in Pittsburgh; from Keefe, "The Empire of Edge."

98 **he started to allow himself certain luxuries:** Nathaniel Popper and Bill Vlasic, "Quiet Doctor, Lavish Insider: A Parallel Life," *The New York Times,* December 15, 2012.

98 **the medical profession was being infiltrated by Wall Street:** Eric Topol and David Blumenthal, "Physicians and the Investment Industry," *Journal of the American Medical Association,* June 1, 2005.

99 **Gilman was recruited by Elan:** *U.S. v. Martoma,* GX 20, also testimony of Gilman. Gilman had been chair of the safety monitoring committee during the test of bapi's predecessor, AN-1792, in 2005. Having seen the disastrous side effects of that drug, which had caused a dangerous swelling in the brain, Gilman felt apprehensive about the safety of the new set of patients. Gilman's fee was $350 an hour, up to a maximum of $25,000.

99 **Everyone involved in the bapi trial:** *U.S. v. Martoma,* January 13, 2014, testimony of Allison Hulme, Elan Corp., testimony of Gilman. Two hundred thirty-four Alzheimer's patients from around the country were enrolled in bapineuzumab's Phase II trial. Twenty physicians were contracted to serve as investigators in the study and to give the drug to their patients and closely monitor their reactions.

99 **"Analysts, hedge fund employees":** *U.S. v. Martoma,* testimony of Hulme, testimony of Gilman.

99 **"Trading in Elan or Wyeth":** *U.S. v. Martoma,* GX 7, also testimony of Hulme, Gilman.

100 **This time seemed like it might be different:** *U.S. v. Martoma,* GX 103, testimony of Gilman, memo to Enchi Liu of Elan.

100 **"Bapsolutely!":** Keefe, "The Empire of Edge."

100 **Martoma reminded him of his first son, Jeff:** *U.S. v. Martoma,* testimony of Gilman.

103 **Martoma referred to Holman:** *U.S. v. Martoma,* Defense Exhibit 269, email from Martoma to Chandler Bocklage, introduced during testimony of Chandler Bocklage.

103 **Cohen contributed $800 million:** *U.S. v. Martoma,* testimony of Peter Nussbaum, SAC general counsel.

103 **Holman signed a consulting agreement:** Deposition of Steven Cohen before the SEC, In the Matter of: Elan Corporation, plc, File No. NY-8152, May 3, 2012.

103 **Martoma was "tagged":** *U.S. v. Martoma,* GX 297, Cohen sector position-alert email, introduced during testimony of Katie Lyndon.

104 **"I think Mat is closest to it":** *David E. Kaplan, et al., v. SAC Capital Advisors, et al.,* No. 12 Civ. 9530 (VM) (KNF), exchanges on March 28, 2008, and April 6, 2008, cited in Elan Shareholder Second Amended Complaint.

7. STUFF THAT LEGENDS ARE MADE OF

108 **an application to wiretap Raj Rajaratnam's cellphone:** *U.S. v. Rajaratnam,* No. 09 Cr. 1184 (RJH), October 6, 2010, Franks Hearing, testimony of FBI Special Agent B. J. Kang.

109 **They must show that a wiretap:** Title 18, United States Code 2518, (1) (c), statute regarding wiretapping.

109 **"Unless oil trades down":** *U.S. v. Mathew Martoma,* No. 12 Cr. 0973 (PGG); Defense Exhibit 505, dated July 7, 2008, introduced during testimony of Timothy Jandovitz.

109 **Martoma arranged a private dinner:** *David Kaplan et al., v. SAC Capital, et al.,* No. 12 Civ. 9350 (VM) (KNF), Elan Shareholder Second Amended Complaint, pp. 80-81.

110 **Elan and Wyeth announced:** "Elan and Wyeth Announce Encouraging Topline Results from Phase 2 Clinical Trial of Bapineuzumab for Alzheimer's Disease," press release dated June 17, 2008.

110 **Cohen also had a large position:** *U.S. v. Martoma,* GX 298, 299.

111 **"The hair on my head":** *U.S. v. Martoma,* GX 53, testimony of Gilman.

112 **On July 15, Gilman flew by chartered plane:** *U.S. v. Martoma,* GX 9.

112 **everything he was about to see had to remain secret:** *U.S. v. Martoma,* testimony of Allison Hulme.

113 **"ICAD presentation confidential":** *U.S. v. Martoma,* GX 11.

113 **"Dear Sid," it read:** *U.S. v. Martoma,* GX 12.

113 **At home that evening:** *U.S. v. Martoma,* GX 710, testimony of Gilman.

114 **Just after 10 A.M.:** *U.S. v. Martoma*, testimony of Nathan Brown, University of Michigan, re campus-access control system.

115 **he boarded a 4 P.M. Delta Airlines flight:** *U.S. v. Martoma*, GX 1307, introduced during testimony of Mark Manhan of Delta.

116 **They talked for twenty minutes:** *U.S. v. Martoma*, GX 459.

116 **After they hung up:** *David Kaplan, et al., v. SAC Capital, et al.*, No. 12 Civ. 9350 (VM) (KNF), Elan Shareholder Second Amended Complaint, p. 86. Before the market opening on July 21, 2008, the portfolios held 10.6 million Elan ADRs, worth $366 million, and 19 million Wyeth, worth roughly $900 million.

117 **They'd sold roughly 1.5 million shares:** *U.S. v. Martoma*, GX 431, introduced during testimony of Phillipp Villhauer.

117 **"400k at 34.97 all dark pools":** *U.S. v. Martoma*, GX 432, introduced during testimony of Villhauer.

117 **Cohen shorted 4.5 million shares:** Elan Shareholder Second Amended Complaint, p. 86; see also *SEC v. CR Intrinsic Investors, Mathew Martoma and Dr. Sidney Gilman, and SAC Capital Advisors*, No. 12 Civ. 8466 (VM), Amended Complaint, March 15, 2013.

117 **Harvey Pitt arrived:** *U.S. v. Martoma*, GX 595, introduced during testimony of John Casey, SAC compliance officer.

118 **One of SAC's compliance officers:** *U.S. v. Martoma*, some details from lawyer discussion at bench, January 16, 2014; others from testimony of Casey.

118 **"Stop and think before trading":** *U.S. v. Martoma*, GX 595, Harvey Pitt talk email invitation, and GX 591, Pitt slide presentation, introduced during testimony of Casey.

119 **Dennis had learned about:** *SEC v. Matthew G. Teeple, David T. Riley, and John V. Johnson*, Complaint, United States District Court, Southern District of New York, March 26, 2013.

119 **When Foundry went up:** *SEC v. Ronald N. Dennis*, No. 14 Civ. 1746, March 13, 2014.

121 **Ross said goodbye:** This account is drawn largely from Ross's trial testimony, *U.S. v. Martoma*.

121 **He'd had a series of chemotherapy treatments:** *U.S. v. Martoma*, chemotherapy treatment schedule elicited during Gilman cross-examination.

121 **his twenty-two slides:** *U.S. v. Martoma*, GX 19, introduced during testimony of Hulme.

122 **"I can remember gasping":** Nathaniel Popper and Bill Vlasic, "Quiet Doctor, Lavish Insider: A Parallel Life," *The New York Times*, December 15, 2012.

122 **"I saw what u did with WYE":** The stock symbol for Wyeth. *U.S. v Martoma*, GX 294, Martoma Lyndon email, introduced during Katie Lyndon testimony.

124   "We'll catch up over a beer": *U.S. v. Martoma*, Defense Exhibit (hereafter "DX") 328/GX 313, testimony of Jandovitz.

126   "Anyway," he added, "no need to call": *U.S. v. Martoma*, GX 235, email date September 28, 2008, introduced during testimony of Gilman.

126   Diamondback Capital, was paying Goyal for his Dell tips: *U.S. v. Michael Steinberg*, No. 12 Cr. 121 (RJS), testimony of Jesse Tortora. Goyal's source, it turned out, worked in Dell's investor-relations department. In 2015, charges against Goyal were dismissed, after the reversal of the Newman and Chiasson convictions.

126   "Dell checks": *U.S. v. Steinberg*, GX 214.

127   his weekend house in the Hamptons: *U.S. v. Steinberg*, GX 631.

128   "Interesting . . .": *U.S. v. Steinberg*, GX 631.

130   The next day, the stock dropped: Laurie J. Flynn, "Dell's Profit Drop Surprises Investors," *The New York Times*, August 28, 2008.

130   His boss covered his short: *SEC v. Dennis*; Patricia Hurtado, "Former Level Global Analyst Says Two SAC Friends Got Inside Tips," Bloomberg News, November 29, 2012.

8. THE INFORMANT

134   Tactical Behavior Assessment training: Eamon Javers, *Broker, Trader, Lawyer, Spy: The Secret World of Corporate Espionage* (HarperBusiness, 2010).

135   referring to the friend, who worked at the Blackstone Group in London: Michael J. de la Merced, "Blackstone Executive Is Charged with Insider Trading," *The New York Times*, January 14, 2009.

136   as if he were a gangster: Peter Lattman and Ben Protess, "How Pursuit of Billionaire Hit One Dead End," *The New York Times*, January 14, 2013.

141   Lee had been wiring $2,000 payments: *U.S. v. Richard Choo-Beng Lee, et al.*, No. 09 Cr. 0972 (PKC), information filed October 13, 2009; also see Sentencing Submission by government.

141   "This is your one chance": Anita Raghavan, *The Billionaire's Apprentice* (Business Plus, 2013), p. 302.

142   The fund had been doing relatively well: Susan Pulliam, "How Associates Helped Build Case," *The Wall Street Journal*, October 20, 2009.

142   The only way to satisfy them: *U.S. v. Choo-Beng Lee*, Sentencing Submission.

145   PGR, was one of the worst offenders: In the Matter of: Application of the United States of America to Authorize to Intercept Certain Wire Communications, 11 Cr. 00032 (JSR), filed July 12, 2011. PGR Wiretap Application,

pp. 20–25. Kang's suspicions had been corroborated by Karl Motey, who was working with FBI agents Dave Makol and James Hinkle. Motey, a married father of three, was a consultant who had five portfolio managers at different hedge funds paying him a total of $500,000 a year for his insights on the technology industry, and some of what he passed on to them was inside information. When Motey was asked if there was anything he had observed in the financial industry that struck him as shady but that he wasn't necessarily involved in himself, he answered: "Expert networks." *U.S. v. Motey*, 10-cr-1249.

145 **PGR's biggest customers:** Patricia Hurtado, "SAC Trial Seen by Probe Convict as Latest Abusive Tactic," Bloomberg News, January 7, 2014.

145 **Dave Makol and James Hinkle, started gathering evidence:** PGR Wiretap Application.

150 **getting permission to send out subpoenas:** Devin Leonard, "The SEC: Outmanned, Outgunned, and on a Roll," *Bloomberg Businessweek*, April 19, 2012.

155 **It was 3 A.M.:** *U.S. v. Raj Rajaratnam, Rajiv Goel, and Anil Kumar*, No. 09 Mag. 2306, October 15, 2009.

155 **At 6 A.M. the following morning:** Danielle Chiesi, a trader at New Castle Funds; Chiesi's boss, Mark Kurland; an IBM senior vice president named Robert Moffat; and Raj's friends Rajiv Goel, an Intel executive, and Anil Kumar, from McKinsey. Chiesi had allegedly been having affairs with both Kurland and Moffat, whom she'd milked for leaks about IBM. Michael J. de la Merced, "Hedge Fund Chief Is Charged with Fraud," *The New York Times*, October 16, 2009.

9. THE DEATH OF KINGS

158 **"If you got a 98":** Ed Beeson, "When U.S. Attorney Preet Bharara Speaks, Wall Street and the World Listens," *The Star-Ledger*, August 19, 2012.

158 **"School, studying, grades":** Carrie Johnson, "Family Ties," *Columbia Law School Magazine*, Fall 2011.

158 **Michael Mukasey:** Also the father of Marc Mukasey, Dr. Sidney Gilman's defense attorney.

158 **inspired Bharara to become a prosecutor:** Benjamin Weiser, "For Manhattan's Next U.S. Attorney, Politics and Prosecution Don't Mix," *The New York Times*, August 9, 2009. Preet wasn't the only Bharara son with the overachiever gene. The younger Bharara brother, Vinny, also attended Columbia Law School, three years behind his older brother. He co-founded an Internet retailer that

sold diapers, which was sold to Amazon for $540 million in 2010; see also Johnson, "Family Ties."

158 **"Schumer Aide Is Confirmed"**: Benjamin Weiser, "Schumer Aide Is Confirmed as United States Attorney," *The New York Times*, August 8, 2009.

159 **"Greed, sometimes, is not good"**: *U.S. v. Raj Rajaratnam, et al.*, 09-Mag-2306, October 16, 2009; prepared remarks for U.S. Attorney Preet Bharara in press conference announcing charges.

159 **Rengan had even worked at SAC**: Rajarengan Rajaratnam testimony before the SEC, In the Matter of: Sedna Capital Management, file No. NY-7665.

160 **People could only speculate**: Just three days after Raj's arrest, *The Wall Street Journal* posted an article on its website that publicly identified C. B. Lee and Ali Far, for the first time, as government cooperators. It was hugely damaging to the investigation. Susan Pulliam, "How Associates Helped Build Case," *The Wall Street Journal*, October 20, 2009.

160 **Biovail's lawsuit against SAC had been dismissed**: Valeant Pharmaceuticals eventually bought Biovail, and in 2010 settled claims brought by SAC Capital for vexatious litigation by agreeing to pay SAC $10 million. Shira Ovide, "SAC Capital, Biovail Finally Bury the Hatchet," *The Wall Street Journal*, November 4, 2010.

160 **SEC had charged the company with fraud**: Judith Burns, "SEC Charges Biovail Officers with Fraud," *The Wall Street Journal*, March 25, 2008.

161 **In the course of reading the SEC files about Cohen**: *Patricia Cohen v. Steven A. Cohen, et al.*, First Amended Complaint, No. 09 Civ. 10230 (WHP), April 7, 2010.

161 **Lurie was bankrupt, a wrecked man**: *Steven Cohen and SAC Trading Corp. v. Brett K. Lurie and Conversion Trading Corp.*, No. 8981/87, Affidavit in Support of Order to Show Cause, N.Y. State Supreme Court, May 12, 1987. See also Douglas Montero, "Slippery Scammer an Elusive Daddy, Too," *New York Post*, October 26, 2004, and "Agents Catch Up with U.S. Citizen on the Run," *A.M. Costa Rica*, Vol. 5, No. 224, November 11, 2005.

162 **she demanded $300 million in damages**: *Patricia Cohen v. Steven A. Cohen, et al.*, December 16, 2009.

162 **The son of a nurse and a fighter pilot**: Story of the Riely family: Virginia Grantier, "Four Boys Thank Her for Courage After Husband's Death," *Bismarck Tribune*, May 11, 2002.

163 **Martoma had received a $9.38 million bonus**: *U.S. v. Mathew Martoma*, No. 12 Cr. 0973 (PGG), GX 555, Dan Berkowitz testimony.

164 **whether Esbriet would obtain FDA approval**: Andrew Pollack, "FDA Rejects InterMune's Drug for Fatal Lung Disease," *The New York Times*, May 4, 2010.

164 **almost 4.5 million shares:** Suzy Kenly Waite, "Hedge Funds Hemorrhage on InterMune," *Institutional Investor*, August 31, 2010.

166 **"Federal authorities, capping a three-year investigation":** Susan Pulliam, Michael Rothfeld, Jenny Strasburg, and Gregory Zuckerman, "U.S. in Vast Insider Trading Probe," *The Wall Street Journal*, November 20, 2010; Ernest Scheyder and Matthew Goldstein, "U.S. to Lift Lid on 'Pervasive Insider Trading': Report," Reuters, November 20, 2010.

166 **he became friends with another SAC portfolio manager in Boston named Noah Freeman:** Steve Eder, Michael Rothfeld, and Jenny Strasburg, "They Were Best of Friends, Until the Feds Showed Up," *The Wall Street Journal*, February 17, 2011.

167 **Freeman was so intense:** Eder, Rothfeld, Strasburg, "They Were Best of Friends, Until the Feds Showed Up."

167 **"the log":** FBI notes from interviews with Noah Freeman, hereafter Freeman 302s.

168 **his numbered Gmail accounts:** Details of Longueuil's Gmail accounts; Freeman 302s.

168 **most of his instant-message chats through Skype:** Longueuil use of Skype; FBI notes from interviews with Samir Barai, hereafter Barai 302s.

168 **They didn't get home until 2:30 A.M.:** *U.S. v. Samir Barai and Donald Longueuil*, No. 11 Mag. 332, February 7, 2011; reference to video surveillance, exit and return times from affidavit filed by FBI Special Agent B. J. Kang. See also Eder, Rothfeld, Strasburg, "They Were Best of Friends, Until the Feds Showed Up." Note: Longueuil's fiancée was never charged with any wrongdoing.

169 **Barai and Longueuil had developed a close, if nasty, friendship:** The three of them merged all their ill-begotten information every quarter, a week or so before earnings season, by meeting at the Santa Clara Hilton, which they referred to in emails as planned "threesomes" or as "Don, Sam, Noah—sex"; Barai 302s.

169 **increasingly ugly divorce:** Bree Sposato, "One Enchanted Evening: Bhavana Pothuri & Samir Barai," *New York*, April 15, 2006; Barai 302s.

170 **Pflaum had only a minimal understanding:** Barai 302s; also, FBI interview notes with Jason Pflaum, hereafter Pflaum 302s.

170 **"You should not ask":** Barai 302s.

171 **Then, a minute later: "Fuuuuuck":** *U.S. v. Barai, et al.*

172 **Kang took pictures of the entire exchange:** Pflaum 302s.

10. OCCAM'S RAZOR

175 **across the street from Carnegie Hall:** Level Global address, 888 Seventh Avenue; Level Global Search and Seizure Warrant, November 21, 2010.

176 **they had a search warrant:** Warrant authorized them to search the offices of Ganek, his partner Anthony Chiasson, and two analysts, Sam Adondakis and Greg Brenner; Level Global Search Warrant.

176 **That Saturday night:** Ganek was scheduled to appear on a panel that weekend with SEC chair Mary Schapiro, a fellow graduate of Franklin & Marshall College; Peter Lattman, "In Insider Case, the Odd Couple Won't Meet," *The New York Times*, November 23, 2010.

176 **making images of the firm's servers:** Level Global Search Warrant. See also *David Ganek v. David Leibowitz, Reed Brodsky, David Makol, et al.*, No. 15 Civ. 1446, February 26, 2015.

176 **he had worked out a deal:** Katherine Burton, "Goldman Sachs Fund Buys Stake in Ganek's $4 Billion Hedge Fund," Bloomberg News, April 2, 2010.

176 **had attempted to turn his life around:** *U.S. v. Noah Freeman*, 11-Cr.-116 (JSR), Sentencing submission on behalf of Noah Freeman, filed January 28, 2015, letter from Silas Bauer.

177 **blood doping with Epo:** Freeman 302s.

178 **"I understood that this involved":** Freeman 302s.

181 **"Everything's gone":** The exchange recounted in *U.S. v. Samir Barai and Donald Longueuil*, 11-Mag-332, February 7, 2011.

184 **Sullivan was a former advisor:** Tory Newmyer and Kate Ackley, "Sullivan's Hiring Hedge Bets on Sully," *Roll Call*, April 18, 2007.

184 **Sullivan argued to the senator's investigators:** Some details in Jenny Strasburg and Michael Siconolfi, "Senator Probes Trades at SAC," *The Wall Street Journal*, May 21, 2011.

184 **On May 24, Grassley released another letter:** Letter to the Honorable Mary Schapiro, Chairman, U.S. Securities and Exchange Commission, from Charles E. Grassley, Ranking Member, Committee on the Judiciary, May 24, 2011.

188 **"you are only a grain of sand":** *U.S. v. Mathew Martoma*, No. 12 Cr. 0973 (PGG); cross-examination of Sidney Gilman.

190 **a five-bedroom, $1.9 million house at the Royal Palm:** The Martomas spent $1.9 million on the house, according to Florida real estate records.

190 **Mathew and Rosemary Martoma Foundation:** According to records, the foundation was incorporated in Florida with $1 million on December 10, 2010; according to its Form 990, the foundation donated a few hundred dollars in $50 or $100 increments to a handful of local charities in 2011 and charged more than $20,000 in expenses. There are no 990s filed for subsequent years.

190 **"Your former business partner, Stephen Chan":** Bob Van Voris and Saijel Kishan, "SAC's Martoma Harvard Expulsion Revealed as Trial Starts," Bloomberg News, January 10, 2014.

191 **Martoma fainted:** This account, based on interviews with people directly familiar with what occurred, conflicts with a version that Rosemary Martoma
provided to *The New Yorker*: Patrick Radden Keefe, "The Empire of Edge," October 13, 2014. In that version, she said that when Kang and Callahan approached, Kang told her to "Get inside the house," but she refused. She said that
Kang then turned to Martoma and said, "Do you want to tell her or should I?"
Martoma told Kang, "You can go ahead and tell her if you like." According to
Rosemary, Kang said to Martoma, "We know what you did at Harvard," and
Martoma then fainted. According to my reporting, Rosemary was not present
when Martoma fainted during the encounter and did not hear what Kang said
before Martoma passed out.

11. UNDEFEATABLE

193 **he presented his son with a plaque:** *U.S. v. Mathew Martoma*, No. 12 Cr. 0973
(PGG), GX 65, Mathew Martoma Sentencing Memo, filed May 28, 2014; letter
from Bobby D. Martoma.

193 **Martoma spent the year after graduation:** *U.S. v. Martoma*, GX 106, Martoma
Sentencing Memo, letter from Manju Varghese.

193 **"He was ambitious":** Patrick Radden Keefe, "The Empire of Edge," *The New
Yorker*, October 13, 2014.

194 **The clerk tried again, on February 4:** *U.S. v. Martoma*, January 9, 2014, Disciplinary Hearing on Charges Against Ajai Mathew Thomas, Findings of Fact
and Decision of the Administrative Board, May 12, 1999, filed as exhibit to
Government's Motion in Limine to Admit Evidence Concerning the Defendant's Expulsion from Harvard Law School in Response to Potential Defenses.

195 **Kane had expelled a Harvard Law student:** Jal D. Mehta, "Law Student Expelled for Forging Transcript," *The Harvard Crimson*, January 30, 1997.

195 **The letters were all dated January 31:** *U.S. v. Martoma*, Exhibit to Government's Motion to Admit Harvard Evidence.

197 **In its final report:** *U.S. v. Martoma*, Exhibit to Government's Motion to Admit
Harvard Evidence, Disciplinary Hearing.

197 **His father took out a second mortgage on their house:** *U.S. v. Martoma*,
Mathew Martoma's Memorandum of Law in Support of His Motion to Exclude
Evidence Concerning Events Unrelated to the Charged Offenses and Preceding
Mr. Martoma's Employment at SAC, filed under seal, January 9, 2014.

197 **a talented young programmer named Stephen Chan:** *Ajai Mathew Thomas
v. Stephen K. Chan*, MICV-2000-0010, June 2, 1999, affidavit submitted by
Mathew Martoma; some details of genesis of Computer Data Forensics.

198 **It was signed by three "Case Analysts":** Computer Data Forensics report filed as an exhibit to Government's Motion to Admit Harvard Evidence.

198 **Martoma also took a polygraph test:** Martoma Motion to Exclude Evidence.

199 **He admitted that he had faked his Harvard transcripts:** *Thomas v. Chan,* affidavit of Stephen K. Chan, January 20, 2000.

199 **their employees hung around the office:** Bob Van Voris, "SAC Capital's Martoma Defense May Be Hurt by Partnership," Bloomberg News, January 28, 2014; also *Thomas v. Chan,* affidavit of Robert Owens.

199 **"We were like rent-a-friends":** Van Voris, "SAC Capital's Martoma Defense May Be Hurt by Partnership."

199 **The aggrieved employees collaborated on a letter:** *Thomas v. Chan,* employee group letter, dated December 26, 1999.

199 **Martoma filed for a restraining order against Chan:** *Thomas v. Chan,* Interlocutory Order Continuing Restraining Order in Force.

199 **bruises all over his body:** Complaint filed in *Thomas v. Chan.*

200 **Chan and six partners had been charged with fraud:** *U.S. v. Chan, et al.,* U.S. District Court, District of Massachusetts, Criminal No. 98-10277-GAO, August 12, 1998. The sham company allegedly entered into millions of dollars in leasing agreements for business purposes, to buy computer equipment and office supplies for a business that didn't exist.

200 **Chan pleaded guilty:** Van Voris, "SAC Capital's Martoma Defense May Be Hurt by Partnership."

201 **he had legally changed his name:** Name change occurred on August 29, 2001, per the Clerk of the Circuit and County Court, Brevard County, Florida.

202 **"We want Steve Cohen":** Some of the details of the FBI encounter come from Rosemary Martoma's account in Keefe, "The Empire of Edge."

202 **some tangible victories to show for its investigation:** Rajat Gupta, the former head of the McKinsey consulting firm and a former Goldman Sachs board member, had been arrested and charged with leaking information about Goldman to Rajaratnam. The Primary Global expert network had been shut down. Noah Freeman was still cooperating with prosecutors. Samir Barai had pleaded guilty and started cooperating. Donald Longueuil had pleaded guilty too and was sentenced to thirty months in prison: "Longueuil Pleads Guilty to Conspiracy, Securities Fraud," Bloomberg News, April 28, 2011; Patricia Hurtado, "Ex-SAC Manager Longueuil Sentenced to 30 Months in Prison," Bloomberg News, July 29, 2011.

204 **why should he cooperate with the FBI?:** *Securities and Exchange Commission v. Jonathan Hollander,* No. 11 Civ. 2885, Southern District of New York, April 28, 2011. In April 2011, Hollander settled with the SEC on civil charges that he

had purchased 5,600 shares of Albertsons stock in his personal account based on inside information. He agreed to pay $192,000 in fines and was barred from the securities industry for three years.

204 **Donald Longueuil, the former SAC trader:** Hurtado, "Ex-SAC Manager Longueuil Sentenced to 30 Months in Prison."

204 **preparing to charge two traders at the hedge funds the FBI raided:** Makol had two cooperators, Jesse Tortora and Sam Adondakis, former analysts at Diamondback and Level Global. On the basis of the information Makol was getting from them, the prosecutors were preparing to charge Todd Newman and Anthony Chiasson, Tortora and Adondakis's bosses, with insider trading. Inside information about Dell's earnings had allegedly passed from a Dell investor-relations employee to a former Dell employee to Tortora, and from Tortora to his boss, Todd Newman, and to Tortora's friend Adondakis. Adondakis had in turn passed it to *his* boss, Anthony Chiasson, at Level Global. Both Newman and Chiasson had ties to SAC. See also Patricia Hurtado, "Newman Calls FBI Inside-Trading Agent as Last Witness," Bloomberg News, December 11, 2012.

204 **"I have a 2nd hand read from someone at the company":** *U.S. v. Michael Steinberg,* No. 12 Cr. 121 (RJS), GX 634, introduced during testimony of Jon Horvath. Full text of the email: "I have a 2nd hand read from someone at the company—this is 3rd quarter I have gotten this read from them and it has been very good in the last two quarters. They are saying GMs [gross margins] miss by 50-80 bps [basis points] due to poor mix, opex [operating expenses] in-line and a little revenue upside netting out to an EPS [earnings per share] miss. Even if they have some flexibility in the opex/other income to offset the light GMs and report in-line EPS or even a penny upside I think the stock goes down (I know they said the headcount reductions last quarter were backend loaded). Please keep to yourself as obviously not well known."

205 **It appeared that Steinberg had then turned around and made $1 million:** *U.S. v. Todd Newman, Anthony Chiasson, Jon Horvath, and Danny Kuo,* No. 12 Mag. 0124, sealed complaint, January 17, 2012.

12. THE WHALE

206 **Sid Gilman bent over the security table:** Just two weeks earlier, on January 18, 2012, Todd Newman, from Diamondback, was arrested in Boston, and Jon Horvath was arrested in New York. Anthony Chiasson, David Ganek's partner at Level Global, found out that his arrest was imminent and checked in to a hotel. Half a dozen FBI agents stormed his Upper East Side apartment building,

only to find that he wasn't home. He turned himself in later that morning. Preet Bharara announced charges against them, alleging that together they'd made $61.8 million in illegal profits trading on inside information in Dell and Nvidia, $53 million of which came from a single massive short of Dell stock by Chiasson at Level Global: Jenny Strasburg, Michael Rothfeld, and Susan Pulliam, "FBI Sweep Targets Big Funds," *The Wall Street Journal*, January 19, 2012.

206   **Gilman was appearing for his first meeting:** *U.S. v. Mathew Martoma*, No. 12 Cr. 0973 (PGG), GX 741, dates of proffer meetings introduced during testimony of Dr. Sid Gilman.

207   **"Mat Martoma will call me re SAEs in bap":** *U.S. v. Martoma*, GX 751.

211   **SEC attorneys were openly discouraged:** See Gretchen Morgenson, "SEC Settles with a Former Lawyer," *The New York Times*, June 29, 2010.

212   **He had just spent $20 million to buy a 4 percent stake in the New York Mets:** Svea Herbst-Bayliss, "SAC's Cohen Buys Small Stake in New York Mets," Reuters, February 23, 2012.

212   **assemble a bid for the Los Angeles Dodgers:** Bill Shaikin, "Billionaire Aims to Own Dodgers," *Los Angeles Times*, December 28, 2011. See also David Ng, "Dodger Suitor on Museum Board," *Los Angeles Times*, January 14, 2012; Ronald Blum, "MLB Approves Dodgers' Finalists," Associated Press, March 27, 2012.

213   **a $2 billion bid from Guggenheim Partners:** Ronald Blum, "Dodgers Reach Deal with Magic Johnson Group," Associated Press, March 28, 2012.

213   **One of Guggenheim's most significant investors was Michael Milken:** Leslie Scism and Craig Karmin, "Guggenheim Gets SEC Scrutiny on Milken Ties," *The Wall Street Journal*, February 27, 2013.

213   **he was sorely disappointed:** Steve Fishman, "The Taming of the Trading Monster," *New York*, June 3, 2014.

214   **a few minutes later, when Cohen pushed through the door:** The date was May 3, 2012.

217   **" 'I am just getting uncomfortable with the Elan position' ":** In re: Elan Corporation, plc, SEC File No. NY-8152, *U.S. v. Martoma*, 12-Cr.-0973, government motion re Cohen SEC testimony.

13. KARMA

221   **Martoma's arrest was being covered by every major news organization:** Michael Rothfeld, Chad Bray, and Susan Pulliam, "Trading Charges Reach SAC," *The Wall Street Journal*, November 20, 2012.

221   *The New York Times* ran a story on the front page: Peter Lattman, "Insider

Inquiry Inching Closer to a Billionaire," *The New York Times*, November 20, 2012.

221 **a high-concept sandwich shop:** *U.S. v. Mathew Martoma*, No. 12 Cr. 0973 (PGG), testimony of Tim Jandovitz, January 10, 2014.

221 **"Karma is a bitch":** *U.S. v. Martoma*, mentioned by Arlo Devlin-Brown during sidebar discussion.

223 **Bharara had appeared on the cover of *Time*:** Massimo Calabresi, "U.S. Attorney Preet Bharara Is Taking Down Wall Street," *Time*, February 13, 2012.

223 **In total, it would be one of the largest settlements the SEC had ever extracted:** Details on CR Intrinsic/Elan settlement: "CR Intrinsic Agrees to Pay More than $600 Million in Largest-Ever Settlement for Insider Trading Case," SEC press release, March 15, 2013. Details on Sigma/Dell settlement: "SEC Charges Hedge Fund Firm Sigma Capital with Insider Trading," SEC press release, March 15, 2013.

224 **Anthony Chiasson and Todd Newman:** The case was so convoluted—with the two portfolio managers having been the fifth people on a chain of emails about Dell's earnings—that it looked shaky. Defense lawyers thought that the government was testing the limits of what criminal insider trading could be. Chiasson and Newman professed not to know where the Dell information had come from and fought the case vigorously. Despite the complexities of the case and the sometimes-bewildering evidence, though, a jury convicted them after two days. Jon Horvath had flipped and started cooperating six weeks before he was set to go on trial with them. Patricia Hurtado, "Ex-SAC Analyst Horvath Pleads Guilty in U.S. Insider Case," Bloomberg News, September 28, 2012. Chiasson and Newman's convictions were overturned on appeal in December 2014.

228 **The SEC hypothesized a likely scenario:** It should be noted that Plotkin and Vaccarino were never charged with any wrongdoing.

229 **He attended the World Economic Forum in Davos:** Katherine Burton, "Cohen Travels to Davos for Lesson in 'Resilient Dynamism,'" Bloomberg News, January 23, 2013.

229 **In 2005, he'd made several significant purchases:** Carol Vogel and Peter Lattman, "$616 Million Poorer, Hedge Fund Owner Still Buys Art," *The New York Times*, March 26, 2013.

230 **"the width of a pencil tip":** Kelly Magee, "Wynn's $troke of Luck," *New York Post*, October 15, 2008.

230 **"This is a painting that has haunted Steve":** Peter Lattman and Carol Vogel, "Suit by Ex-Wife of SAC's Cohen Revived on Appeal," *The New York Times*, April 3, 2013.

230 **"When you stand in front of it, you're blown away"**: Lattman and Vogel, "Suit by Ex-Wife of SAC's Cohen Revived on Appeal."

230 **When news of the purchase, for $155 million, appeared:** It turned out that Cohen might have actually purchased *Le Rêve* several months before, in early November of 2012, just three weeks before Martoma was arrested. His advisors tried to undo the effects of the news coming out when it did: "The timing was bad," Heller said, referring to the press reports about the Picasso purchase and clarifying that the price Cohen had paid was actually $150 million. "We're correcting the chronology." Lattman and Vogel, "Suit by Ex-Wife of SAC's Cohen Revived on Appeal."

14. THE LIFE RAFT

234 **Berke thrived on situations like this:** Berke's statement after Steinberg's arrest: "Michael Steinberg did absolutely nothing wrong. At all times, his trading decisions were based on detailed analysis as well as information that he understood had been properly obtained through the types of channels that institutional investors rely upon on a daily basis."

236 **it was much safer to file cases that were close to a sure thing:** For more on the subject of the chilling effect losses had on the Justice Department, see Jesse Eisinger, "Why Only One Top Banker Went to Jail for the Financial Crisis," ProPublica and *The New York Times Magazine,* April 30, 2014.

239 **In 1988 Michael Milken's lawyers:** James B. Stewart, *Den of Thieves* (Simon & Schuster, 1991), p. 441.

241 **Klotz then revisited some of the facts:** See *In the Matter of Steven A. Cohen,* Administrative Proceeding File No. 3-15382, order filed July 19, 2013.

244 **that crime could be attributed to the company he worked for:** "9-28.000—Principles of Federal Prosecution of Business Organizations," *U.S. Attorney's Manual,* "Title 9: Criminal."

245 **Klotz called the head of the securities unit:** Ben Protess and Peter Lattman, "Cohen Declines to Testify in SAC Insider Case," *The New York Times,* June 28, 2013.

245 **Since the beginning of the year, almost $2 billion had been redeemed:** Peter Lattman and Ben Protess, "SAC Starts to Balk over Insider Trading Inquiry," *The New York Times,* May 17, 2013.

245 **Executives at the firm had been watching as the investigation developed:** Matthew Goldstein, "Blackstone Notifies Cohen's SAC It Intends to Pull Money," Reuters, May 25, 2013.

245   **He felt that the Obama administration:** Jonathan Alter, "Schwarzman: 'It's a War' Between Obama, Wall St.," *Newsweek*, August 15, 2010.

245   **he didn't want to abandon Cohen:** Peter Lattman, "Blackstone Keeps Most of Its Money with SAC," *The New York Times*, February 14, 2013.

248   **SAC's own compliance department had sanctioned someone:** *U.S. v. SAC Capital Advisors, et al.*, No. 13 Cr. 541 (LTS), Sealed Indictment, July 25, 2013.

250   **"Today we announced three law enforcement actions relating to the SAC group of hedge funds":** Preet Bharara press conference, July 25, 2013.

251   **"A lot of people were thinking":** Fishman, "The Taming of the Trading Monster."

252   **jokes that he "looked good in stripes":** Michael Rothfeld, Jenny Strasburg, and Susan Pulliam, "Prosecutors Pursue Big SAC Settlement," *The Wall Street Journal*, September 24, 2013.

15. JUSTICE

255   **He made a point of being there by 8 A.M.:** Michael Rothfeld, Jenny Strasburg, and Susan Pulliam, "Prosecutors Pursue Big SAC Settlement," *The Wall Street Journal*, September 24, 2013.

255   **major investment banks:** Morgan Stanley, JPMorgan Chase, and Goldman Sachs continued to do business with SAC; Deutsche Bank did pull a line of credit from the firm after the indictment. Jenny Strasburg and Rob Copeland, "SAC Reconsiders Industry Relationships—and Its Name," *The Wall Street Journal*, December 12, 2013.

255   **"They're an important client to us":** Gary Cohn interview with Kate Kelly, CNBC, July 31, 2013.

256   **the company had "trafficked in inside information on a scale without any known precedent":** Preet Bharara prepared remarks, July 25, 2013. See also Peter Lattman and Ben Protess, "SAC Capital Is Indicted, and Called a Magnet for Cheating," *The New York Times*, July 25, 2013.

258   **"The tiny fraction of wrongdoers":** Peter Lattman and Ben Protess, "$1.2 Billion Fine for Hedge Fund SAC Capital in Insider Case," *The New York Times*, November 4, 2013.

262   **"Dress conservatively":** Kaja Whitehouse and Michelle Celarier, "Steinberg Wife to Pals: No Wearing Bling Near Jury," *New York Post*, December 16, 2013.

263   **When Horvath was led into the courtroom:** Horvath was born in Sweden, grew up in Toronto, and graduated from Queen's University with a degree in commerce. *U.S. v. Michael Steinberg*, No. 12 Cr. 121 (RJS).

263 **how much money Steinberg had made:** *U.S. v. Michael Steinberg,* GX 2004, 2005, and 2006, introduced during testimony of Daniel Berkowitz, November 21, 2013.

264 **a group that included a former postal worker:** Christopher M. Matthews, "SAC's Steinberg Convicted in Insider-Trading Case," *The Wall Street Journal,* December 18, 2013.

267 **At 2:59 P.M. on December 18, 2013, the jury took a vote:** Alexandra Stevenson and Rachel Abrams, "Insider Jury-Room Demonstration Persuaded Holdouts in Ex-Trader's Trial," *The New York Times,* December 19, 2013.

267 **guilty on all counts:** In October 2015, charges against Michael Steinberg were dismissed in the wake of an appeals court decision. See Matthew Goldstein, "U.S. Prosecutor to Drop Insider Trading Cases Against Seven," *The New York Times,* October 22, 2015.

16. JUDGMENT

268 **Richard Strassberg, was on the line:** Martoma replaced Charles Stillman as his defense lawyer on the case in 2013. Peter Lattman, "Martoma, Former SAC Employee, Changes Lawyers in Insider Case," *The New York Times,* April 4, 2013.

270 **On the front page was a headline:** Matthew Goldstein and Alexandra Stevenson, "Ex-SAC Trader Was Expelled from Harvard Law School," *The New York Times,* January 9, 2014.

271 **this was almost more painful:** Martoma said he was devastated. *U.S. v. Mathew Martoma,* No. 12 Cr. 0973 (PGG), Mathew Martoma Sentencing Memorandum, GX 101, letter from James Tierney.

276 **Martoma, then, became something of a surrogate child:** Todd, as it happened, had his own theories about why Gilman became so deeply, destructively enmeshed with the handsome young Martoma. As the trial was unfolding, Todd, who had not spoken to his father since 1991, started writing a proposal for a book about his father. Todd had cut off his relationship with Dr. Gilman because he felt that his father had rejected him for being gay, as was Todd's older brother, Jeff. The book proposal suggested that Dr. Gilman was "deeply disturbed that both of his sons were gay," as Todd put it. It then juxtaposed that fact with the ongoing mystery of Dr. Gilman's decision to jeopardize his reputation and life's work in furtherance of his relationship with Martoma. "Not My Father's Keeper: Unveiling the Skeletons in Dr. Sid Gilman's Closet," a book proposal by Todd Gilman, Ph.D., October 6, 2014.

280 **"And I think we all agree that that is not a path":** More on Judge Gardephe's

mindset: "From the Trenches: High Profile Trials 2014," Practicing Law Institute, September 2014.

281 **the word *guilty* after every count felt like three bullets:** *U.S. v. Martoma*, Martoma Sentencing Memo, GX 65.

282 **the case had left Martoma financially ruined:** *U.S. v. Martoma*, Forfeiture Request, GX A.

282 **after establishing the foundation as a nonprofit:** Mathew and Rosemary Martoma Foundation, Form 990, 2011; the foundation did not file 990s for 2012 and 2013.

283 **"There is not, and never was, and never will be":** Patrick Radden Keefe, "The Empire of Edge," *The New Yorker*, October 13, 2014.

283 **Stanford stripping Martoma of his business degree:** Melissa Korn, "Stanford B-School Strips Diploma of SAC Capital's Martoma," *The Wall Street Journal*, March 5, 2014.

284 **"Given this sequence of events":** *U.S. v. Martoma*, Memorandum Opinion and Order, September 8, 2014.

EPILOGUE

287 **One of the paintings going up for sale:** Katya Kazakina, "Billionaire Cohen Said to Sell $25 Million Dubuffet 'Paris,'" Bloomberg News, April 7, 2015.

288 **"Steve is a very serious, very astute collector":** Carol Vogel, "Steven A. Cohen Was Buyer of Giacometti's 'Chariot,' for $101 Million," *The New York Times*, November 10, 2014.

288 **moved on and started his own hedge fund:** Saijel Kishan, "Ex-SAC's Kumin Said to Gather $1 Billion for Hedge Fund Startup," Bloomberg News, January 14, 2015.

288 **"advisory board":** Juliet Chung and Jenny Strasburg, "Steven A. Cohen's Point72 Asset Management to Create Advisory Board," *The Wall Street Journal*, November 16, 2014.

289 **Cohen's "family office" was earning him hundreds of millions of dollars a year:** Matthew Goldstein, "Profit at Point72, Cohen's New Firm, Outshines Many a Hedge Fund's," *The New York Times*, January 5, 2015.

290 **It is widely considered one of the artist's greatest works:** "Giacometti's iconic *L'Homme au doigt* (Pointing Man)," Impressionist & Modern Art Auction Preview, Christie's, April 16, 2015.

290 **It was the most money anyone has ever paid for a sculpture at auction:** Eileen Kinsella, "Billionaire Steve Cohen Goes on a $240 Million Giacometti Buying

Spree," *Artnet News,* June 8, 2015; Kelly Crow, "Steven A. Cohen Was Mystery Buyer of $141 Million Sculpture," *The Wall Street Journal,* June 8, 2015.

291 the **"Newman decision":** See On Petition for a Writ of Certiorari to the United States Court of Appeals for the Second Circuit, Brief for Todd Newman in Opposition, *USA v. Todd Newman and Anthony Chiasson,* No. 15-137, filed by Stephen Fishbein, John Nathanson, and Brian Calandra of Shearman & Sterling.

291 **"Yesterday's decision":** Interview with Richard Holwell, Bloomberg Television, December 11, 2014.

291 **had their guilty pleas dismissed:** In addition to those of Steinberg and Horvath, Bharara dismissed the guilty pleas of five other cooperating witnesses: Jesse Tortora, Spyridon Adondakis, Sandeep Goyal, Danny Kuo, and Hyung Lim. Matthew Goldstein, "U.S. Prosecutor to Drop Insider Trading Cases Against Seven," *The New York Times,* October 22, 2015.

292 **"This creates an obvious road map":** Gina Chon, "Preet Bharara Warns of Insider Trading 'Bonanza,'" *The Financial Times,* October 5, 2015.

292 **In his opinion granting:** *David Ganek v. David Leibowitz et al.,* 15-cv-1446, Memorandum and Order, 03/10/16

293 **"People are going to be lining up out the doors":** Aruna Viswanatha and Juliet Chung, "Deal Ends SEC's Pursuit of Steven Cohen," *The Wall Street Journal,* January 8, 2016.

294 **The general counsel for Point72:** Simone Foxman and Tom Schoenberg, "Steve Cohen's General Counsel is Part of Trump Transition Team," *Bloomberg News,* November 14, 2016. See also Neil Vigdor, "Connecticut's Former Top Prosecutor Off Trump Transition Team," *Connecticut Post,* November 16, 2016.

INDEX